IDENTIFY AN

JOSEF TEBOHO ANSORGE

Identify and Sort

How Digital Power Changed World Politics

OXFORD
UNIVERSITY PRESS

OXFORD
UNIVERSITY PRESS

Oxford University Press is a department of the University of Oxford.
It furthers the University's objective of excellence in research, scholarship,
and education by publishing worldwide. Oxford is a registered trade mark of
Oxford University Press in the UK and certain other countries.

Published in the United States of America by Oxford University Press
198 Madison Avenue, New York, NY 10016, United States of America.

Published in the United Kingdom in 2016 by
C. Hurst & Co. (Publishers) Ltd.

Library of Congress Cataloging-in-Publication Data
Names: Ansorge Josef Teboho, author.
Title: Identify and sort : how digital power changes world politics / Josef
Teboho Ansorge.
Description: New York, NY : Oxford University Press, 2016. |
Includes bibliographical references and index.
Identifiers: LCCN 2015047818| ISBN 9780190245542 (hardcover) |
ISBN 9780190245559 (pbk.)
Subjects: LCSH: Information technology—Political aspects. | Digital
communications—Political aspects. | Technology and state.
Classification: LCC JF799.5 .A67 2016 | DDC 303.48/33—dc23 LC record
available at http://lccn.loc.gov/2015047818

1 3 5 7 9 8 6 4 2
Printed by Webcom, Canada

This book is dedicated to my son, Daniel, and my wife, Nana Akua.

It could not have been written without the unflagging support of the most wonderful family, friends, and teachers.

CONTENTS

CONTENTS

1

THE SOVEREIGN'S DATA

We live in an identified world. Our reality is rich in names, signs and codes. Number plates, house numbers, passport numbers, tags, and credit card numbers are all around us, waiting to be read. This identifying information is stored in myriad databases with varying levels of access. Identifying and subsequently sorting entities is essential for consciousness and coordinated human activities. Before forces can be mustered for any coordinated activity—be it to invade a city or ban landmines—they need to be constituted, arranged, collated, sorted, ranked, and directed. Before anybody can be disciplined and punished they need to be identified and sorted. Lists are made. Individuals have to be recognised, placed into a hierarchical relation, and aggregated into groups. Prior to any state effectively levying taxes it has to assess the wealth of its citizenry and translate it into a common value system. Numbers are crunched and spreadsheets are tabulated. Before international policy is enacted, organisations produce vast records and written assessments. To make political claims corporations and foundations generate complex methodological indexes and rankings of governments and countries. Transformation indexes, democracy indexes, corruption perception indexes, transparency indexes, failed state indexes, business friendly indexes, political risk indexes, press freedom indexes, happiness indexes, health indexes, and prosperity indexes all vie for position, advocating different approaches to measuring and sorting. Taken together these indexes comprise a way of knowing—an epistemology—of planetary life. By way of these indexes social and political life is rendered legible, seen, and known. In some instances, our planetary life is constituted by these indexes. Such global uniformity is the result of powerful forces of standardisation. Metrics generated by indices are the product of, and input for, information technologies and systems that seek to provide more knowledge about social and political life.

How did we end up in this identified world?

The sovereign hungers for data. Authority demands information-generating processes to understand the social order and act on it. The sovereign desires a reliable process to *identify* and *sort* our visceral, constantly reproducing, dying, and migrating mass of humanity into stable, legally constructed categories and socially meaningful gradations. '[M]uch of the point of most laws is to sort people out for differential treatment, often quite seriously differential treatment.'[1] Depending on the level of intricacy—as well as the preferred amounts of control and legibility—different constructions are possible. The basic, most common, and preferred categories are citizen, subject, criminal, enemy, and foreigner. Each of these categories can be subject to further multiple divisions. For instance, the foreigner can be the undocumented immigrant, the political refugee, the permanent resident, or the visiting student. The enemy can be the privileged belligerent or the terrorist, the pirate, the rebel, the partisan, the insurgent, etc. The criminal can be further identified by the class of the crime they committed: the murderer, the rapist, the embezzler, the thief, the robber, etc. Engaged in this perpetual identifying and sorting labour, putting individuals into these and many other categories, the sovereign regularly encounters serious problems of the ontological and epistemological sort. What is there to know? How do I know it? What is society comprised of?

Races, sexes, nationalities, cultures, classes, political parties, linguistic groups, communities, generations, professions, religious groups, free men, individuals, and networks have all—at one time or another—been used as the primary ontological category by those seeking to understand society. What accounts for the behaviour of individuals? Race, genetics, personality type, head shape, sex, fear, will to power, passion, honour, birth order, diet, early childhood, family life, utility maximisation, morality, social norms, wealth, education, incentives and behavioural priming have all—at one time or another—been advanced as principal explanations by those seeking to act on the social order. In a rich intellectual history, the sovereign's information needs produced copious instrumental models and techniques to better understand and act on the social and political order. While the functional categories, systems, processes, organising principles, and regulative ideals of these identifying and sorting practices changed historically, their underlying animating inquiry always remained the same:

Who the hell are all these people?

This book is about the solutions developed to answer that transhistoric and transcultural question of the sovereign. Information technology and political authority are deeply intertwined in this story.

The historical responses to the sovereign's question—Who are all these people?—can be structured into three different modalities, organised around rituals, archives, and digital tools. Each represents a cluster of technical practices and a type of political power. Each is a way to generate the sovereign's data. Using these instruments a variety of substantive answers could be produced and the mass of humanity consistently identified and sorted into useful categories. Occasionally this led to some striking similarities. For instance, the popular quadripartite classificatory schema of priests, warriors, merchants, and peasants was present in Hindu, Buddhist, and Persian law.

In some societies, such as our own, the *longue durée* story is one of political authority gradually monopolising the identification and sorting of individuals. Here, priests, administrators, and judges—or their functional equivalents—authorised by a centralised power and deploying a stable technical process would be the ones to help determine who you were, what purposes you would serve, what resources you would access, whether you were socially sanctioned to procreate, whether you could migrate, whether you were saved, whether you were going to be punished, how you would be punished, and so on.

Frequently these identifying and sorting practices were shrouded in mystery. Often they achieved heightened authority and legitimacy precisely because they were obscured and hidden. They functioned because the population was led to assume, whether erroneously or correctly, that the sovereign had great secret powers and higher forms of knowledge, regardless of whether these stemmed from experience, accumulated resources, cultural awareness and technocratic expertise or a privileged intimacy with the spirit realm. It is hard to second-guess the sovereign when you don't know what the sovereign knows—when all you know is that the sovereign knows more. These are the kind of beliefs that generate deep order and obedience to a prevailing structure of political authority.

The National Security State's Rabbit Hole

In May 2013 a hitherto unknown and unimportant analyst named Edward Snowden disturbed a variant of this order when he began to reveal the most updated information collection processes of the U.S. National Security Agency (NSA). Years of Hollywood movies had prepared the global public for a coming hyper-informed state, yet there was still surprised, halting outrage as the lavish dimensions of the global collection efforts were broadcast. Foreign allies were spied on, the public's emails and text messages were stored, and GPS location was tracked, not once or twice, or based on any specific suspicion—let alone probable cause—but categorically, systematically and *en masse*. The sovereign's appetite for data had led to an attempt at the total appropriation of information. Despite these disclosures it remains difficult to fully appreciate the industrial (and thereby also banal) scale of the ongoing information collection processes. When the storage capacity of facilities is measured in the yottabytes[2] it means nothing less than that every day entire libraries' worth of information are being captured and sifted, regularly requiring novel linguistic terms to be fashioned to account for this new world. Were we to only focus on that aspect—the gross (in both senses of the word) amount of data circulated and processed—this Sisyphean technological feat would have to be celebrated as one of humanity's greatest intellectual-industrial achievements. But there was no celebration, only cognitive dissonance.

An unspoken agreement exists in our modern, digital age: the sovereign may look at and collect as much information as it can find, as long as it only uses the information to protect and prosecute—not persecute—and as long as it does so competently. Most people are fine with their privacy being invaded so long as everybody else's is also invaded to the same degree and that invasion is done in a professional and detached manner. We feel no shame before a database. Snowden's public presence disrupted this sentiment and made it difficult to maintain. His pasty, sullen face brought the inherent frailty and fallibility of the sovereign's sorting and identifying machinery into sudden focus. If the NSA could make such patent mistakes in their hiring, contracting, and internal control—what kind of hidden and deadly blunders were they committing with all of our information? For now the gaze had shifted from admiring the quasi-omnipotent technical assemblages to seeing the tired and highly imperfect bureaucrats manipulating the dials, in some cases to spy on their love interests.[3]

With the human, all too human, desires and imperfections of the operators looming in our field of vision the privacy-invading nature of these state activities achieved momentary public salience. This is because in the Anglo-American tradition sentiments about privacy are constructed around fears of police physically breaking into your home, peeping toms spying on your naked wife, gossip, and embarrassment. It is easy for this legal and political tradition to see and understand privacy violation when the surveillance is personified and exercised by a visceral, red-blooded, and identifiable individual. It follows that the Anglo-American tradition knows how to respond to corrupted surveillance— the use of the *public* surveillance apparatus to satisfy personal desires. Snowden's disclosure helped draw attention to the humans surveilling society, which in turn raised the consciousness of privacy violations. But most of all Snowden's campaign of revelations confirmed the sovereign's insatiable appetite for information—a craving triggered by the falsely simplistic yet ultimately disordering question:

Who are the terrorists?

In offering answers to this question the NSA opted to follow the Google/Borges[4] paradigm all the way to the bottom of the rabbit hole.

Get all of the data > store it all permanently > make it all available to the user.

This mass archiving of information is a unilateral modification of the social contract between individuals and political authority.

We live in a totalitarian digital present in which state organs capture virtually all of our machine-mediated communications. How did this Stasi-fantasy manifest in a system that imagines itself as anti-totalitarian? Future historians will have to tell that story. For now, recall that the great communist vs capitalist ideological debate of the twentieth century could be, and frequently was, reduced down to the practical question of whether the political control of society should extend to a control of its economic forces, a control of the market. Behind the superstructure of normative arguments—with the two camps drawing on discourses of freedom and equality respectively—there was always a base of feasibility assessments. Could this even be done? For one economist, whose defence of capitalism remains extremely popular, it was not possible. In 1945 Hayek assuredly wrote that 'the "data" from which the economic calculus starts are never for the whole society "given" to a single mind which could work out the implications and can *never* be so given'.[5] Here it was agreed that the knowledge apparatus of the state had met its match in the form of the market. Now, what is it about the modern national security state that it ignores its own previous truisms on the impossibility of centralised knowledge and regulation? Why should the sovereign, whom we cannot trust to set the right price of butter, be in a privileged position to determine how threatening each individual on earth is?

Many important lessons lie in the past. Looking at previous solutions to the sovereign's persistent question—Who the hell are all these people?— few would believe that our ancestors' and predecessors' processes or categories were correct, natural or neutral. Instead, most recognise the political significance of these practices and intuitively understand that they helped to shape society. We easily grasp that identifying and sorting practices played crucial constitutive functions in the past. As an analogue, when reading the antique or modern legal traditions regulating the complexities of slave purchase, we don't think that this regime was a neutral representation of social norms, but rather that it did important work in shaping subjectivities and legitimating a slave society. It is more difficult to do the same in the present, to understand the costs of the status quo. Let us gaze upon our time as something strange and terrifying yet, ultimately, incapable of completely sorting and identifying human life.

There is always a remainder, a liminal character that does not belong to any devised category. This character is queer, obscure or appears anomalous but, it must be emphasised, only appears so because the sovereign's schema or taxonomy has no place for it. Automated processes confronted with a liminal character inevitably freeze up and make mistakes, requiring the exercise of human discretion and political decision—this is what linguists, philosophers, and computer scientists call disambiguation protocols. The more complex and automated our identifying and sorting architecture becomes, the more disambiguation protocols we need. When too much is demanded of the sovereign's sorting and identifying machine, governing practices as a whole are in danger of appearing incoherent and illegitimate. The central challenge for the sovereign in our digital era is to maintain this element of discretion and decision, while having the brunt of the political labour of identifying and sorting be undertaken by normalised, juridified, and automated processes before which the human subject feels no shame and to which it assigns no responsibility. This balance becomes difficult, verging on the impossible, to maintain in a time of accelerating computing power and perpetual innovation of the technical means of identifying and sorting.

The sovereign hungers for data, but what it really needs is stability. These contending drives produce legitimacy crises and 'constitutional moments'[6] during which fundamental questions of social order become unsettled, and the relationship of central authority and knowledge to individual subjects can be renegotiated. '[T]echnological innovations are similar to legislative acts or political foundings that establish a framework for public order that will endure over many generations.'[7] The window for political action can however be brief and limited to the initial planning and construction of the technical system.[8] Political scandals and technological innovation have conspired to create an opportunity to contest the planetary arrangement of the sovereigns' data.

Our political and legal discourses are not well prepared for this constitutional moment. If you detect some urgency in this book, it is because I fear that we may miss this moment or make unintended concessions during it. To arm ourselves we need to follow de Tocqueville's injunction from a different context: a 'new science of politics is needed for a new world'.[9] Let us begin to move toward this new science with an appreciation of political power in the digital era.

Digital Power

Industrial information technology provides the sovereign with a new kind of political power—digital power—that permits it to 'know' each of its subjects with unprecedented detail and confidence, as well as attach a permanent identity to them. Digital power is, first, the ability of an actor to collect and combine various bits of information into an artificial representation of an individual (which this individual does not have access to). Second, digital power is the ability to compare that representation against the rest of the population. Third, digital power is the ability of an actor to develop strategies and activities that target the individual associated with the artificial representation.

For identified and sorted individuals, the circuitous layers of information and loss in anonymity change the way they behave and see themselves, as well as the way they remember and communicate with each other. For the technically enhanced sovereign, the experience of proto-omniscience brings significant changes of specificity and scope. Digital power enables novel approaches and policies to prevent crime, control immigration, run election campaigns, combat terrorism, run development programmes, and fight wars. Digital power permits the technically enhanced sovereign to eavesdrop on the telephone conversations of entire countries. Because of digital power we have need for the concept of national privacy. The advent of digital power changes the way political authority imagines and acts on the world.

What does it mean to 'see like a state'[10] when the state looks at computer screens? First of all, information becomes cheap and responsive. The world converts into a reservoir of data with everything, in principle, being readable and permanently storable. Hyper-legibility abounds. Identifying and sorting operations that were prohibitively expensive, politically difficult, impractical, or embarrassingly quixotic some years ago can now be executed with a few discrete keystrokes. Digital power produces two novel strategies to understand and act on populations.

Radical Individuation ⇒ Instrumental Aggregation:

Through digital power, the sovereign and other actors can achieve a level of granularity that goes beyond salient groups defined by race, religion, gender, or political affiliation. Instead they see a society constituted by individuals with astonishingly unique combinations of measured attributes. These individuals can then be clustered into new groups defined by whatever the desired particular attribute, constellation of attributes, or probability of a future attribute is. Through this operation a population can continuously be segmented into useful categories and unique strategies can be developed for dealing with each of them. Digital power first disaggregates a population into individuals and then reaggregates them into instrumental categories.

Discovery by Exclusion:

Digital power permits the sovereign to amass a comprehensive and complete model of society. Once this is in place a novel type of search operation becomes possible. By repeatedly excluding individuals that are known to *not be* in the group one is interested in, it becomes possible to whittle down and discover the desired group. This is what the Germans call a *Rasterfahndung* and the Americans call a digital dragnet. As an analogue, digital power is like having a list of a population on which names can be crossed off until so few names are left that you can efficiently concentrate your resources on those to find who you are looking for. This process of exclusion becomes more useful the more complete and detailed the record of a society is and the more sophisticated the information technologies at its disposal are.

Through these strategies taxonomies and ideal types—limit-shapes—of 'supporters', 'terrorists', 'recruits', and 'citizens' are created. Crucially, both of these strategies enable a dynamic categorisation and recategorisation of human individuals that does not have to correspond with how they regard themselves, or each other. The sovereign sees a very different world than the citizen, subject, criminal, enemy, or foreigner. These taxonomies can always be subverted by what they exclude. The sorting and labelling operations, initially deployed as practices of particular organisations for specific purposes, begin to find wider resonance through ritualised use in the construction of modern societies, up to the point where they play key roles in the way society is imagined and constituted. Predicates turn to subjects; means are transformed into ends. Put differently, through repeated use a shift occurs from an actor who sorts and labels subjects, to a situation in which the definition of political agency is given by the ability to identify and sort, and the very notion of political subjectivity by being identified and sorted.

The modern networked relational database is only the latest member in a large class of political technologies. It does not replace or overcome standardised surnames, tattoos, cadastre, censuses, passports, registries, ID cards, and fingerprint classifications, but rather draws on and incorporates them into one large layered system of meaning. The database derives its utility from integrating all of these sites of information. This system is characterised by an unprecedented capacity for retention, combination, duplication, iteration, recall, and communication of information. Like other political technologies preceding it, the database serves a crucial social and political function in hierarchising society while insulating and uniting it against outsiders—it polices borders and maintains internal orders. Yet it does all of this removed from the public gaze and scrutiny by recourse to a putatively neutral technical apparatus and automation. This leads to the increasingly important legal and ethical question of who is responsible for automated and autonomous activities?[11] Within the columns of a database it is possible to organise populations into virtual classes without any consciousness, as well as establish more sophisticated means for identifying and determining who should be part of the mobility: that class of individuals who can easily cross international borders.

Digital power creates a space for political activities away from the public eye, within the internal, bureaucratic identifying and sorting processes. The state's vision of society can thereby be radically disassociated from the public's vision of society. Put differently, digital power has the potential to fully liberate the sovereign from the identity constructions of the people it is identifying and sorting. When this occurs, digital power affords an experience of extreme legibility to those looking at computer screens—watching the flow of images and strands of data in the matrix—while those subject to the sorting and identifying experience are alienated from their representations. This, in turn, contributes to a profound inequality of legibility.

The experience of hyper-legibility has its own, seldom emphasised, drawbacks. For one, visibility is not the same as legibility. Seeing more does not mean understanding more. Actually the opposite appears to be the case. A number of psychological studies have found that making it more difficult to read information—what psychologists call disfluency—can lead to higher cognitive functioning, better understanding, and better educational outcomes.[12] The ease of accessing and reading information provided by digital power may therefore come with a tragic tendency to degrade the quality of the operator's understanding of that information.

Moreover, digital power does not transcend fundamental difficulties of identifying and sorting human life. The first problem—and this is a persistent, acute and deep one not remedied but exacerbated by more information—is that the connection of constructed category to human individual permits of many different possibilities and permutations. Quite frequently fine distinctions between influential categories are arbitrary and subject to more or less violent fluctuations in interpretation, dependent on fluid intellectual fashions and innovations in information technology. As an illustration consider how minute, even haphazard, the difference is between the worst applicant accepted and the best applicant rejected from a civil service. Here the categorisation creates facts on the ground that are of more weight and permanence than the facts the categorisation is based on. The technical and hidden process of identifying and sorting obscures this contingent and constitutive element. Put differently, because legal and social categories such as 'criminal' and 'terrorist' are founded on social interaction and not physical reality any technical means of identifying them is necessarily built on shifting sands. Technical solutions to political and social problems are attractive because they represent a depoliticised resolution, but ultimately technical solutions to political problems fail to deliver what their purveyors promise because there is no such thing. There is no depoliticised resolution. This of course only leads to a search for more technical solutions...

The digital improvement and monopolisation of identifying and sorting processes does not erase two further fundamental paradoxes of political technologies of identification. The first is that individual identity can only be established through a prior identity paper. To receive a piece of identification one requires a previous one: a birth certificate for a passport, an ID card for a driver's licence, a social security number for a diploma, a marriage licence for a marriage certificate, etc. This Kafkaesque circularity of identity, the manner in which it is always already caught and framed by prior recursive systems of symbols, exists at all levels of identification, from medieval letters declaring rights of passage to biometric ID cards. For most individuals the founding moment of this web of signification is a birth certificate, which usually requires no other documentation to be validated. From this point onwards an individual's identity is always deferred back to such a founding document. Improving biometric ways of 'reading' the human body, such as fingerprints, face recognition, retinal scans, or DNA tests, does not disrupt this circularity or neutralise the recursive system. As Saussure teaches us, the relationship between sign (identity) and signified (body) is arbitrary.[13]

The second paradox is that radical individual identity is always established through recourse to a layering of various group identities: tall, B+ blood type, 'Jewish', high IQ, and so on. The singular is serialised through the addition of characteristics. An individual can only be known to the sovereign through supra-individual categories. Therefore systems of individual identity and modern database technics do not simply disaggregate an entire population, but rather re-arrange by categories and re-aggregate it into new groupings and hierarchies. This means that improving the legibility of individuals in a population always entails the constitution of smaller groups, sometimes even the 'discovery' or invention of new groups.

'Control over technique and control over society go hand in hand in the modern world.'[14]

WHAT THIS BOOK IS ABOUT

This book is an exploration of those technics—constellations of techniques (practices) and technological artefacts (tools)—used by states and other political actors to make legible, sort, and order human individuals and populations, what Michel Foucault has called the 'bio-politics of populations' or 'bio-power'[15] and James Scott refers to as 'state simplifications'.[16] Such technics can be understood as ways of seeing—or forms of visuality[17]—which have been constructed by political power. These practices usually entail mathematical expertise; they belong to what Max Weber identifies as 'techniques by which life—both external things and the behaviour of people—can be ruled through calculation'.[18] One animating principle of these kinds of practices is Jean-Jacques Rousseau's idea that a society's 'number and population ... increasing and multiplying' is a clear indication of the value of a government. This gives an indication of how growth is built into the valuation of a political community as well as the reliance of these practices on a mastery of numbers. Rousseau declared, 'Statisticians, it is now up to you; count, measure, compare.'[19]

The political technologies I consider in this book develop through difference at the international level and fulfil an important role in recreating the international system's conditions and characteristics. I situate political technologies—or technics of politics—as being engendered at interfaces of public and private and arising from the power differentials of the international system, in particular between the global North and the global South, in response to the challenge of the illegible other. Through a few of these technologies categories of national identity and statehood are regularly, sometimes at great cost, stabilised and reproduced in a worldwide field of dynamic and uneven relations, flows and circulation. Because assumptions which structure the ontology of the modern individual and the international system are folded within persistent data-mining practices—while also establishing the borders of what counts as private, public, and legitimate knowledge—the database, if interpreted properly, can offer up the cognitive building blocks of an imagined international relations. In this way, databases, and other technologies, function as sovereignty machines: imagining and performatively enacting the units of an international order.

The approach I pursue is one that repeatedly asks how politics and the world are constructed, in both senses of the word: by what means and in what shape. This turn from 'what' and 'why' to 'how' questions is itself indicative of a technical orientation that has been gaining ground since the late middle ages.[20] My argument is that part of the answer to 'how' can be found in the type of knowledge produced about the individual and the international, and another part in the technological artefacts used to achieve population legibility and order—which co-constitute each other. In the course of this book, I seek to display some important second- and third-order political effects of technical processes, most of which can occur independently of the knowledge or intent of their multifarious technicians and operators. To understand and contribute to theorising the power relations extant in information technology, I introduce a range of analytic concepts: technics of politics (ritual mode, archival mode, and digital mode), digital power, limit-shapes, arithmetising the other, disambiguation protocols, and sovereignty machines. To develop these terms, I cover a broad range of historical cases, from Aztec rituals to Barack Obama's election machinery, to counter-insurgency campaigns and post-conflict reconstruction programmes in Liberia.

Throughout, I draw inspiration from the anthropology and philosophy of religion, by regarding databases as fulfilling modern functions of oracles, Fordist production lines as appropriating and harnessing the power of the ritual, and modern technical artefacts as taking the place of the fetish.[21] This book embeds technological artefacts in social, political, and economic contexts to see them in a totality of relations and not as separate categories. Because technology is socially constituted we can only properly understand technological artefacts if we consider them in concrete social and political situations.

There is a rich tradition that has long grappled with many related issues of technology, rationality and power. In the course of this book I pursue a number of different lines of thought coming out of this tradition. Through the use of a variety of thinkers intellectual resources are engendered for critically discerning the modern database and its uses in world politics. Engaging with the political thought of individuals who lived in different times and cultures is always an exercise fraught with methodological pitfalls.[22] In this book, I seek to neither neutralise the tensions within and between the thinkers I deal with, nor to properly contextualise their writings. Instead I undertake readings of select texts in which I outline and focus on particular aspects of a strong and connected tradition that deals with issues of technics. These sections are simply bringing 'buried intellectual treasure back to the surface, dusting it down and enabling us to reconsider what we think of it'.[23] Maybe they can help us in our current predicament.

Except where indicated otherwise, all of the translations are my own.[24]

Ten Theses on Information Technology and Political Power

i. *Digital power is on an individualising trajectory, permitting the state to create finer and finer gradations and categorisations of individuals.* This tendency permits political power to act at a level of specificity that evades group consciousness and traditional public discourses surrounding discrimination and civil rights.

ii. *Technics of politics are pioneered and developed in the periphery by the metropole, before flowing back to the metropole.* Political technologies arise from the interaction of actors with different levels of technological development and power in response to the problem of security, illegibility, economic underdevelopment and otherness.

iii. *Technics of politics are constituted by a 'technical code' that embodies hegemonic political values and beliefs.*[25] Much like culture or background radiation, technical codes are difficult to detect because of their ubiquity.

iv. *Advanced technologies used to identify individuals replace the need for conspicuous and public markers of identity.* This creates circumstances in which states of hyper-legibility exist for the operator plugged into a network and drawing on information, while the everyday experience of an individual is increasingly deprived of the markers of individual identity.

v. *The modern state is framed as a type of machinery that produces goods for its subjects and can be reconstructed if it fails to do so.*[26] One of the areas in which this becomes apparent is in 'state-building' and 'responsibility to protect' discourses.

vi. *Technics of politics are the frame of politics, acting as a field of truth that reveals and elides particular meanings.*[27] A political technology is a symptom of the underlying political and economic order that maintains it, as well as one of the practices which regularly enables and rearticulates this order.

vii. *The experience of warfare resists the rationalising impulse of the technics of politics, which spurs actors to more radical attempts at rationalisation.* While war has historically been the grounds for some of the most radical advances in technology, the friction[28] experienced in war repeatedly demonstrates the limits of technical solutions to social and political problems.

viii. *Modern technics is marked by theological characteristics; it fulfils a similar function to religious systems of dominance.*[29] The anthropology and philosophy of religion are particularly useful bodies of knowledge for thinking through the various roles—sacral, fetish, oracle—modern technics play in the global order.

ix. *Sovereign is (s)he who can sort and rank their population.* To remain sovereign one must have control of a society's identifying and sorting mechanism. With politics framed by modern technological artefacts, it is a crucial function of power to stabilise and integrate modern technologies into old political orders, as well as maintain control of the most sophisticated representations (elaborate databases) of society.

x. *Technics inherently produces technological solutions and formal knowledge in response to dynamic social and political problems.* This minimises the need for consensus and displaces the responsibility of political actors. Due to this tendency a permanent critique is required that attempts to democratise and bring politics back in to technics.

The overall emphasis on technics for the study of world politics serves two related functions. First, it focuses on an understudied aspect of the international: the how-to of its information technological manifestations. Second, it helps to denaturalise political and academic processes that appear technical and factual.

To begin our study of technology and political power in earnest it helps to start with the capacious, instructive, and evocative idea of the ship of state.

2

THE SHIP

Imagine a ship at sea, perilously twisting in the wind and rain. It's a frequent metaphor. But what does it mean? Does it inspire confidence or concern? In the history of political thought it has been deployed to justify an extensive range of political forms and allude to a huge variety of themes.

Ships are closed systems that feature strict social organisation and division of labour. In principle, everybody on a ship has a defined task and the captain represents a unified site of authority. Often the image of a ship is used to underline the importance of technical expertise for political stability. In book VI of Plato's *Republic* technical skill plays such a role. He uses the craft of handling a ship as a metaphor for running a state.[1] The point Plato makes is that although the ship-hands might not appreciate their captain and might wish to supplant him, they overlook the fact that 'any genuine sea captain has to study the yearly cycle, the seasons, the heavens, the stars and winds, and everything relevant to the job'.[2] For Plato the technological artefact of the ship, along with the social organisation and particular expertise required to operate it, serve as a tidy argument for technocracy and subordination to anti-democratic authority, all the while underlining the existential need for properly guiding the vessel of the Polis. Here the knowledge of the captain and the technical apparatus of the ship are significant ordering symbols helping to 'securitise' centralised political power.[3]

This conception of the 'ship of state' repeatedly surfaces as a regulative ideal in poetry, political philosophy, and journalism. Horace has a famous ode which seems to treat the ship as an allegory for the Roman state threatened by civil wars—'Do you not see how your side bare of oars and mast stricken by the swift South Wind and sail-yards groan, and without riggings your keels can hardly endure the sea too.'[4] Nearly two millennia later Henry Wadsworth Longfellow wrote:

> Thou, too, sail on, O Ship of State
> Sail on, O Union, strong and great!
> Humanity with all its fears,
> With all the hopes of future years,
> Is hanging breathless on thy fate![5]

In these renditions the ship continually serves as a powerful icon evoking a range of sentiments: courage, ingenuity, purpose, danger, but also authority and expertise. One gets the sense that everybody's fate is intertwined and failure would be the failure of all.

There is an intriguing variation of this theme in Tommaso Campanella's utopia *The City of the Sun* (1623), which grafts mystical prophecy with political authority and technical competence. One of the curious characteristics of Campanella's utopia is that practical skill and technical expertise are, unlike in Plato's *Republic*, not overlooked but highly treasured and valued. Campanella's book places technology, and especially the skill of individual craftsmen, on a pedestal.[6] At the end of *The City of the Sun*, 'a large ship appears, which without oars or sails is driven by a mechanism which the holder of an "absolute authority" controls.'[7] The goal of the ship is to travel the world and convert everybody to the enlightened ways of its people. Automation and technical supremacy, on this account, lead to absolute authority and benevolent colonialism. For Friedrich Engels, too, a ship at high sea was an example used to discredit anarchist notions of freedom and demonstrate the persistence of authority in socialism. 'But the necessity of authority, and of imperious authority at that, will nowhere be found more evident than on board a ship on the high seas.' In these settings 'the lives of all depend on the instantaneous and absolute obedience of all to the will of one'.[8]

With the advent of industrialisation a new technological form is used to make similar points. Lenin writes about the importance of running the revolution like a factory:

It must be said that large-scale machine industry—which is precisely ... the foundation of socialism ... calls for absolute and strict unity of will, which directs the joint labours of ... tens of thousands of people ... But how can strict unity of will be ensured? By thousands subordinating their will to the will of one … We must learn to combine the public-meeting democracy of the working people … with iron discipline while at work, with unquestioning obedience to the will of a single person, the Soviet leader, while at work.[9]

Read together these examples constitute a history of technical practices used to legitimate different forms of political domination. There is a curious permanence to presenting technical capacity as a basis of political authority.

From the British philosopher Michael Oakeshott we receive a different idea, one in which democracy is like ship-hands on a 'boundless sea' with 'neither harbour nor shelter nor floor for anchorage, neither starting point nor appointed destination' where the most important 'enterprise is to keep afloat on an even keel'.[10] The ship is lost and going nowhere, yet its entire purpose is to keep on moving. Its sole mission is survival.

A whole range of types of political organisation, oligarchy, empire, socialism, and democracy, can be represented and legitimated with the metaphor of the ship. The sociologist Paul Gilroy moves us into a different direction from the examples above; for him the 'image of the ship' is a:

living, micro-cultural, micro-political system in motion [that] focus[es] attention on the middle passage, on the various projects for redemptive return to an African homeland, on the circulation of ideas and activists as well as the movement of key cultural and political artefacts: tracts, books, gramophone records, and choirs.[11]

Here the ship is embedded within a complex field of global relations; it is a slaver, a vehicle for repatriation and a conduit of information. In their radical global history from below Peter Linebaugh and Marcus Rediker see something emancipatory in a ship where many others do not. According to them the 'pirate ship was egalitarian in a hierarchical age'.[12] From this perspective, the ship is a channel for resistance and a vector of democratic politics and emancipation.

The complex of themes which a 'ship' is used to allude to—technical expertise, authority, domination, existential danger, automation, disorientation, globalisation and colonialism—are central subjects of this book. In the wide use of the metaphor for totally different purposes one catches a glimpse of the undetermined relationship of technology to politics. The quotes above indicate that technology does not have a fixed or stable political meaning, but that there is a tendency to treat technical expertise as a justification for political authority. My interest lies in how and when technological artefacts and expertise mediate political relations. Or put differently, how does 'the ship' fit into global social and political relations? In our world politics there is no captain of a global 'ship of state'. In most introductory texts in the field of international relations the absence of a central hegemon to enforce consistent common rules is identified as the perennial problem and cause for an anarchic international system. Not only is there no captain of the global ship of state, but the ship is also constantly undergoing construction. The philosopher of science Otto Neurath has a beautiful image of building a ship at sea:

> We are like sailors who on the open sea must reconstruct their ship but are never able to start afresh from the bottom. Where a beam is taken away a new one must at once be put there, and for this the rest of the ship is used as a support. In this way, by using the old beams and driftwood, the ship can be shaped entirely anew, but only by gradual reconstruction.[13]

The ship of state is an ancient image combining technological and political themes. I would like you to think of the ship of state as an interface of technology and politics, one that is closely concerned with the ability of a captain, or sovereign, to understand and act on their crew. As such, the ship requires identifying and sorting practices. To begin to understand how the identifying and sorting practices of this ship have changed over time, it helps to switch registers and focus on something that has physically been stable from the oldest to the newest ship, but has still evolved, in the sense that it has been used for a variety of legal and political purposes: ears. By considering the ear, we will begin to appreciate how practices of identifying and sorting have changed over time across species barriers and how these practices fulfil important functions for authority. We will then be in a better position to create models and ideal types of the ritual mode, the archival mode, and the digital mode.

3

THE EAR

What is the political history of the ear? The ear resides at the margin of the face, ever-present, but our eyes are not naturally drawn to it. It is not typically an object of focus in our encounters with each other; that is unless there is something unusual about the appendage: an earring or other adornment, or some disfigurement, notching, or mutilation. What has it meant to cut an ear, not by accident, but on purpose? There is a rich global history of intentionally boring, slicing, severing, cropping, or notching the ears of domesticated animals and peasants, as well as the ears of slaves, vagrants, captives, deserters, and criminals. The ear is a prominent site of identifying and sorting practices. Ear cutting is a practice that has been applied across species barriers and great cultural divides. What problem does cutting an ear solve?

The ear is more public than a flogged back or a tattooed wrist but less public than a severed or slit nose, tattooed forehead, or a gouged-out eye. The ear lends itself as a broadcast canvas and permanent trace to advertise and deter through signalling recidivism, criminality, penalty, shame, and property. The ear is a site at which authority can inexpensively yet indelibly mark the human head without severely harming the person, diminishing their labour-power, or requiring a long period of recuperation. It is therefore an expedient grid for the expression of disciplinary and classificatory power. The cut ear is a public record fused to one's face. It is an information technology that works 'like sumptuary laws, to make status legible to any observer'.[1] This short chapter surveys diverse

21

practices of ear marking and offers an interpretation of their evolving function: from a concern with punishment, torture, humiliation and classification to evidence of ownership and a method of individual identification, one that is being replaced by ever-more sophisticated techniques to reliably recognise an ear from afar.

Focusing on the political history of the ear provides a good entry point to the changing nature of domination exercised on mammalian bodies through the technics of politics. In the history of the ear we find a shift from ritual, to archival, to digital means of identifying and sorting. It shows how a practice, at once ancient and widespread in its application to animal and human ears, was essentially abandoned for humans in the nineteenth century (along with other mutilation punishments),[2] and for a range of animals in the twentieth and twenty-first centuries. My thesis is that this occurred due to a revolution in the identification and sorting regime—initially of humans and subsequently of domesticated animals—that made ear mutilations appear crude, egregious, and ultimately unnecessary. Understanding how this happened requires considering some of the miscellaneous uses and limitations of ear cutting in history.

Ear Cutting as a Punishment Technology

Ear cutting was generally a punishment reserved to shame low-status individuals who could not pay a fine. The oldest systematic set of legal rules we know of—the Babylonian Code of Hammurabi (1772 BC)—prescribes ear cutting only for slaves who transgress. 'If the slave of a freed man strike the freed man, his ear shall be cut off.'[3] Cutting or cropping of the ear has the potential to be a meaning-laden punishment, suggesting that a person has failed to listen to authority. Like most mutilation punishments such a sentence's repetition is limited to the amount of body parts to be cut off. Put differently, what did the Babylonians do when a slave struck a freed man for the third time? In ancient Egypt mutilations were combined for more severe offences. The records of the Harem Conspiracy against Ramses III (1167 BC) document that the conspirators had their noses and ears cut off. One of them, a 'former ... butler', subsequently committed suicide because 'he was left alone'.[4] Cutting of (and off) the ear was primarily a punishment for low-status individuals—the slaves and butlers above—but it could also be used as a symbol of a person's permanent transition to low-status. Amongst those whose noses and ears were cut off as a result of the Harem Conspiracy were also a 'scribe', an 'officer of infantry', and a 'captain of police'.[5]

A nineteenth-century history of the Hebrew people describes a priest at the time of Herod who, as punishment, had 'his ears cropped, and was thereby rendered incapable of ever being high priest again'.[6] There is a similar passage in Tacitus's *Annals* (109 AD), where a reigning king has the ears of a challenger to the throne cut off—thus making him permanently unfit.[7] To assume elevated offices in these societies the incumbent had to be holy and 'holiness' was 'exemplified by completeness'.[8] This is the broader cultural context in which we should read the biblical passages in which the disciple Simon Peter cuts off the ear of Malchus, the high priest's slave, after the betrayal of Jesus.[9] In such circumstances an intentionally cut ear could function as a perpetual bar and disqualification for positions of religious and public authority. The cut ear identified persons and sorted them into crude categories. This superficial survey of ear cutting in antiquity already provides us with two conceptually distinct, yet in practice overlapping, functions: (i) ear cutting as punishment and symbol of transgression, and (ii) ear cutting to identify an entity barred from higher office and certain locations. The first is retrospective, responding to a violation or act; the second is prospective, preventing future access to specific positions. To make more sense of the first function it helps to consider the ear cutting of animals.

The earliest records of ear cropping dogs date back to ancient Rome.[10] A lot of different reasons have historically been offered for ear cropping dogs, such as: a cropped ear is more hygienic, will make the dog tougher, or is more aesthetically appealing. In our era cropping a dog's ears is only accepted for cosmetic reasons. Curiously, in some periods and cultures ear cropping of dogs and other animals served similar punishment, deterrence, and exclusion functions as it did for humans. Three examples regarding different animals in diverse contexts (agrarian and hunter-gatherer) illustrate this use. An early twentieth-century anthropology text describes the practice amongst the 'Hudson's Bay Eskimo'. Dogs are not permitted to eat the deer-meat, 'lest the guardian spirit of the deer be offended'. If a dog does get into the deer-meat, his 'tail is cut off, or his ear cropped'.[11] The same practice, without the religious content, is reported in a nineteenth-century text about Scotland. The challenge for the highlanders 'was how a cream-stealing cat was to be turned from its evil ways without actually killing him, or so maiming him as to render him worthless in his legitimate feline pursuits'.[12] The solution deployed to cure cats of cream stealing was cutting off their left ears. A picture taken in 1901 of the Moqui (Hopi) Indians shows a donkey with his ears removed. The accompanying text explains that when a donkey eats some corn that is not meant for him, he is punished with ear cropping. In what is described as a proto-trial, the donkey 'is brought before the heads of the pueblo, formally tried, convicted … and condemned'. As punishment the donkey's ear is cropped, 'serving the double purpose of punishment and of a brand'.[13] This dual logic of the ear crop—'punishment and brand'/retrospective and prospective—was formalised and applied broadly to humans convicted of minor infractions in England during the medieval period.

In thirteenth-century London human ears were cut off for petty theft. A judicial finding that the theft was minor led to four possible responses: 'dismissal, finding pledges for good behaviour, internal exile or ear cropping'.[14] As concrete examples, three persons individually convicted of stealing—one took a cloak of 'little value', one 'two caps', and another stole a 'canvas and other small things'—all 'lost an ear'.[15] Ears were also cut off as punishment for vagrancy and begging. In 1538, during Henry VIII's reign (a time of agrarian revolts directed against enclosures), an 'act for punishment of sturdy vagabonds and beggars' was proclaimed.[16] The vagrancy laws were amended to extract labour from the unemployed masses. A penalty system was established in which first-time violators were whipped, second-time violators had an ear cropped, and third-time violators were hanged.[17] The place of ear cutting in Henry VIII's escalating punishment sequence is worth reflecting on.

First, these vagrancy laws are used to make more fine-grained distinctions between persons (first-, second-, and third-time offenders) than the code of Hammurabi (slave who strikes or insults a master). Second, the persons targeted with this punishment are obviously impecunious, like the slave in the code of Hammurabi. In crass terms, as homeless people, they are judgment-proof against both fines and imprisonment. How does the sovereign efficiently discipline and punish a person who has nothing? As we will see further below, this is a persistent problem that also animates the logic of ear cropping of slaves. Third, the cut ear here acts both as a warning to the vagrant and as a means of identifying vagrants who should be hung the next time they are caught. The cut ear stores and displays the information that a person is a vagrant recidivist currently between their first and third punishment.

Over on the European mainland, the *Carolina* of 1532—Emperor Charles V's criminal code—also prescribed ear cutting for lesser offences, such as 'assisted infidelity'—i.e. trafficking in prostitution. The punishment sequence is described as, 'Publicly placed in the pillory, both ears cut off, and exiled from the land until granted permission to return.'[18] Here the act of ear cutting is explicitly a highly public affair: binding, torturing, and mutilating the accused in the heart of the community. The physical pain of having an ear cut off is only one component of a communal ritual inflicting the psychological pain of humiliation and shame, culminating in exclusion. Engels' account of the German Peasant's War (1524–5), written in 1850, places special emphasis on the barbarity and ubiquity of cutting off the ears of peasants. 'None of the chapters of the *Carolina* which speaks of "cutting of ears", [etc.] … was left unpractised by the lord.'[19] 'A host of prisoners were executed … the rest were sent home with cut off noses and ears.'[20] Like the English vagrant recidivist, the cut ear serves as a *Schandmal* ('mark of shame') signalling that this subject is to be, or has been, set apart from the community and thereby permanently damages their reputation. To this day, to refer to somebody as a *Schlitzohr* ('slit ear') in Germany is to imply that they are untrustworthy.

It is noteworthy that for the famous English jurist of the eighteenth century, Sir William Blackstone, cutting off an ear was treated as a lesser offence than cutting off a finger and did not rise to the level of a felony. Unlike removing a finger, an eye, or a 'foretooth', 'cutting off his ear, nose, or the like, are not held to be mayhems at common law'.[21] Blackstone's reasoning was that depriving humans and 'animals' of finger, eye or foretooth 'abates their courage' and weakened them while severing an ear only 'disfigured him'.[22] Blackstone's material distinction between mutilations of the ear and other body parts is alien and counter-intuitive to us, but helps to appreciate the intellectual history of this practice. Cutting off an ear was a crime, but was not understood to significantly harm the individual. The empirical question of how often these 'mere' disfigurements were actually committed by courts and whether such punishments 'worked' is a thorny issue that cannot be acceptably resolved in this book. 'How many had their ears cropped … no historian has told us.'[23] In England, the repeated revision of Henry VIII's vagrancy laws in subsequent reigns indicates that these harsh systems did not satisfactorily solve the problem they were addressing. Moreover, a hard look at the digitised proceedings of the Old Bailey (London's Central

Criminal Court) from 1674–1913 reveals, surprisingly, no single instance of ear cropping[24]—showing that, whatever the legal form said, the practice of ear cropping of criminals had disappeared from use in London by the late seventeenth century.[25] A handbook of German law published in 1762 also states that ear cutting had 'almost entirely' fallen out of use as a punishment.[26]

By all accounts, this was not the case in pre-colonial Ashanti society or colonial America. First, the Ashanti. According to Rattray's descriptions—a colonial British anthropologist writing in 1929—the intentionally cut ear (*Aso twa*) fulfilled a similar function in Ashanti society as many of the examples listed above. It was meted out as a punishment for lesser offences. A person with a cut ear had their status changed to become a different kind of, subaltern, subject. Right ears were cut to ensure that nobody could hide their mutilated ear behind the bundled *kente* cloth Ashanti traditionally wear on their left shoulder—demonstrating that the permanent legibility produced by the cut ear was a primary purpose of the practice, with real consequences for social mobility. The cut ear was designed as a means of social discrimination, as a tool to identify and sort Ashanti. Ear cutting required authorisation from the very highest level. It was possible for an uncle, when given permission by the King of the Ashanti, to cut a piece of the ear of an unruly nephew.[27] This practice of ear cropping as punishment for a lesser offence was also used in the new world.

Ear cropping is first found in seventeenth century Massachusetts law as penalty for theft committed 'on the Lord's day'.[28] During deliberations on the Eighth Amendment of the U.S. Constitution (that is the one prohibiting 'cruel and unusual punishment') in the first Congress, Samuel Livermore, the Senator from New Hampshire, voiced his concern about how the proposed text could come to delimit the range of necessary punishments. Cutting off the ear was seen as a vital tool of government for Livermore:

> No cruel and unusual punishment is to be inflicted; it is sometimes necessary to hang a man, villains often deserve whipping, and perhaps having their ears cut off; but are we in the future to be prevented from inflicting these punishments because they are cruel?[29]

Despite this defence the punishment does not seem to have been very frequent in this period. A prominent legal historian informs us that '[d]ozens [not hundreds or thousands] of detached ears ... litter the record books'.[30] With time, ear cropping of common criminals fell out of use and is now primarily associated with the colonial era. In a return to the law of the Hammurabi Code, however, ear cropping was used freely to punish slaves in the early American Republic up until the abolition of slavery in the mid-nineteenth century. The ear cropping of slaves as punishment in North America bleeds over into agricultural practices of ear cropping as a symbol of property and ownership.

Ear Cutting to Identify Property

Ears have been cut and marked to designate property in two different ways: (i) to classify an entity as property, and (ii) to identify the owner of the property. In the book of Exodus (ca. 500 BC), taking on a slave for life required the owner to 'take him to the door or the doorpost and pierce his ear with an awl'.[31] This ear marking fell into the first category. The person with the pierced ear was now a slave, permanently. In North America this type of ear marking existed up until the nineteenth century. Often ear cuts were exacted on slaves for minor transgressions or no transgression at all. A New York abolitionist publication from 1839 explains that an 'inhuman method of marking slaves, so that they may be easily described and detected when they escape, is called cropping'. Descriptions of these slaves describe them as 'cropt', 'notch cut in the ear', or 'part or the whole of the ear cut off'.[32]

This practice of ear cutting led to perverse forms of litigation, contractual disputes over who carried the costs if a slave—after his sale but before his delivery—had his ears cropped:

> [T]he negro before the sale had committed a burglary, for which he was afterwards tried, convicted, and punished; by reason of which punishment, his ears being cropped, his value was greatly impaired. The fact of the commission of the offence was unknown to both parties at the time of the sale. ... [T]he jury found a verdict for the plaintiff, for the whole amount of the note.[33]

Note here that the cropped ear reduces the value of the slave, but also reproduces their status as a slave. This identification is more significant than the physical punishment itself—being permanently classified as a slave is of more weight than having one's ear cut off. The social meaning ascribed to the cut ear is the truly devastating punishment. Ear mutilations were also used to more closely document the individual identity of a slave, and thereby the identity of their owner. For instance, one advertisement in *The New Orleans Bee* published on 27 August 1837, read: 'Fifty dollars reward, for the negro Jim Blake—has a piece cut out of each ear.'[34] In this way, the ear crop functioned as a means of classifying the slave, as a slave, and of assisting in their individual identification as 'Jim Blake' slave of X (the advertisement does not say who the owner was). This secondary dual function of ear cropping practices—not just punishment and brand, but classification and identification—crosses the species barrier.

There is an interesting history to cutting sheep, pig and cow ears to signify their property status and the identity of their owners. How were animals to be kept apart with poor fences, prior to the invention of barbed wire?[35] Their ears were cropped in unique ways. A sizable vocabulary was developed to describe the different symbols created through ear cutting. Crop, smooth crop, split, notch, nick, underslope, overbit, underseven, half-penny, swallow-tail, swallow fork, round under, upper slope, sharpened to a point, and hole punched all referred to particular cuts of the ear. Descriptions were made more specific by organising cuts into four quadrants on two axes—left ear, right ear, upper ear and lower ear. Ear-mark descriptions were then registered, like patents, and granted to individuals.[36] In New England, town records from the late eighteenth and early nineteenth century stored this information. 'Edmond Hinckley—a half penny upper side the right Ear.'[37] 'James Comstock … crop of left ear, slit in right.'[38] 'Joseph Chandler … Swallow's tail in the top of the near Ear and a half penny under the Side of the Same Ear.'[39]

The property status of domestic livestock could thereby be fixed along with the identity of the possessor. Animals that had strayed from their enclosures could readily be identified and returned to their rightful owner. The ear crop acted as a signature classifying the animal and identifying the owner. One prominent shortcoming is immediately apparent: this identification system does not lend itself well to a change of ownership, to the sale and purchase of livestock. For domestic animals to become proper fungible commodities they need to be disassociated from the signs and realities of permanent ownership, or the signs of ownership must be edited. To mark animals for the market it makes more sense to classify them as belonging to a herd, than to an individual. Consider these illustrative descriptions of steers sold in the late nineteenth century, as an example. '95 head of steers, one year old this spring, marked as follows: Right ear cropped, and notch cut out of the under side of the left.'[40] 'Fourteen steers one year old, crop off left ear, and slit in same ear; four heifers one year old, marked on ear as above steers.'[41] Here the ear crop is not tied to an individual owner in perpetuity, but rather serves to better identify a transferable commodity.

A second problem—only visible when considering historic case law on the ears of domestic animals—is that this cropped ear order is a poor defence against theft. As should be apparent by now, ears can easily be removed and cut. There is a whole line of cases about the mutilation of domestic animals' ears committed with the alleged intent to obscure the identity of their original owner.[42] Ears and heads would be chopped off to prevent identification through ear crop. With the ear serving as a prominent site of identity, descriptions of stolen animals read similar to the descriptions of runaway slaves. 'A white-face Hereford bull weighing about 750 pounds, marked overbit and underbit and crop in left ear, and marked split and underbit in right ear.'[43] The kind of cropping of the ears of domestic animals described in this section primarily serves to identify the animal's relationship to its owner.

Today, one cannot wilfully pierce the ears of pet cats,[44] the cutting of the ears of sheep is controlled,[45] one definitely cannot disfigure a horse's ear,[46] and cropping a dog's ears without anaesthetic qualifies as cruelty against animals.[47] There is an international movement to ban the cropping of dogs' ears underway. In other words, cutting of animals' ears for punishment, torture, and aesthetic reasons is no longer permissible or is becoming increasingly impermissible. This tracks with the history of the cutting of human ears. Cutting animal ears for the purpose of classification and identification, however, is still permitted. The next section considers the ear as a site of individual identification for domestic animals and humans.

The Ear as a Site of Individual Identification

How much can we really tell by an ear? Different systems of knowledge—Chinese face reading, phrenology, etc.—have all responded to the biological fact that the human ear is an intricate and unique structure, which remains remarkably stable over a person's lifetime. Human ears are like fingerprints, entirely individual, even across identical twins. '[I]t is impossible to discover two ears alike.'[48] This individuality permits the ear itself to act as a means of identification, requiring no marking or cutting to classify the person. This natural individuality of the ear has to be translated into a reliable system with standardised notation to be

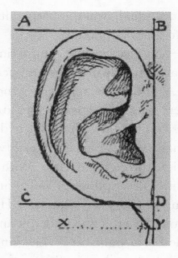

Take the stem of the instrument in the left hand, place it horizontally about half a centimeter above the upper edge of the ear, so that the narrow fixed branch is turned downwards and rests in front of the tragus, against the cartilaginous part of the auditory conduit, parallel with the line of junction of the ear with the cheek.

Figure 1: Bertillon's Instructions for Measuring the Ear

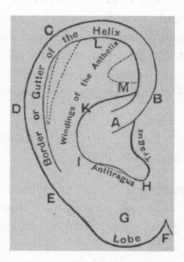

The measurer, holding the instrument horizontally with his left hand, rests the extremity against the subject's tragus, the projection turned away from the auditory conduit, and with it draws the rod along until it just touches cartilaginous band D E K I, without depressing it in any way.

Figure 2: Bertillon's Detailed Analysis of the Parts of the Ear

made useful. And just like with fingerprints, the unique structure of the ear is also what makes it difficult to create a universal and useful classification system.

Enter the nineteenth-century biometric practice of *Bertillonage*, designed to identify recidivists. Just like in Henry VIII's system and the *Carolina*, the ear holds a privileged position in Alphonse Bertillon's system to identify the recidivist—'no organ is superior to it for assuring recognition of a subject after an interval of many years'.[49] For Bertillon the ear served as a linchpin of an individual's identity. The pattern of the ear is a 'necessary and sufficient condition for the confirmation of the individual identity'.[50] In Bertillon's system a complex set of dimensions is captured and precision dictates each and every measurement (Figures 1 and 2). The handbook, *Signaletic Instructions*, exhorts, in its section on ear measurement, in bold: 'At 3 millimetres the mistake becomes inexcusable.'[51] Alphonse Bertillon had a vision of the precise ear measurement of all humans being stored in national 'signaletic' offices designed for this purpose:

> [I]n order for society to reap its full benefit, every human being should be partially signalized (especially by that part of the descriptive signalment relating to the ear) at about the age of ten years, and completely so at the age of maturity; and every country should have a national signaletic office where all the signalments of its inhabitants should be filed.[52]

The breakthrough necessary to making ears useful as sites of individual identification is a splitting of the population into smaller sub-categories for the purpose of minimising the comparisons to be made. The twentieth-century discipline of *Earology*[53]—that is the real name—seeks to achieve this by first classifying all ears into four types and then categorising them into smaller groupings, and so on.

Contemporary animal husbandry, like every professional field in modernity, is a highly data-intensive vocation. To produce the best livestock detailed records have to be kept of domestic animals. Which pigs have been vaccinated, which were sick recently, what was the average weight of the pigs of that litter, and so on, are organising questions for these kinds of data-production. 'In order to keep such records, producers must be able to identify pigs from birth.'[54] It may well be that the ears of pigs, cows and sheep are as unique as human ears. For now, however, a far cheaper method has been developed to individually identify pigs (Figure 3). The ears are notched to create two different numbers. The right ear is notched to create a litter number and the left ear is notched to create a number to represent the individual pig. This way, the pig-farmer can count the notches on a pig's ears to know, track, and record its individual identity.

The left ear is used for notches to show an individual pig's number in the litter. Each pig will have different notches in the left ear. The left ear is divided into three sections, with values of 1, 3, and 9. To develop a number, make notches in different parts of the ear in such a way that their numerical values will add up to the desired number.

The ear, here, has become a resource for something very different from its early history. It is no longer a canvas on which political authority draws lines of punishment and property but is rather a means to create a stable identification regime for sites of power. What is lost in this shift? For one, having human ears measured instead of cut takes some shame and humiliation out of the equation. Secondly, this shift to ear surveillance represents an internalisation of the signs of legibility. Here the cut ear no longer acts as a sumptuary law, resulting in a highly visible order for the entire community, whether it is an English or an Ashanti town. Instead, the ear is only decipherable to those with the technology to read it and the records to compare it to. There are few actors with these kinds of resources, thereby leading to a radical inequality of ear legibility.

The Technological Future of the Ear

What is the future of the ear? It is poised to be both, (i) a site at which people continue to express their individual identity through innovative body-modification and piercing, and (ii) a site of increasing individual identification by automated systems. In 2004 the European Commission funded the multi-year Forensic Ear Identification (FearID)—also the real

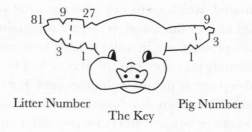

Litter Number   Pig Number
The Key

Figure 3: Ear Notching for Pig Identification

32

name—research project to contribute to an automatic identification of ears. The newest forms of ear measurement take place at a distance, and are no longer prone to Bertillon's operators taking faulty physical measurements or imprints[55] or earologists making visual comparisons. In the language of the engineers, '[i]ncreasingly stringent security requirements call for more robust, convenient, user-friendly personal identification systems.' 'Acquiring the biometric data at a distance … make[s] the ear biometric an appealing candidate for video surveillance and non-contact biometric recognition.'[56] Through the help of video surveillance and algorithmic mapping—digital power—Bertillon's vision of the national storage and retention of a population's ears is becoming feasible.

In this approach, each subject's ear is modeled as an adjacency graph built from the curve segments in a Voronoi diagram, which is extracted by edge detection as shown. An Error Correcting Graph Matching algorithm is then used for authentication, which takes into account the erroneous curve segments which can occur due to changes in the ear image.

Bertillon described one of the 'transcendent merits of the ear for purposes of identification' that one can swear in a court that comparing a photograph 'is well and duly applicable to such and such a subject here present'.[57] Criminal courts have begun to respond to this idea that the ear is, like a fingerprint, a valid form of identification and evidence. In 1999 in the United States, in *State v. Kunze*, the Washington Court of Appeals

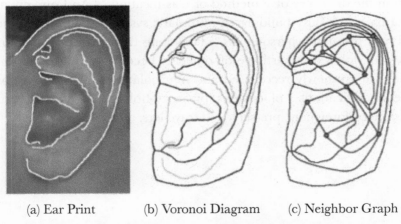

| (a) Ear Print | (b) Voronoi Diagram | (c) Neighbor Graph |

Figure 4: Stages in Building the Ear Biometrics Model

reversed a defendant's conviction that had been based on latent earprints discovered at the scene of the crime. The court held that 'latent earprint identification is not generally accepted in the forensic science community.'[58] Thirteen years later, however, in *People v. Lawson*, the Michigan Court of Appeals upheld a conviction for felony murder, which was based, in part, on a forensic expert examining and comparing features of the ear taken from surveillance footage with the defendant's ear. As the prosecutor said at trial—'That's his ear ladies and gentlemen.'[59]

Consider the journey of the ear. The history of changing identification practices related to the ear illustrates that sorting is an expression of power that helps to make sovereign power reasonable, ritualised, and predictable. But at the same time, the identifying practice must also fulfil applied functions and requirements for political authority. The ear has been a great resource for these practical requirements. From public punishment and coarse categorisation for slaves, criminals, vagrants—to identifying the individual owner of domestic livestock—to now identifying the individual attached to the ear—the ear has been a site of information, power, and individualisation. It has cycled through ritual, archival, and digital systems. The history of the ear is a record of punishment, property, and individuality; as such it is a record of changing concerns of power and of the evolution of an identification and sorting regime. What comes next after this personalising trajectory? To be useful for centralised power, these must always be a form of re-categorisation. As Bertillon already stressed, 'the problem of judicial identification consists less in the search for new characteristic elements of individuality than in the discovery of a method of classification.'[60] And sure enough, researchers are busy building an automatic system to identify ethnicity and race through a person's iris.[61] How long then until the curvatures, crevasses, lobes and cartilage of our ears become the means through which we are newly recognised and interpolated into social groups— state simplifications—of citizens, property-holders, ethnics, criminals, consumers, foreigners, pre-screened travellers, and security risks?

4

TECHNICS AND TOWERS

Can we theorise that through which the sovereign identifies and sorts populations? To do so, I propose we take on the concept of technics of politics as well as three distinct architectural designs: the obelisk or pillory, the panopticon, and a manual registry.

TECHNICS OF POLITICS

Technics is the modern English equivalent of the ancient Greek term τέχνη (*tekhne*); it makes 'no distinction between industrial production and "fine" or symbolic art'.[1] At the same time *tekhne*, as technical knowledge, is pitched against and contrasted to the more philosophical *episteme*,[2] ethical *phronesis*,[3] and practical *metis*.[4] In the *Nicomachean Ethics*, Aristotle provides the following description:

> Every art [*tekhne*] is concerned with bringing something into being, and looks for technical and theoretical means of producing a thing which belongs to the category of possibility and the cause of which lies in the producer and not in what is produced. ... *Tekhne* operate[s] in the sphere of the variable.[5]

At its most basic, a technics of politics makes a population legible to a central authority, and thereby helps to regulate and order it. To do this the technics of politics must identify and sort individuals. This is as fundamental to state politics as a profit-seeking logic is to capitalism. What I take from its classic etymology is that technics is a term that combines ideational and material factors—practices along with built artefacts. The construct enables one to treat the phenomena of technical artefacts and practices or techniques as belonging to the same order, all the while emphasising the variable and political nature of their application. I differentiate technics from the far broader term technology, which can refer to all human application and knowledge of tools.[6]

The wider definition of technics of politics, which I propose, is that of an underdetermined means disembodied from its originary inventor and context that exerts influence over entities through the use of abstraction and procedural repetition that shrouds sovereign power. Technics always entails a technological artefact and a technique;[7] together they constitute assemblages of social control, legibility, and domination. Technics are concerned with identifying individuals, retaining information, and regulating the circulation of goods and individuals. For a technics of politics to function it requires an effective training mechanism through which it is disseminated and reproduced as well as a class of operators—such as priests, land surveyors, statisticians or database managers—who are motivated by an ideology—be it animist religion, Marxism-Leninism, National Socialism, Modernisation, or even anti-hierarchical principles. Technics can exist as both means and ideology, in the same way that a religious ritual is both the reason and plan for a course of action.

In that sense technics is a revelation of underlying power structures, in a similar manner in which language is not merely a means to the 'end' of communication, but also a system of knowledge. We can say that technics of politics is a grammar of power which establishes the parameters of dominance and resistance, private and public, positive and negative liberty. Technics of politics usually arrange and taxonomise individual identities for different purposes. These power structures and practices of social control and domination (ranging from micro to macro) are, in turn, not widely recognised or analysed because they are legitimated by a technical or theological rationality that is constructed as above and beyond politics or political interests.

According to Niklas Luhmann technics can be understood as 'functional simplifications',[8] which are marked by a reduction of complexity. James Scott has also written about such practices in *Seeing Like a State* (1998):

> State simplifications ... represent techniques for grasping a large and complex reality; in order for officials to be able to comprehend aspects of the ensemble, that complex reality must be reduced to schematic categories. The only way to accomplish this is to reduce an infinite array of detail to a set of categories that will facilitate summary descriptions, comparisons, and aggregation.[9]

Keeping North–South relations in mind, and situating all of our preliminary conceptual work in a global context, it is worth noting that Bernard Cohn's main argument on the knowledge practices of the British in colonial India is very similar to Scott's point here. Cohn notably concludes that the British 'reduced vastly complex codes and their associated meanings to a few metonyms'.[10] In both cases sovereign power necessarily reduces complex realities into schematic formulaic knowledges to facilitate the rule of peoples and territory. In both cases the state simplifications—whether they are surnames or caste characteristics—are animated by being operationalised and repeated. They combine to constitute whole technics of politics. As we can see here, the practice of abstraction and simplification is required to make societies 'legible' and prepare them for benevolent governance, domination, or exploitation.

The upshot of this, and a permanent source of tension, is that for state simplifications to work and be applicable they have to be constructed and are therefore 'false' in one way or another. Focusing on one form of this kind of simplification, the map, Mark Monmonier has argued that '[n]ot only is it easy to lie with maps, it's essential.' This is an important point. He goes on to explain that for a map to 'portray meaningful relationships for a complex, three-dimensional world on a flat sheet of paper or a video screen, a map must distort reality'.[11] In this way, for a state simplification to be effective, it must be exaggerated at some points and cannot be too exact. It must also feature disambiguation protocols to deal with complexity. Disambiguation protocols are rules of thumb to help operators classify confusing data they encounter into available categories. Once state simplifications and schematic categories are constructed, disambiguation protocols become necessary to place ambiguous cases into these schematic categories. Such protocols do the hard work of categorising reality.

Scott goes on to claim that the extent and depth of a state's intervention is dependent on the quality of its legibility:

> Legibility is a condition of manipulation. Any substantial state intervention in society … requires the invention of units that are visible. The units in question might be citizens, villages, trees, fields, houses or people grouped according to age, depending on the type of intervention. Whatever the units being manipulated, they must be organized in a manner that permits them to be identified, observed, recorded, counted, aggregated, and monitored. The degree of knowledge required would have to be roughly commensurate with the depth of the intervention. In other words, one might say that the greater the manipulation envisaged, the greater the legibility required to effect it.[12]

37

A tendency of placing primary analytic focus on technology and technique, or technics, is that it may appear as if periods and peoples without modern technological artefacts have less politics. This is problematic, both as a statement of fact and as a political orientation. An added theoretical difficulty of placing emphasis on technics is that these kinds of artefacts change quite radically over time. Ptolemaic maps are invented at one point or another, as are statistics, as are passports, as are complex data-mining algorithms. To deal with these issues the technics of politics needs to have three properties: (1) a deep historical ontology that extends past a present technical configuration (which may also include ritual and other means of governance); (2) a subdivision which can organise different technical configurations and add further insight to each of them; and (3) an account of why change occurs. A small excursion into Carl Schmitt's writings helps provide a rough framework to meet these requirements.

Periodisation and the Drive to Technification

Carl Schmitt (1888–1985) provides an intellectual clearing for the technics of politics when he writes of the rise of a 'religion of the technical miracle, human accomplishment and domination of nature' and claims that 'magical religiosity goes over into a just as magical technicity'.[13] While much has been published about Schmitt's relationship to Nazism[14] and post-war Germany,[15] his ideas concerning the concept of the political, sovereignty and the state of exception[16] in political theory and international relations,[17] relatively little attention has been paid to his conception of technics.[18] In what follows, I present Schmitt's most important idea about technics from his lecture, 'Das Zeitalter der Neutralisierung und Entpolitisierung' (1929) and his text *Leviathan* (1938).

His first move in the quote above is that aspects of religiosity can be found in technicity; implying that more is at work in technology than just the practical purposes for which it is deployed. According to Schmitt, periods of history are dominated by central organising concepts that define the way everything else is seen. He lists the succession as moving from the 'theological, to the metaphysical and moral, to the economic'. For instance, in our current period of economic and technical thought, progress is naturally understood as economic or technical in nature—such as judging the development of countries by their internet connections—while in the humanistic-moralistic belief of the eighteenth century progress was regarded as one of moralistic enlightenment. With every preceding period having a different kind of intellectual class (cleric, enlightenment philosopher, economist), Schmitt believes that an intellectual class is no longer possible for the technical age.[19] Today's class of wealthy digerati would appear to contradict this prediction.

What is important to note for this simple succession of periods is that it 'simultaneously meant that there was a progressive neutralisation of the areas from which the centre [theology, metaphysics, etc.] was moved'.[20] Schmitt's point here is that a 'centre' such as theology is left/moved on from because it is politicised, becomes a point of conflict, and a newer, more neutral, territory, such as metaphysics, is constructed, until it too must be superseded by moving on the 'centre' which is abandoned, marginalised and thus neutralised. In this sense one can read a tendency to neutralisation and depoliticisation within European history. 'Hence since the seventeenth century a neutralisation process has taken place', Schmitt repeats in his *Leviathan*, 'which with internal consistency ends in the general technicisation'.[21] While 'it belongs to the laws of dialectic' that on every new field assumed to be neutral a new battleground is created, he points out that there is a 'widespread belief that one has found the absolute and final neutral ground in technics'.[22] Schmitt agrees that the technical appears to be neutral, but he adds the crucial element that the 'neutrality of technics is different from the neutrality of all preceding areas'.[23] This is because while technical progress can be put to use in the name of any preceding belief system, it does not inherently entail moral, or any other kind of, progress. It is like the 'ship of state' being used to legitimate a huge range of different political forms.

Schmitt's argument provides a conceptual apparatus for our understanding of different modes of technics. In this configuration the repeated politicisation of realms that appeared to be neutral are drivers of change in technics of politics. This provides an account for the observed politicisation and depoliticisation of particular domains of life such as the ritual, the archive, and the database. In each instance, a new, more authoritative, field of political arbitration is sought until it too becomes politicised and subject to conflict.

The tendency for depoliticisation can also be connected to a propensity for technification at a deeper lever. Niklas Luhmann does precisely this when he writes that 'technical arrangements' appear to be preferred in 'societal evolution' because they 'spare the need for consensus' as well as the 'always difficult and conflict prone coordination of human action'.[24] One of the implications of this technification is that political arguments increasingly need to be made in neutral depoliticised terms on technical matters. Indeed, for Jürgen Habermas our contemporary age is characteristically marked by 'manifest authoritative domination being replaced by the manipulative forces of a technical operational administration'.[25] Furthermore, it is precisely 'the role of technics and science [that] can explain and legitimate', according to Habermas, 'why in modern societies a democratic decision-making process loses its function over practical questions and is replaced by plebiscites about alternative administrative personnel'.[26]

Despite differences and depoliticisations all modes of technics necessarily focus on making populations—domestic and foreign—legible through identification and sorting for taxation (or tribute), representation, and conscription. This is a central problem of human political organisation, which is so constant that we can grasp the bureaucratic state as machinery constructed for dealing with it. For Schmitt, in a similar vein, the 'State' is treated as the 'first product of the technical age'.[27] If this first product of the technical age fails to find an adequate solution to the problem of legibility, identification, and sorting, it breaks, disappears, or is appropriated. Both history and a survey of the contemporary political field are littered by failures and examples of peoples 'who *don't demonstrate this technical competency becoming protectorates*'.[28]

The state drive for legibility and order manifests as various tools in different periods for the documentation of individual identity, assessments of material wealth and productive processes, means for hierarchising society, as well as the establishment of who is inside and outside of society. These technics are astoundingly standardised in the contemporary international system, pointing to a powerful historical homogenisation. This could also be called the globalisation of technics of politics and can be organised into waves and different modes: ritual mode, archival mode, and digital mode. The underlying logic of these tools in turn— whether ritual, archival, or digital—come to dominate as central organising concepts for political progress. In this way practical tools and techniques, technics, are joined up with whole periods and systems of sovereign power. Instead of disciplining and surveillance, which has received plenty of academic attention,[29] I especially emphasise identifying and sorting as fundamental practices of sovereign power.

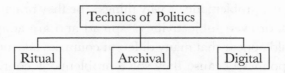

Figure 5: Modes of Technics

The three different modes of technics introduced here do not come to replace each other in a neat chronology; instead every mode includes aspects of that which has preceded it, and all belong to the same genus of the technics of politics. To fully analyse the currently prevalent digital mode of the technics of politics, it is useful to read it next to peculiarities of previous forms of political ritual and archival administration. It is important to note that different 'technics of politics' function more as 'ideal types', heuristic devices, and analytic categories than as statements or measurements of empirical fact. Like all ideal typical analysis I underline and emphasise my object of analysis.

This sub-categorisation and clustering still lends itself to a rough periodisation, since each mode provides different strategies for some of the same problematics of human governance: centralisation, circulation, and collective action. The shared problem of how to maintain, understand, and control a population unifies all of the disparate historical examples and modes of technics—what differentiates them is that they each exhibit different strategies for the storage, retention, control and communication of information to achieve this end. In the following section I sketch out particularities of the ritual mode and provide examples of its function for communities such as the Inca and Aztec empires.

Why the Technics of Politics Spread

One of the most fundamental questions concerning the technics of politics in international relations is why and how a technical standard may spread. Why do governments undertake the same techniques of wall construction for the purposes of border control?[30] Why do states institute similar, or even identical, means of passport control? Technics of politics seem to share the universalising tendencies of the Western legal tradition and Christianity. It is possible to work through a variety of academic disciplines to generate a number of answers and developed explanations that speak to the problematic of why things—be they practices, artefacts, commodities, or even subjectivities—spread and are adapted. At first glance it would appear that many different countries take on a particular technics of politics because they solve problems of coordination and depoliticise processes, thereby sparing the need for consensus. But once looked at more closely a whole host of other explanations come into focus—explanations that help to make sense of our highly homogenised state of affairs. Read together these accounts provide a powerful interpretation of the dynamics of standardisation.

Let us begin with Foucault, who describes a migration and standardisation of the technics of politics:

> While, on the one hand, the disciplinary establishments increase, their mechanisms have a certain tendency to become 'de-institutionalized', to emerge from the closed fortresses in which they once functioned and to circulate in a 'free' state; the massive, compact disciplines are broken down into flexible methods of control, which may be transferred and adapted.[31]

A supplementary account of why this 'de-institutionalisation' and 'circulation' occurs can be found in writings that are seldom quoted with Foucault, Schumpeter's work on economic change:

> [A]s soon as the various kinds of social resistance to something that is fundamentally new and untried have been overcome; it is much easier not only to do the same thing again but also to do similar things in different directions, so that a first success will always produce a cluster.[32]

A number of deeply political processes are taking place here: mechanisms are de-institutionalised and resistance to them has been overcome. A different response to why the technics spread, one which a functionalist political scientist might offer, would be that identical internal pressures are leading to 'institutional diffusion' which in turn is manifesting this world of similarity, meaning that governments share the same problems (illegal migration, illegible population, terrorism) and simply find the best solution to them.[33] There is no intellectual patent regime that applies to disciplinary apparatuses or the technics of politics as a whole, although individual technologies are of course protected.

But this account, in which the technics are just a tool rationally applied, does not mesh well with mystical rituals fulfilling the same stabilising functions. A promising idea can be found in some anthropological and historical writings on Southeast Asia, where one encounters the interesting notion of 'self-Hinduisation', which refers to early 'court centers in Cambodia and Java' using 'the ritual technology afforded them by Indian merchants'.[34] Here, one reading of why the Hindu religion was appropriated is because it was observed to be part of an effective technology of rule. Leaning on the notion of self-Hinduisation one could argue that it is because particular technics—such as border practices and ID cards for individuals—are practised by some of the most powerful actors in the world today that they are imbued with authority and emulated, past the point of functional necessity. More to the point, it is precisely because powerful actors use these technics that they symbolise authority and thereby function. If the most powerful actors were using technics more anchored in the ritual or archival mode, these too would be adopted and spread. This idea meshes well with the sociological notion of 'anticipatory socialisation', referring to behaviour by an individual that mimics the behaviour of a group it wants to join, be they the Davos elite, marine corps soldiers, humanities professors, or state managers.[35]

Finally we must also consider the imagined and experienced reality of external pressures and benefits. The thickening of international law and norms that place particular requirements on states—such as the registration of citizenry, establishment of stable property ownership systems, and holding of elections—help to mainstream specific technological solutions to these problems. Along with such formal requirements there is the more blurry force of what economists call 'positive externalities', which means that benefits can be accrued through the actions of others.

An example of a positive externality in the technics of politics could be large and powerful states doing the painstaking and expensive labour of reliably documenting the identity of each individual citizen and creating a requirement for all of them to carry IDs, followed by a smaller state merely having to construct an apparatus to read this information. This kind of positive externality would also feature a tendency to standardisation. Or, a further example, if powerful states invest a large amount of time and resources into establishing safe and efficient mechanisms of information retention and communication, then a smaller state only needs to copy or purchase the established system. Once set up as efficient, legitimate, and authoritative, technics of politics can be de-territorialised and applied by any number of countries. Gradually what was a condition of free choice can be transformed into one of impersonal domination.

Many of the ideas of the different disciplines discussed so far are characterised by what could be called a simple form of feedback; the more people use the standard, the more powerful and widespread it becomes, therefore leading to more people using it, etc. Ideas of feedback and self-regulation are expressed in many different fields with a variety of terms: the invisible hand, the balance of power, supply and demand, checks and balances, self-regulation, and so on. Cybernetics as a subject was specifically established to research regulative systems and such types of feedback in both nature and technical arrays. Recalling the mythical power of the ship, it is interesting to note that Norbert Wiener, the founding figure of cybernetics, drew particular inspiration from it.

> ... we have been forced to coin at least one artificial neo-Greek expression to fill the gap. We have decided to call the entire field of control and communication theory, whether in the machine or in the animal, by the name *Cybernetics*, which we form from the Greek χυβερνήτης or steersman. ... We also wish to refer to the fact that the steering engines of a ship are indeed one of the earliest and best-developed forms of feedback mechanisms.[36]

The cybernetic contribution to thinking through the dynamics of the spread of the technics of politics is that their adaptation can be thought of in terms of 'black boxes' and understood as a circular process, in which an earlier input changes the position and calls for a different input. In both nature and technical systems there are forms of feedback which function, as well as others that do not and break down—such as feedback on a stereo or a 'purpose tremor'.[37] From a cybernetic view, one could see the appropriation of standardised technics of politics by different states as a circular adaptive process, a feedback loop that a polity uses to regulate its symbols and practices of authority and control, one that is coupled to the scripts and technologies of more powerful actors.[38]

In the case of a weak government appropriating, mimicking, or emulating the technics of politics of more powerful states a fascinating dynamic can be observed. The weaker a government is the more dependent it is on the technical apparatus and techniques of a powerful country, and the more it will be forced to create a compatible technics of politics. At the same time, as has become apparent in the Arab revolts of 2011, the less digital power a government has the more it can be impacted by citizens organising themselves with new social media; weak governments cannot afford to make their own 'great firewall'. This particular combination of dependence and vulnerability leads to a recapitulation of the innovation of new technics in the periphery; just like the census initially was, novel practices of censorship and data managing deployed in the periphery are regarded as illiberal.

This is not the only kind of feedback at work in the spread of technics of politics. Because the digital mode relies so heavily on networked computers, it is worth briefly touching on the economics and dynamics of information technology. The forces and tendencies at work in the contemporary information technology industry are similar to the telegraph, telephone, broadcast radio, and television industries when they were first developed.[39] These industries are characterised by 'high fixed costs and low marginal costs or production, large switching costs for users, and strong network effects'.[40] As with everything that is run for a while, one would expect what economists call 'increasing returns to scale'—which means that the output increases by more than the proportional input of time and capital; this tendency is especially strong with information technology.[41] To this type of feedback we can also add the modern information age's equivalent of Malthus's insight on geometric and arithmetic increases: Moore's Law and Metcalfe's Law. Moore's Law postulates that every two years the size of computer processors is halved; this prediction has proven to be remarkably accurate over time, leading to exponential miniaturisation of processors and computing devices. Metcalfe's Law postulates that a network's strength can be measured as the square of the amount of connections it has.[42] These 'laws' have remained remarkably stable and are actually quite astounding when considered together. They tell us that not only will the material basis of information technology become exponentially physically smaller and more powerful, but that the networking of these information technologies will result in an exponential increase of power. With such a doubly exponential and dynamic increase in computing power at hand the desire for, and belief in the feasibility of, technical fixes to political problems is sure to remain a permanent presence.

OBELISK, PANOPTICON, CUNTZ'S TOWER

Our three modes of the technics of politics coincide with three different architectural designs. The ritual mode is most closely represented by an obelisk or a pillory: a tower in the heart of the community carrying the description of the rules or symbols of the sovereign or a place where the accused can be tied, punished and presented, maybe for an ear-notching. The archival mode is most closely represented by the Panopticon, an architectural design in which each prisoner is filed away and everything is arranged to maximise the legibility for the sovereign eye at the centre. Finally, the digital mode is best represented by a tower to which only the sovereign has access and in which information representing the population is stored.

The Panopticon

One of the most elegant and widespread tropes of a technics of governance is Michel Foucault's (1926–84) discussion of the Panopticon, which is based on a model for a prison that Jeremy Bentham (1748–1832) designed in 1785. The basic idea of the Panopticon is a series of cells organised around a tower in a circular fashion. This placing of the cells in regard to the watchtower produces a situation of constant possible surveillance for the inmates. Below is Bentham's description of the Panopticon:

> The building is circular. The apartments of the prisoners occupy the circumference.... These cells are divided from one another, and the prisoners by that means secluded from all communication with each other, by partitions in the form of radii issuing from the circumference towards the centre and extending as many feet are thought necessary to form the largest dimension of the cell. The apartment of the centre occupies the centre.... Each cell has in the outward circumference a window, large enough not only to light the cell, but, through the cell, to afford light enough to the correspondent part of the lodge. The inner circumference of the cell is formed by an iron grating, so light as not to screen any part of the cell from the inspector's view.... To cut off from each prisoner the view of every other, the partitions are carried on a few feet beyond the grating.[43]

Bentham had great hopes for any institution that would implement this architecture. He expected no less than to see, 'Morals reformed— health preserved—industry invigorated—instruction diffused.'[44] But the history of the Panopticon would prove to be very different. As a construction project it was an utter failure, never having been built the way Bentham had planned and not working when implemented in part. Yet as an intellectual edifice, institutional design, academic idea, and meme the Panopticon has been incredibly successful. A vast amount of books and articles have mentioned it in one form or another. It is necessary to resort to statistics to provide an adequate notion of the frequency of this term. The Panopticon as a concept experienced radical, practically exponential, growth within the academic literature after the publication of Foucault's *Discipline and Punish* in 1975.[45] While it was practically ignored

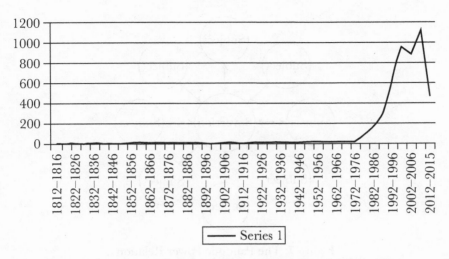

Figure 6: Number of Journal Articles Referencing the Panopticon

before, there are close to fifty articles from 1975–1980 referencing the Panopticon available on JSTOR today. This number rose dramatically until it peaked at about 370 articles from 1995–2000. It has slowly been falling ever since.

This popularity is undoubtedly related to its elegance—the Panopticon represents a very neat blueprint and vision of an institutional order entirely organised around surveillance—but is also a statement on the rising and sinking sociological significance of French thought in the post-war Anglo-American academy.[46]

Foucault's description of this technology of power emphasised the visibility and individualisation of inmates:

> By the effect of backlighting, one can observe from the tower, standing out precisely against the light, the small captive shadows in the cells of the periphery. They are like so many cages, so many small theatres, in which each actor is alone, perfectly individualized and constantly visible. ... Hence the major effect of the Panopticon: to induce in the inmate a state of conscious and permanent visibility that assures the automatic functioning of power.[47]

Whereas for Bentham the level of intervention for the Panopticon was a small and closed community—a prison, hospital, or factory—Foucault's point was not only that the 'panoptic schema spread throughout society' but also that it represented a whole 'new physics of power': 'a society penetrated through and through with disciplinary mechanisms.'[48]

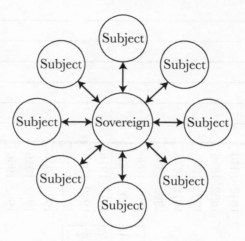

Figure 7: The Panoptic Power Relation

This model of the sovereign gaze surveilling the subject and thereby leading to individualisation and self-discipline is usually accepted as the essence of the Panopticon. Such a reading of the Panopticon has become widely used by social scientists today as a metaphor for excessive control and surveillance in modern society. However the use of this concept appears to have reached a tipping point at the turn of the millennium with an increased number of calls for 'post-panopticism' and thinking beyond the Panopticon.[49] While many suggestions for alternatives have been forms of variation on Foucault/Bentham's theme—such as Metapanopticon, Ban-opticon, Synopticon, Oligopticon—in this book I attempt an entirely different architectural metaphor. However, first there are four, often ignored, aspects worth mentioning in regard to Bentham's writings on the Panopticon and its wider potential as a metaphor for political power in the archival mode.

The first is of particular value in an age of pervasive privatisation: Bentham placed much emphasis on the use of contractors for running the Panopticon:

> The contractor was the key to Bentham's scheme, and in more than the sense that is by now all too obvious. ... The final turn of the screw, the final pitch of perfection, is the discovery that Bentham himself actually intended to be the contractor and the governor of the prison.[50]

The second is that Bentham did consider practices applied to entire populations. He was, for instance, concerned with establishing a stable system of names in England. Yet his suggestion was not for multiple or meta-Panopticons. His solution was far more pragmatic: individuals' names were to be tattooed on their wrists.[51] This needs to be read as a precursor to biometric IDs and a different technology of power, one based around identification and sorting. The third and most important point for the comprehension of the development of these kinds of tools of governance in a world of multiple states and uneven power relations is that the Panopticon has an intimate relationship with the periphery. Like many other innovations in the technics of politics it was first developed there. Jeremy Bentham's panoptic principle was devised and refined by his brother, Samuel Bentham (1757–1831), who spent some time running and experimenting with the organisation of factories in Russia.[52] Not only was the Panopticon designed in the periphery, it would also find most application there.

As Governor of the Bombay Presidency, Montstuart Elphinstone had a number of Panopticons built in the 1820s.[53] This developmental path of the panoptic mode inverts the way technology diffusion is usually thought of, as moving from the core to the periphery, and characterises the history of other tools of governance and innovations of management. It also establishes the widespread use of the most modern forms of biometric data gathering in peripheral zones as a typical trajectory of these kinds of technologies, and not an outlier. Biopolitics are innovated in the colony. The fourth and most crucial aspect in regard to modern information technology is that we can detect the desire for automation in the plans of the Panopticon. The Panopticon functions as a giant machine that distributes the sovereign's gaze equally across the subjects. It can be operated by anybody; it is even foreseeable that nobody operates it. The Panopticon can run smoothly simply through having the inmates assume that the sovereign is in the tower—much like the discovery in *1984* (spoiler alert) that Big Brother is not even real.

While these four factors offer valuable further characteristics to the Panopticon, it is important to emphasise that the prevalent reading of panoptic individualisation, surveillance, and internalisation leave much out about the full extent of power in the archival mode. It is difficult to be in two Panopticons at the same time, but through different forms and representations the archival mode easily produces circumstances in which we can be measured and represented by multiple sovereigns. Furthermore, surveillance in the Panopticon looks like it works; the sovereign really can see the individual subjects. But, as I have sought to stress so far, the categorisations and models of humans produced to make them legible are always, to some extent, false. An over reliance on the metaphor of the ocular-centric Panopticon, up to the point where it saturates the relevant academic discourses, forms a stumbling block to grasping important aspects of the technics of politics.[54] Direct visual surveillance, public identification, and probing questionnaires are no longer strictly necessary in a world of active databases where information can be gleaned from a variety of sources and exchanges. With the archive, state simplifications have moved out of the public space and into the sovereign's machine. As we will see in the subsequent discussion of databases, state simplifications can be far more dynamic, groups might not have time to internalise them. All this points to quite a different form of power than that of the Panopticon.

Foucault was aware of this tension. He said the following in a lecture three years after the publication of *Discipline and Punish*:

> The idea of the Panopticon is a modern idea in one sense, but we can also say that it is completely archaic, since the panoptic mechanism basically involves putting someone at the center—an eye, a gaze, a principle of surveillance— who will be able to make its sovereignty function over all the individuals [placed] within this machine of power. To that extent we can say that the Panopticon is the oldest dream of the oldest sovereign: None of my subjects can escape and none of their actions is unknown to me. ... *The government of populations is, I think, completely different from the exercise of sovereignty over the fine grain of individual behaviours*. It seems to me that we have two completely different systems of power.[55]

Foucault himself was not convinced of the application of the Panopticon to entire populations; he felt that this area was better understood as bio-power. If bio-power is the recognition of humanity as a species, then digital power goes one step further and is the proposition of that species as consisting of individuals that can be categorised and sorted into dynamic groups with machines. In that sense the basic category for digital power is the same as that for the Panopticon, the individual. But the scale and practices deployed are different. The panoptic mode and surveillance are not sufficient for grasping the modern procedures that store information, construct categories, and sort and identify individuals. There are strong heuristic limits to the Panopticon. If the analyst only considers direct surveillance and emphasises self-discipline, then they are in danger of missing large parts of the sovereign's tools and techniques. A more appropriate paradigm for these processes can be discovered in a technical proposal from the Third Reich.

Cuntz's Tower: The Manual Database

Erwin Cuntz (1878–1977) was a freethinker, pacifist, avid chess-player and lawyer who—apparently out of a sense of civic duty—concocted a scheme for centrally storing the data of all Germans. In a short letter to Adolf Hitler, dated 22 November 1934, he describes his proposal and presents a pencil sketch of it. Stuck in a folder at the Prussian Secret State Archives (Geheimes Staats Archiv) in Berlin, between pages of detailed and heavily edited discussions about German registry laws and practices, Erwin Cuntz's vision has gone relatively unnoticed.[56] It is unknown if, but unlikely that Hitler ever replied to him. From the archival record it also appears as if the proposal was never seriously considered, although it was filed with the relevant letters discussing registry reform. However, Cuntz's plan is worth translating and analysing in some detail; not because it is the first or only instance of a national registry design, but because it serves as a particularly elegant blueprint for *digital power*—a power relation once imagined and now ubiquitous.[57]

Cuntz begins his proposal, which is translated and reproduced in full in the appendix of this book, with the problem of identification and centralisation: 'there is no office where one could find out the address of every German and other worthwhile information about him in a single step'. He continues that this kind of useful office could be easily constructed and achieved if one:

> advance[s] to the insight that the human is a movable, itself moving, being [*Wesen*], that one therefore should not select as the basis for an organisation something which can continuously change and continuously changes for millions, namely domicile and address, but something which is solid and always remains the same, namely date of birth and place of birth, and, in a more developed framework, race and family origin.

This shift from a system that files according to address to one based on an unchanging identity is more revolutionary than it may at first appear. It is, using Foucault's words, a new physics of power, one that moves from observed reality to managing its representation. Cuntz explains further:

> Instead of the territorial principle, one must apply the personage principle [*Personalitätsprinzip*], for which I have fought for years. It is the bringing into line [*Gleichschaltung*] with technology that is the challenge.

This is an example of the shift Foucault identifies from a 'territorial state' to the 'state of population', here presented as a technical solution to the problem of identifying individuals. In his letter Cuntz refers to the registry as a dream no longer relegated to fantasy. What kind of a dream does he mean? It is a dream that stands at the beginning of our latest tools of governance and deeply informs the contemporary configuration of digital power: an automated labour of surveillance and sorting, producing knowledge of each subject for the sovereign. Cuntz's vision is that of a shift from a simple archival and ledger technology of legibility to what can only be described as a huge manual database with individuals as its primary category. The shift is as significant as that from spectacular punishment to surveillance or a tributary system to one of regulated taxation.[58]

The cavalier statements that humans need to be brought into line with technology and that a '*Gleichschaltung*' is necessary are particularly harrowing when one recalls the various uses of that word in Nazi Germany. More than just an obscure historical document, Cuntz's tower is a valu-

CUNTZ'S TOWER

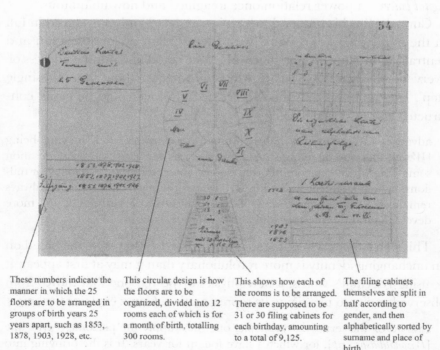

| These numbers indicate the manner in which the 25 floors are to be arranged in groups of birth years 25 years apart, such as 1853, 1878, 1903, 1928, etc. | This circular design is how the floors are to be organized, divided into 12 rooms each of which is for a month of birth, totalling 300 rooms. | This shows how each of the rooms is to be arranged. There are supposed to be 31 or 30 filing cabinets for each birthday, amounting to a total of 9,125. | The filing cabinets themselves are split in half according to gender, and then alphabetically sorted by surname and place of birth. |

Figure 8: Cuntz's Sketch for a Tower Storing a Card for Each German Citizen

able theoretic schema of the kind of labour and power relations at work in databases of populations. Why consider a pre-computer age design to understand digital power? Due to its simple design this diagram brings into stark outline a fundamental power relation inherent to the database. Cuntz's Tower also forms a missing link of spatial architecture to data architecture; it is both a data storage structure and a blueprint. As data storage it indicates how society needs to be represented to fulfil the desire of the sovereign for an individual identification of *all* subjects; as a blueprint it impresses upon us the fantastic enormity of sorting 60 million cards. There is no sovereign in Cuntz's tower watching, but rather a cadre of bureaucrats labouring. Index cards representing citizens replace cells holding inmates. The power of the Panopticon is based on the principle that subjects might be observed at any given time and therefore self-discipline is induced, thus integrating the external power—a Hegelian might refer to it as a negation of the negation. The principles at the heart of Cuntz's Tower on the other hand are individuation, identification, and grouping; particularly identification and grouping which take place without the subject's knowledge. It is an architecture that is designed to facilitate the sorting of individuals. But instead of the actual individual, such as in the Panopticon, an abstraction of the individual (the name card) is organised into a fashion that makes the population legible and the individual discernible. A copy of the entire population is made, with each human corresponding to a card ordered and incarcerated in a tower that acts as a primitive databank. These index cards are like effigies of individuals, copies incorporated into one grand system.

In this way, the humble card index, which led to so many revolutions in library management systems, accounting practices and the storing of knowledge, is a precursor to the modern database.[59] The immediate content of the registry cards is, just like the content of a ritual, negligible. It is the repeated sorting and labelling operations that undertake the important political labour. This helps produce particular forms of knowledge and domination. The most subversive and pervasive political labour the registry card does is to multiply the operations of power through standardising its processes, thereby making it appear technical and factual. Moreover, when a technical and bureaucratic apparatus mediates decisions, the responsibility and accountability of individual operators can be diminished. Technical processes that make its agents appear less liable legitimate sovereign power.

5

THE RITUAL

One of the main questions this book asks is: What is new and what is old about the drive to identify and sort? How might we contextualise this current moment into a long history? In that vein, how does ritual fulfil similar identifying and sorting functions? First off, an obvious but necessary caveat: dividing past practices of identification and sorting into three categories (ritual, archival, digital) is more of a heuristic device and ideal type than a historical reality. However, this sub-categorisation and clustering still lends itself to a rough periodisation, since each mode provides different strategies for some of the same difficulties of human governance: centralisation, circulation, and collective action. The shared problem of how to maintain, understand, and control a population unifies disparate historical examples and modalities of identification and sorting. What differentiates them is that they each exhibit distinctive strategies for the storage, retention, control, and communication of information to achieve this end.

Consider a ritual. Hierarchic and classificatory distinctions do the heavy lifting of identifying and sorting processes. They can be grounded in a ritual order, just as much as they can be anchored in a bureaucracy or a bill of rights. The convenient thing about the ritual mode is that it does not require mass literacy to function. Think of ritual as 'prescribed formal behaviour for occasions not given over to technological routine'.[1] In all societies ritual signifies and symbolises the transition of individuals from one social category to another. As anthropology has taught us, ritual is a rehearsed performance that does crucial social labour. It thereby helps sort and identify an undifferentiated mass of humanity into finite categories. Initiation rituals mark the transition from youth to adulthood, coronation rituals symbolise the establishment of a reign, warrior rituals identify members of the fighting class and so on. By doing so, *rituals process and generate information*. Many rituals go hand in hand with a public symbol signifying that the person now has a different status: a wedding ring, a tribal mark, a papal tiara, a uniform, and so on. Such signifiers and practices abound. Indeed, the history of human innovation is marked by a wealth of ritual invention and innovation.

Ritual has become an object of increased scholarly interest overall;[2] recently the study of the significance of ritual to politics has developed into a flourishing subfield of its own.[3] Thinking through rituals in relation to politics can occur at many different levels, such as in the study of obvious contemporary political rituals (state funerals[4] or coronations)[5] or in the interpretation of coded political symbolism in rituals that appear non-political (the Swazi Newala).[6] Ritual can also be studied as constitutive and symptomatic of a political order and a mode of technics of politics. In such an approach, which this section pursues, ritual rules and classifications are understood to fulfil practical purposes in the production of order and legibility. As Bruce Lincoln observes:

> The social order, like that of an army, depends on the preservation of certain hierarchic and classificatory distinctions along with a full complement of behavioural rules through which these are made operational.[7]

These distinctions and behavioural rules can be grounded in a ritual order, just as much as they can be anchored in a bureaucracy or a bill of rights. In his seminal *Elementary Forms of Religious Life* Émile Durkheim (1858–1917) explicitly defines rite in distinction to belief as 'a particular mode of action' and rites as 'rules of conduct'.[8] Taken individually a ritual, or a rite, is no more than a specific type of action, yet taken collectively, as a system, these aggregated types of action arise as a structure of rules governing human behaviour. The cultural anthropologist Victor Turner (1920–1983) describes ritual as 'prescribed formal behaviour *for occasions not given over to technological routine*, having reference to beliefs in mystical beings and powers'.[9] It is significant that Turner defines ritual in opposition to technological routine through reference to the beliefs that motivate it, thereby belying some of the underlying similarities ritual holds to modern routinised bureaucratic practices. It opens a possible interpretation not only of ritual as a type of 'primitive' automation, but of modern technological routine as fulfilling some of the same stabilising societal functions as ritual does. This is in keeping with the sociologist Jeffrey Alexander's suggested approach when he claims that 'the modern intellectual disciplines taken as a whole ... have lived under the debilitating illusion that post-religious society is ontologically different from the religious social orders of earlier times'.[10] Most recently Catherine Bell has provided a valuable understanding of ritual that integrates the notion of time and deferral:

> People generate a ritualized environment that acts to shift the very status and nature of the problems into terms that are endlessly retranslated in strings of deferred schemes. The multiplication and orchestration of such schemes do not produce a resolution; rather, they afford a translation of immediate concerns into the dominant terms of ritual.[11]

Ritual here anchors reality and, much like automation, depoliticises. It becomes a register for responding to novel and dynamic problems with established and rehearsed forms, deferring agency and responsibility from the sovereign to a recapitulating routine which reproduces fundamental order. Reading these definitions in conjunction illuminates aspects of what ritual does and helps to 'perceive ritual as a human labour, struggling with matters of incongruity'.[12] In all of these accounts, I am most interested in the political labour ritual engages in: how with ritual 'early man built up habits of absolute control over his own conduct';[13] how through ritual human relations were stabilised, exchanges mediated, and identities reinforced. In what way could it have been used to constitute and render different societies? Where does it reproduce internal hierarchies, property relations, and structured encounters with the other?

Unfortunately many past inventions and innovations of the ritual technics of politics have been lost to us, as they were mainly practised by homeostatic oral cultures.[14] As Lewis Mumford (1895–1990) underlines in his *Technics and Human Development*, though, this does not mean that they were not of great significance in the evolution of human organisation and society, and we ignore them at our peril:

> Which, then, is the greater error—the failure to appreciate the basic importance of ritual before man's life had acquired any other mode of significant expression, or the failure to understand the threat to human development in contemporary mechanical mass rituals?[15]

We do however have a prominent example of a political system regulated through the careful distribution and application of ritual in the Americas and featuring curious technological artefacts. This case is especially valuable because it entails one mode of technics, the ritual mode, encountering another, the archival mode. It is useful to contrast these different modes because 'conventions are most conspicuous when partial'. Without a historical trace of difference or real encounters with different systems it is difficult to understand the contemporary standardised conventions of the global technics of politics. 'A universal standard may often prove inconspicuous, appearing to its users simply as a social fact with its actual function in social coordination obscured.'[16]

Administering Inca and Aztec Ritual

For the Inca Empire (1438–1533) offering maize beer (*chicha*) in exchange of labour was a tool for the extraction of surplus value.[17] Much of the empire was built around the circulation of and access to copper (from Peru) and spondylus shells, which were harvested in coastal Ecuador and also used for rituals. The successful redistribution of *chicha* and spondylus shells required that labour was 'continuously undercompensated', as in modern capitalism.[18] Crucial for our understanding of the technics of politics in this period is that both the Aztec and Inca emperor were regarded as deities and perceived by their subjects as divine sources of wealth and power.[19] This wealth and power was displayed and regulated through the administered use of ritual. The Aztec Empire (1325–1521) featured such a vast array of rituals that it required functional differentiation: 'it was not possible for a single minister to attend to all ... The nation had a special official for each activity, small though it were.'[20]

Between sun rituals, harvest rituals, and sacrificial rituals, the system was so complex that it needed specialised knowledges and a division of labour to administer. A particular class of operators was required and empowered to administer all of these tasks and a framework of laws and taboos put in place to help maintain them. Amongst its various taboos it was forbidden for the subjects to lay their eyes on the emperor.[21] It is obvious why such an injunction is useful in a society organised around the belief that the emperor is divine. The taboo here does three things: it indicates divinity, constructs the experience of divinity through repeated use, and hinders the discovery of a non-divine emperor. It is therefore means and ends, cause and effect. This is an example where 'by describing awful penalties for breaking a taboo, early man built up habits of absolute control over his own conduct'.[22]

Through the use of a central sacred fetish—the emperor himself—and a composite array of rituals these large and complex empires were ordered and maintained. What I wish to propose is that these rituals should be understood as technics of politics, which worked to regulate the circulation of 'capital' and goods, and the identification and sorting of individuals. There was great political utility in what appeared to many of the first conquistadors as the confused actions of superstitious people. The Inca and Aztec empires are valuable cases for thinking about the technics of politics because they responded to problems of centralisation, legibility, and information without recourse to writing, as we understand it. Not having a society that writes provides the ritual mode with particular restraints, but also certain benefits. For instance, how else are we to appreciate that, '[i]n the first days of empire Itzcoatl had taken the precautionary measure of destroying tribal records' but as a sophisticated intervention in history enabled by the fact that records were centralised and the majority of society was non-literate? This historical erasure would then 'allow the construction of a past more compatible with the Aztec present'.[23] In a world in which the written form does not exist as a retention device, the past is more malleable and great feats of memorisation are more necessary and frequent.

Consider how the need for identifying and sorting individuals manifested in visual markers of identity. Inca officials bore titles and regalia that corresponded to how many men they could muster, in stark contrast to the aristocratic titles in Europe at the time which usually indicated a control of territory. This practice can also be discovered in the history of Southeast Asia in general, and in particular the area now called Thailand, thereby indicating that the primary problem for these political societies was a 'shortage of labour rather than of cash'.[24] The proliferation of visual markers of identity comes to its most radical expression in the tattooing of a population.[25] For Lewis Mumford, 'body decoration was an effort to establish a human identity' without which 'all other acts and labours would be performed in vain'.[26] For our purpose tattoos, as well as regalia and special clothing, can be read as a political technology responding to the problems of mobile populations and illegibility. It functions by making visual surfaces of the human body represent and correspond to political categories, it acts as a visual index of human categorisation, and it has the potential to result in a highly legible order. This practice of individual identification would serve the Aztecs poorly when facing Spaniards on the battlefield—generals could easily be picked out of the crowd by their dress.[27] Near the end of the military confrontation a high-ranking Aztec leader, Cuauhtémoc, is only captured 'because he tries to escape in a boat richly decorated with royal emblems'.[28]

All human political communities encounter challenges of identification, communication, and information management. As communities grow in scale and become more complex these problems become qualitatively more difficult. As Duncan Bell has put it 'the problem of constructing and governing an integrated political system over large distances' is 'one of the most persistent yet overlooked themes in the history of political thought'.[29] For the Incas the problem of quick communication was solved through constructing posthouses along highways. A message was sent by having a runner take it from one posthouse to the next. 'As he approached, he called out for attention and then passed the message on: a new runner took the message the next few miles.'[30] According to the sixteenth-century Spanish traveller Cieza de León this system was superior to one relying on horses or mules, since runners could negotiate mountain passes in a quicker fashion.[31] In the case of the Aztecs we learn that for the purposes of sending and gathering information there were 'men of great agility who served as couriers to go and come, whom they did nourish in this exercise from their youth, labouring to have them well-breathed'.[32] For the Inca Empire, the problem of records was solved in a more ingenious manner. Data was stored in binary codes on assemblages of cotton or wool strings, called *khipus*.[33]

The Khipu

The artefact of the *khipu* serves as an important precursor to the modern database and disrupts any simplistic understanding of the Inca Empire as 'primitive'. *Khipus* are systems of different coloured strings placed into up or down positions with knots tied into them. Unlike a stone or clay tablet, *khipus* can easily be transported as well as updated by tying and untying the knots. *Khipus* form a non-printed example of what Bruno Latour has, in an entirely different context, called 'combinable and immutable mobiles'.[34]

I discuss the *khipu* to illustrate four related points about the centralisation and retention of data, which, in part, also pertains to the digital mode. The first is that the number reigns in these systems of information retention. Because it is easiest to store quantities and numerical values, other aspects of social reality that do not lend themselves to quantification or arithmetisation are marginalised. The second is that context is everything. Without knowing how and for what the systems are used it is impossible to reconstruct their content. The third is that these systems are most useful and needed in situations that are not legible, such as newly conquered territories. The fourth is that although artefacts characterise these systems they always require a particular class of individuals to operate them.

Recent research has established that *khipus* have a base positional system, with a base of ten. *Khipus* were primarily used to store quantitative information—of goods, individuals, soldiers, etc.—although it is also possible to imagine that numeric values could be used as signs or codes, for events (astronomical, meteorological, or political) as well as individuals, using an Inca equivalent to the Dewey decimal system. Of significance for the study of such technics is that researchers are having difficulty deciphering the meaning of *khipus*; in particular they are struggling with how to read the identity of the quantified objects out of these devices. This is obviously the case because the social and cultural context in which they were embedded has been destroyed and is made even more difficult by the fact that the context was one of an oral culture, which is always far easier to eradicate. The difficulties encountered by researchers indicates that the *khipu* required added oral communication and signification to function, but it is also an illustration of the extent to which the meaning of any technical artefact, whether the *khipu* or a database, is constituted by a particular social and political context.

These data-retention systems were produced by *khipu*-makers: data managers who played an important role in the functioning of the Inca state and bureaucracy. They were placed in various territories that had previously been conquered and sent *khipus* to Cuzco, the capital; this process lent itself to a particular hierarchic bureaucratic organisation.[35] In Cuzco higher-ranking officials then added up the various bits of data received on a larger, statistical, *khipu*. Copying was achieved through multiplying and mimicking the productive operation—by having more *khipu*-makers produce more *khipus* for the same data—which also served as a verification mechanism. For this manual reproduction to function a standardised system of data retention must have been used.[36] Moreover, to ensure that the figures represented by the *khipus* were properly calculated, *yupanas* were deployed. *Yupanas* are impressive boards that look like architectural models of forts, on which calculations are made with maize kernels according to the Fibonacci sequence.[37]

Like the Inca and Aztec ritual systems of classification and signification which have since been lost, the *khipu* and *yupana* were an empire's response to the problem of legibility and communication—which is necessary for central control and always most urgent in newly conquered territories. What the reader needs to take from this brief discussion is that the distribution of *chicha* and the use of ritual and fetishisation of the emperor are not simply religious pre-modern acts, but complex technics of politics which along with the runners and *khipus* calculated with *yupanas* maintained power, identified and categorised individuals, ensured surplus extraction, and regulated the circulation of goods and individuals. They are systems that are produced by and constitute centralised political power and legibility, manifesting different categories of individual identity. On one level, *khipus* and the emperor are artefacts that fulfil concrete daily functions for the empires: they quantify, relate and organise. This leads to an unusual, but interesting, question: Because they combined social technologies with human beings, can we think of Aztec and Inca emperors as a form of cyborg, 'a cybernetic organ, a hybrid of machine and organism, a creature of social reality as well as a creature of fiction'?[38]

What is certain is that ritual technics shape the very form of political interaction. They constitute information systems that determine the nature of political exchanges thereby stabilising and homogenising political power and subjectivity in a given geographic area. This epistemological system and knowledge of how it coded *khipus* would quickly be destroyed along with the empires.

System Failure

The technics of politics mediating the relationship between symbolic and actual worth began to come to a violent close for the Incas with the arrival of Pizarro (1526) and for the Aztecs with the arrival of Cortés (1519).[39] The radical shock of alien invaders entering the ordered societies of the Aztec and Inca empires, which had cosmologies in which all important events were foretold, led to the subsequent underlining of oracles that had been predicting the demise of the empires all along.[40] Contrasting the different technics of politics of the Spanish invaders to that of the Aztec empire provides a good account of how the conquest could take place. It offers an additional response to the truly vexing question of how it was possible 'that a motley bunch of Spanish adventurers, never numbering much more than four hundred or so, was able to defeat an Amerindian military power on its home ground in the space of two years?'[41]

Tzvetan Todorov writes in the *Conquest of America* that a primary reason why the devastation of the Aztec people was so complete at the hands of such a small group of invaders was that the Aztecs 'lost control of communication' and failed 'where they had previously excelled: in gathering information'.[42] Faced with the disorienting arrival of the conquistadors, Montezuma, the Aztec emperor, did not manage to 'produce appropriate and effective messages'.[43] At the same time Cortés, according to Todorov's account, was a master of psychological warfare that was designed to 'leave its interlocutor in perplexity'.[44] He manages to deploy shows of force and violence to effectively intimidate and confuse his opponent. In Todorov's rendition Cortés understands the Aztecs well enough that he can destroy them.[45]

I am sympathetic to the manner in which Todorov extends the notion of communication to say that there are 'two major forms of communication, one between man and man, the other between man and the world' and then claims that the 'Indians cultivate chiefly the latter, the Spaniards the former'.[46] But at this stage I would like to advance this argument into two directions. First, I wish to more clearly aggregate the different manners of communication and information retention into two different technics of politics: ritual and archival. The great differences of the Aztecs and the Spaniards can be read as a fundamental incompatibility of two different systems that regulated politics, two systems that failed to effectively communicate with each other. Secondly but related, I will, along with Inga Clendinnen whose work I draw on heavily in this section, resist the interpretation that everything went according to Cortés's plan. A different reading is possible in which Cortés himself is horrified and alienated by the 'fierce and unnatural cruelty'[47] which he witnesses at the final destruction of Tenochtitlán, the Aztec imperial city.

Instead of thinking that the main difference between the Aztecs and the Spaniards are metal swords and horses, Todorov draws attention to their different information and communication technologies, although he never quite calls them that. In its most simple characterisation, one was constituted by memory, the other by writing. One was a society running its affairs in a highly ritualised and structured manner; the other was a small group of individuals taken out of their familiar world and therefore forced to improvise and permitted to transgress. At one point, in an action pregnant with meaning when read in a tradition of writings about the 'ship of state', Cortés disables his own ships 'to release the sailors for soldiering service and to persuade the faint-hearted against retreat'.[48] As we saw above, the ritual can do all kinds of things. It is a highly effective form of political labour, yet one which does not respond well to novel situations. The kind of technics of politics that are in place can have great consequences for a political entity. A difference of modes—where one party is regulating its affairs orally and through ritual and the other regulating its through the written word and freed of restraints—can lead to significant communication failures in a state of war.

It appears that there was a breakdown in the meanings of violence, a fatal problem of translation. For instance, Cortés regularly said that he wanted to go and see Montezuma. How may the Aztecs have felt about this considering the taboo forbidding that anybody laid eyes on the emperor?[49] For much of the conquest Cortés regards Tenochtitlán as the ultimate prize for a series of dangerous and daring feats. At this stage we should note that Tenochtitlán is larger and a more sophisticated city than any in Europe. It has a complex and ordered social structure; the rulers have zoos—Cortés is impressed by all of this. He seeks to capture the city, to have it surrender to him, as one would with a European city, and with it have the Aztec empire transferred to the Spanish crown. He lays siege to Tenochtitlán. This is an entirely unfamiliar and unfathomable tactic for the Aztecs who in some cases sent supplies to their enemies before a battle to ensure that victory would not be due to anything but warrior prowess.[50]

The Aztecs are accustomed to a strictly ritualised form of battle between warriors. The goal of most battles is to capture a warrior of equal standing on the field; they purposely try not to kill their opponents during battle, but sacrifice them afterwards in a ritual that is a highly structured account of an ideal battle.[51] The Spaniards don't follow any of these rules, regularly exacting massacres on the civilian population. When the Aztecs do have to kill a Spaniard on the field, they are sure to beat the back of his skull in—a dishonourable death reserved for criminals. The Spanish violence is designed for the Aztec authorities to understand the futility of resisting the conquistadors and to capitulate. But this communication does not transact without a severe loss and perversion of fidelity. The signals Cortés and his party are trying to send to the Aztecs are not arriving at their destination, leading to disastrous consequences. Instead the Aztecs have understood the Spaniards to be entirely unpredictable, unreasonable, and barbaric, utterly beyond reaching a settlement with. Cortés writes that 'we each day expected them to sue for peace, which we desired as much as our own salvation'.[52] But they don't surrender. So he continues to attack, even though the city is diminished by famine. 'There was not one man amongst us whose heart did not bleed at the sound.'[53] On one day they kill 12,000 weakened inhabitants, on another 40,000.[54] Finally, Cuauhtémoc is captured in his emblazoned canoe; now, with the city in ruins and their social structure destroyed the Aztecs abandon Tenochtitlan, 'so thin, sallow, dirty and stinking that it was pitiful to see them'.[55] The prize of Cortés's conquest has been ruined.

This is a particularly poignant, if gruesome, encounter between two different cultures, but also two entirely different technics of politics. Not only the forms of information retention and communication were different, but, fatally, the means of interpretation. Writing during the Cold War, Thomas Schelling emphasised how necessary a fundamental mutuality is for bargaining to occur:

> [T]he essence of bargaining is the communication of intent, the perception of intent, the manipulation of expectations about what one will accept or refuse, the issuance of threats, offers, and assurances, the display of resolve and evidence of capabilities, the communication of constraints on what one can do, the search for compromise and jointly desirable exchanges, the creation of sanctions to enforce understandings and agreements, genuine efforts to persuade and inform, and the creation of hostility, friendliness, mutual respect, or rules of etiquette.[56]

In a situation in which the parties to a conflict have sufficiently different technics of politics to not properly exchange communications and interpret the signs of the other, one is rendered to a potential horror in which precisely measured violence, calculated to achieve particular effects, is not intelligible to the other. Instead of conquest Cortés achieves genocide. With the Amerindian empires destroyed, the area would soon become a site of innovation for the archival mode, as modern archival censuses were pioneered by the Spanish and other European powers.

THEORISING THE RITUAL MODE

The repeated and escalated use of technics of politics which have failed—rituals, sacrifices and auguries—as well as the recourse to omens which predicted their demise all along is a common feature of complex ideologies and knowledge systems encountering situations that they cannot easily integrate into their models. On a related note, Bruce Lincoln explains that 'there is nothing that is intrinsically, inherently, and automatically anomalous'. Following this line of thinking, it can be stated that in the ritual mode of technics of politics, as well as other classificatory systems:

> there are only things that appear anomalous within the framework of a given taxonomic system: specifically a system that is incompetent—given the nature of the taxonomizers it deploys—to classify those specific things in a satisfactory manner. One can, in fact, define anomaly in rather neutral terms as any entity, the existence of which goes unrecognized under the terms of a given taxonomy.[57]

Foreign Caucasian invaders did not fit into the Inca and Aztec political taxonomy; more devastatingly the systems of information exchange were not sufficiently compatible for full communication to occur. A taxonomic anomaly does not have to inherently disrupt a system of classification as most systems have a category and coping mechanism for dealing with the uncategorised, the queer, and the liminal. Systems and modes of politics can adapt to a certain degree in the following fashion. Firstly, new disambiguation protocols need to be put in place; new rules for sorting an overwhelming reality into the same schematic categories. Secondly, instead of regarding unexpected liminal outcomes as undermining the model, the outcomes are treated as 'noise' and more of the old input is called for—more data, more ritual, more archive. In this way paradigms and modes of technics of politics are essentially non-falsifiable. Self-same practices can be seen in action after the defeat of the United States in Vietnam, and the fall of the Soviet Union. This 'death drive'[58] of the technics of politics is a reoccurring motif. Ritual as a structure regulating society and politics appears as unassailable for another reason: it commonly follows an apotropaic logic. This means that most rituals are enacted to ward off evil. In that sense, it could appear as if the ritual has worked and done its political labour, by virtue of the fact that *nothing has happened*, that no disaster has befallen the people who enacted the ritual. But what else is particular to the ritual mode of technics?

According to James Frazer (1854–1941), in his magisterial book *The Golden Bough*, many rituals feature the underlying logic of sympathetic magic. This kind of magic relies on contact or a similarity, what is often termed as 'like producing like' and Frazer calls 'homeopathic magic'. Examples of this kind of logic are 'North American Indians' who:

> believe that by drawing the figure of a person in sand, ashes, or clay, or by considering any object as his body, and then pricking it with a sharp stick or doing it any other injury, they inflict a corresponding injury on the person represented.[59]

This basic schema of the ritual can be discovered amongst people of many different times and places. Usually the central logic of these rituals is conceptualised as 'like producing like'. But, as the anthropologist Jonathan Z. Smith argues, in the case of sympathetic hunting magic, the power of the ritual can also be understood to lie in the fact that it is actually 'unlike the hunt. It is, once more, a perfect hunt with all the variables controlled.'[60] Ritual, in this reading, is not just characterised by its similarity to a reality it is seeking to influence, but by the acting out of an idealised fantasy that cannot be realised. In this way a fantasy—of personal violence or the perfect hunt or the perfect battle—is enacted but not implemented. From this reading it can be ventured that ritual practices at the heart of politics play an essential role in the constitution of society through automated repetition, the creation of an ideal image, and the opportunity to performatively act out grievances and fantasies that are the way reality 'should be'. In the fourth chapter we will encounter a modern practice sharing all of these characteristics: the war game. Ritual technics is a forum in which sovereign fantasies of perfect legibility and clean violence can be played out, thereby regulating and framing the day-to-day requirements of power. It is a site at which fantasy and fiction come to play important practical roles in the construction and constitution of society.

It would be a mistake to overstate the coherence or totality of the ritual mode of technics—their effects can be experienced as contradictory and dynamic forces. It is important to recall that one of the central characteristics of technics of politics defined above is that they are underdetermined. The power of ritual for instance, can be used to anchor the regular normalised distribution of bodies and goods, making it appear as if individual actions are part of a larger homogenous and meaningful whole. Yet, individuals can also be identified and singled out through the ritual identification of culprits and establishment of sacrificial scape-goats. In this way ritual technics can serve to both individualise and homogenise, effortlessly moving from the level of the individual to the collective and back again. What these practices share, however, is the appearance of being above politics and individual human agency. There are different techniques for making the ritual mode of technics appear to be beyond politics, which is essential to its smooth operation. As Catherine Bell writes 'in seeing itself as responding to an environment' the ritual process is inherently grasped as exceeding the environment. Thereby 'ritualization interprets its own schemes as impressed upon the actors from a more authoritative source, usually from well beyond the immediate human community itself'.[61] Ritual is legitimated by the past or the deistic to respond to the present.

This characteristic of the ritual mode of technics can also be discov-ered in different forms in the archival and digital modes of technics. Every mode of technics of politics seems at one point or another to be beyond society and immediate politics: whether the logic is theological, factual, or technical. Each of these achieves, in a different way, the same outcome of instituting separate logics and legitimations for large-scale interventions into populations. Their myriad uses—improving taxation, raising militaries, identifying potential supporters, controlling migration, producing fantasies of superiority—establish the parameters of individ-ual privacy, rights, and identity in a community. While most cases in which the ritual mode dominates exist in oral cultures, tendencies of the ritual mode and ritualisation persist in all technics of politics. For instance, in the past two centuries a global stabilisation of identity has occurred, moving from places and families to individual identity fixed in a national framework. This takes place through ritualised repetition of immigration practices and procedures. The ritualised repetitions of these practices also play a role in structuring perceptions of the international, thereby determining the international system—as we will encounter further below.

6

THE ARCHIVE

Some of the oldest forms of writing humanity possesses are accounting lists. It is humbling to consider that the invention of the written form, and all that it entails philosophically and politically, was intimately wedded to the mundane concerns about who owes whom how much livestock. In contrast to the ritual mode, archival modes dominate in written societies and are primarily characterised by the information technology of the book or ledger. With the growth of literacy in a society, novel avenues for the centralised control and homogenisation of human actions are opened up; the archival written form lends itself to a whole new art of legibility and domination. In sixteenth-century Europe, the development of the printing press enabled the mass production of the technological artefact of the book, which had previously required painstaking individual labours to generate, thereby radically multiplying archival forms of data retention and communication. In the nineteenth century, managing this material and cognitive mountain of growing information in libraries, in turn, became one of the drivers for the development of index card systems. This was a breakthrough technology for the activist state, enabling innovative forms of identification and sorting. It was also a precursor to the modern database.

Like any complex iterative process involving many participants, both printing and library management tend towards a strict rationalisation and standardisation. Ideally every page in a book should be the same size, all of the letters should be in a single script, and all cards in a library filing cabinet must have the information on them organised in an identical fashion. The thoroughly regimented card catalogue radically improved information organisation and retention for all of the important institutions of modernity: prison, police, hospital, university, government, military and the border. In fact, it is hard to imagine a modern technocratic, welfarist, or national security state existing without it. Implementing a national ID or passport system, for instance, would entail great difficulty without the physical and intellectual apparatus of the card catalogue.

If maps help to legitimate territorial authority and a binary model of land ownership, and censuses and statistics provide 'intelligence' of foreign lands as well as measure and evaluate 'suspicious' parts of the population, then passports enable states to control the migration of humans and identify individuals to an unprecedented degree. Passports standardise political subjectivity into a global ontopological system—ontopology grafts ontology onto topography, it expresses being and identity in a territorial schema. Out of all of the archival forms, the passport, and the border sites it is evaluated at, are the most frequent manifestations of state power in a modern individual's life. Just as time and space were standardised, and territorial authority and simple land ownership were legitimated, the passport contributes to a specific construction of the world and self.

The daring escape of a political leader or general in disguise is a recurring motif in both literature and history. In revolutionary France in 1791, engaging a tactic entirely opposite to that of Cuauhtémoc, Louis XVI managed to flee, for a little while. By travelling in a party he 'absconded for Varennes disguised as a valet'. He managed to get away with this because 'passports for the nobility typically included a number of persons listed by their function but without further description'.[1] The fact that the king had gotten to Varennes acted as a catalyst for a new regime of identification. Fearing a reactionary émigré invasion, the French revolutionary government began to change the administrative practices, legislation, and archival form of the passport. Now a passport could only be assigned to an individual; the modern identification regime was born.

Contrast the different regimes of identification Cuauhtémoc, Louis XVI, and Edward Snowden sought, or still seek, to move in and one cannot fail to be struck by the previously unimaginable level of centralised control now present in our system. Techniques of identification and sorting transformed from external displays of clothing, regalia, and tat-toos; to artifacts persons carried with them, such as passports, IDs, and letters of entry; to a system of identification where the body itself is the source of information expressed in fingerprints and other biometrics. Perhaps most remarkable about this trajectory is that the sovereign's identifying and sorting practices are gradually disassociated from those of the wider public. A public scene in the ritual mode would not have been much more legible to the sovereign than to a common person. The same cannot be said for the digital mode, where an extreme unevenness of legibility exists between the subjects and the sovereign's operators. Today we don't primarily carry our identity outside our clothing or in our pockets anymore, we are now already known, just the way we are, although how we are known and what we mean to the sovereign is becoming more and more of a mystery.

In the nineteenth and twentieth centuries similar processes of stand-ardisation were at work in the world. New means of transportation (the railway) and communication (the telegraph and the intercontinental cable) contributed to frequently discussed processes of globalisation—'the intensification of worldwide social relations which link distant locali-ties'.[2] For such inter- and trans-continental technologies to work they needed to be uniform. A general tendency towards such homogenisation could also be seen in the establishment of global postage systems, inter-national congresses for standard measurements and units, proposals for world formats, and world languages that all characterised the era. Along with these standards novel communication and transportation technolo-gies also appeared to make different forms of political organisation appear feasible: 'Before the 1870s a highly integrated global polity (let alone one ruling over a single self-conscious nation) was rarely, if ever, considered a feasible political option; afterward, it became a frequent demand.'[3] These interconnecting technologies also led to a great regu-larisation of time and space.

The regularisation of something as substantial as time and space occurs over long periods and in many different instances, yet one can still identify a particular moment and place when these two fields were nor-malised.[4] The International Meridian Conference of 1884, convened by the Scottish born Canadian railway engineer Sandford Fleming, took place in Washington, DC but located the prime meridian at the Royal Observatory in Greenwich, London. At this point, space, which was already cut up into longitude and latitude, was globally stabilised. Before the International Meridian Conference there had been a variety of prime Meridians, running through 'Cadiz, Christiania, Copenhagen, Ferro, Lisbon, Naples, Paris, Pulkowa, Rio de Janeiro, and Stockholm, among others'.[5] At the conference Fleming also promoted the establishment of a terrestrial time not tied to any particular place on earth.[6] Yet, with the subsequent fixing of longitude and latitude, time zones are also established and Greenwich finds itself at the centre of both time and space; a 'convergence' of time takes place.[7] Prior to the setting of Greenwich Mean Time and time zones there had been a great variety of times, with many cities having their own time. This posed significant problems both for coordinating transport and the exchange of scientific data.[8] To regulate this heterogeneous reality, clocks had to be adjusted: in Belfast, Maine, the clocks were 'set twenty-four minutes slow' and in Pittsburgh, Pennsylvania, they were set 'twenty minutes fast'.[9]

At first glance such standardisation may appear to be no more than an innocuous optimisation of communication. As John Maynard Keynes wrote in his *Treatise on Money* (1930), '[e]veryone agrees that there are many fields of human activity in which it is only common-sense to establish international standards.'[10] Yet primarily thinking of this standardisation in terms of inconsequential utility would obscure four significant aspects of it. First, and most apparent, is that the standardisation of time and space marginalised and delegitimised a myriad of contending local conceptions of it. Secondly, the standardisation of time and space elevated precise measurement to a type of expertise and created particular, monopolistic positions of institutional power that curated and legitimated the standard. Third, because time and space were now the same everywhere it became far easier for a central authority to imagine knowing and therefore acting on distant places; in Scott's terms, the standardisation of time and space increased 'legibility'. Fourth, it is always important to note that the content of the standard, whether it is a metre or a second, is negligible: such coordination 'solutions are, of course, arbitrary to this extent: any solution is "correct" if enough people think so'.[11] Bearing these four points in mind I now turn to some archival forms which, I argue, contributed to a great standardisation of political power and human subjectivity in the international system. One of these forms is the map.

Maps and Cadastre

Maps are deeply implicated in many different aspects of international relations. In this section I will touch on their role in the development of the state system, the stabilisation of property relations, as well as colonialism. In its essence a political map is no more than a projection of political power onto a spatial terrain, which in turn is the simplification of the uneven surface of our planet onto a two-dimensional plane. Yet, once it is established as the primary way of understanding the relationship of space to authority, a political map helps anchor and reproduce a specific world-view and visuality[12] of power and identity—one in which states and individuals are ontopological.[13] Here I want to think about the political map as both analogous and connected to the standardisation of time and space, which means that I want to consider how it displaced and delegitimised other forms of political power; enshrined the expertise of mapmaking and created sites of legitimacy; enabled a central authority to understand and simplify complex realities; and was, to some extent, arbitrary.

How is one to begin drawing a map? How great should the scale be, what should be used as symbols, what is the centre, how should it be oriented? What should be included and what should be excluded? A look to the history of mapmaking shows that humanity has come up with a great range of responses to these questions. Yet today the fundamental questions appear to all be settled. Maps are oriented North, longitudinal and latitudinal meridians are set, standard scales are established, and political authority is indicated through covering an area delimited by a territorial line with a distinct, often primary, colour. That this is a particular kind of map that privileges the modern state as well as a certain, Weberian, understanding of it should be apparent—it at once implies homogeneity and complete control within a given territory. Recently it has been argued that it was the medieval recovery of a Ptolemaic tradition of mapmaking that used longitudinal and latitudinal lines which 'helped delegitimate nonterritorial authorities'.[14] Far from a neutral representation of a settled social and political reality, the constraints of the map form tend towards reinforcing highly specific imaginaries of territorial authority. It was 'mapping' which 'gave sovereign statehood its territorially exclusive character, thereby structuring the effects of other causal factors'.[15]

Cadastral maps, which show land ownership on a territory in the same way political authority is displayed, had a similar effect of helping to naturalise notions about the nature of land tenure, all the while helping to enforce and argue for distinct holdings:

> The cadastral map is an instrument of control which both reflects and consolidates the power of those who commission it. ... The cadastral map is partisan: where knowledge is power, it provides comprehensive information to be used to the advantage of some and the detriment of others, as rulers and ruled were well aware in the tax struggles of the 18th and 19th centuries. Finally, the cadastral map is active: in portraying one reality as in the settlement of the new world or in India, it helps obliterate the old.[16]

In this way cadastral maps enable the effective organisation and taxation of a population. Again, this kind of a technics helps to standardise and naturalise something that is actually contingent. Before a cadastral simplification occurs which declares that the territory is owned by a single entity there may exist a great variety of land ownership rules and regulations, entirely exceeding the cadastral form. Scott offers the following hypothetical account which draws on a variety of cases from Southeast Asia: families have 'rights to parcels of cropland', but only 'certain crops ... may be planted', 'every seven years the ... land is redistributed' according to the size of the families, 'after the harvest ... all cropland reverts to common land'. Trees that are 'planted and any fruit they bear' belong to the family, but the 'fruit fallen from such trees' belongs to 'anyone who gathers it', if a tree is cut down, certain parts of it go to the family, other parts to the neighbour, again other parts to the poorest in the community.[17] Scott continues for another page detailing what can be planted when by whom, but the point is already well made: when the cadastral map is applied to such circumstances a complex and locally adapted system carefully regulating communal relations is replaced with a simple, binary, reality. Either one person owns the land, or nobody owns it. Bearing this in mind, it is interesting to note that the establishment of cadastral maps in Afghanistan today is a top priority for the 'international community'. I will return to this issue in a discussion of the contemporary role of digital power in warfare in the fourth chapter.

To these two lenses of understanding particular forms of the map, as both legitimating territorial authority and simplifying ownership systems, we can add a third: the map in international, colonial relations. In the same way that a ritual can be both justification and explanation, maps representing imperial holdings should be understood as a 'model for rather than a model of what [they] purported to represent'.[18] Or put differently, just because large parts of a map are coloured pink does not mean that imperial control or legibility is distributed equally across the parts, rather it indicates a desire for such a state. Despite the naturalising tendency of a map, or perhaps because of it, different moments arise where not only a particular line but the entire standard of mapmaking itself becomes contested and scrutinised. One well-known incident illuminating this is Arno Peters' critique of the Mercator projection. The Mercator projection, named after the sixteenth century Flemish mapmaker Gerardus Mercator, treats the earth's latitudinal lines—the line at the equator and those above and below it—as equal in length, thereby turning the earth into a cylinder. This distortion solves the problem of projecting the area of a sphere onto a two-dimensional plane by increasing the size of territory above and below the equator and decreasing the size of territory at the equator. This operation creates an image of the world in which the global South appears smaller than the global North, Greenland ends up being the size of South America, and, significantly for the Cold War, the USSR looks huge. For Peters, whose academic work is characterised by a deep-seated egalitarianism, the Mercator projection was a disservice to peoples living in the global South. In 1973 he therefore developed a different world map and atlas that had a closer fidelity to area. Here one can begin to get a sense of how what may appear as arbitrary, technical, standardisations can have political effects that move, beyond obvious and intentional acts of carto-propaganda, towards, literally, influencing one's worldview.

Added to this potential for the map form to normalise and produce particular ideas of ownership and authority also lay a deeper animating desire for completion. As Thongchai Winichakul argued, maps with large blank spaces on them helped to concentrate exploratory desires:

Since Mercator invented the latitude-longitude matrix covering the entire globe, the world has been full of blank squares waiting to be filled in. The New World was 'discovered'. African Africa was found. The unexplored places were opened up and inscribed on the map. Indeed, modern mapmaking had inspired innumerable missions to fulfil its desire to plot the entire world.[19]

Marlow, in Joseph Conrad's *Heart of Darkness* (1902), exemplifies this desire for cartographic completion:

I would look for hours at South America, or Africa, or Australia, and lose myself in all the glories of exploration. At that time there were many blank spaces on the earth, and when I saw one that looked particularly inviting on a map (but they all look that) I would put my finger on it and say, When I grow up I will go there.[20]

This collection of sources and arguments enables a historical reading in which representations of political authority in space have been standardised, which, in turn, has led to a standardisation of the very idea of political authority. Such a cycle of tools becoming deeply constitutive, of predicates turning into subjects, is recurring in our study of the technics of politics. Standardised political maps serve practical functions and, more pervasively and obscured, help to frame and legitimate contingent political realities. Apart from maps, the archival forms of censuses and statistics also feature significantly in the modern political imagination; they help to provide a thick description of those large coloured spaces demarked by territorial lines on a map and more directly deal with the problem of identifying and sorting individuals.

Census and Statistics

In this section on census and statistics I seek to more clearly locate the role of the colony in the development of such technics of politics, to identify the importance of specialised knowledge (statistics) for such technics, and show how these forms can be used in a new way to legitimate the persecution of previously illegible population groups.

While there are traces of Egyptian censuses up to 3,000 years ago, as a modern archival technic of the state, the census was primarily deployed and developed in present or recent colonies: Spanish census of Peru (1548), Spanish census of their North American holdings (1576), census in Virginia, Bermuda (1642–5), census in the United States (1780), and census in India (1871), for instance.[21] One could simply count these with other cases where the assessment of society—making it legible—was closely tied to its previous or subsequent exploitation and conquest. Let us return to Cortés for an instant, who claims that before invading a country 'it must be determined whether it is inhabited, and if so by what kind of peoples, and what religion or rite they have, and upon what they live, and what there is in the land'.[22] A further indication that censuses were once widely regarded as state 'intelligence' can be seen in the fact that in England a census at home seemed illiberal: 'A census had been proposed in 1753, but rejected as "subversive of the last remains of English liberty."'[23] This tension, of a technology appearing illiberal at home but emancipatory and illuminating abroad, is reoccurring in the history of the technics of politics. Innovations in census technologies were undertaken by metropole powers in the periphery. Another good example for this tendency is the first case of the inspection of a *national* economy, which took place when 'Ireland was completely surveyed for land, buildings, people, and cattle under the directorship of William Petty, in order to facilitate the rape of that nation by the English in 1679'.[24] This seventeenth-century precursor to a modern day Gross Domestic Product (GDP) was dubbed 'Political Arithmetic' by Petty and served as the intelligence which enabled effective exploitation. For Petty, Political Arithmetic was the application of Baconian science to government; a new type of knowledge representing an innovation in the means of governance and domination.[25]

With the development of new archival forms of the technics of politics different areas of expertise, as well as sites of institutional power, are engendered. This is especially visible in the history of statistics in the territorial area now called Germany. Ever since the birth of Prussia, census technics have played a significant role in the domestic administrative practices of the State in 'Germany'. In 1700 the German mathematician Leibniz wrote to Prince Friedrich of Prussia suggesting the creation of a statistical bureau for the kingdom of Brandenburg–Prussia, which was to be created the following year.[26] Leibniz's main argument was that the purpose of statistics is to measure the power of the state and that the state should set about it, a sentiment echoed by Rousseau when he wrote that, 'Statisticians, it is now up to you; count, measure, compare.'[27] In this sense it also contributes to a particular realist vision of international power: quantifiable centres of influence that make up the international system.

The census and surveying of Prussia only began in earnest in 1730, some thirty years after Leibniz's suggestion. Individuals were identified and sorted into one of nine categories (such as landlords, journeymen, servants, and children), buildings were sorted according to their quality, livestock and lands were measured.[28] A census in the archival mode is extremely tedious. Individuals collect all the information; all tallies are compiled by hand. We should remember that at this point physical reality itself is also less legible, street signage is not standardised, house numbers have not been established—they would be developed in Vienna for the purposes of conscription in 1770—city planning has yet to really come into its own, the world is simply not as tagged as it is today. To these difficulties we can add a particular political-technical problem of censuses and statistics that reappears with reliable frequency: to have any comparative ability over time and space the same categories need to be used. Yet, this obviously constrains the capacity to update one's model of society—what if Prussian administrators decided that there were now more than nine categories for individuals?—and through reiteration leads to constitutive effects—the Prussians learn that there are nine categories for individuals. With the growing importance of censuses to provide legibility for the state, statistics, which was understood as 'remarkable facts about the State', was born as a university field.[29]

With demography and statistics it became possible to construct tallies of suspicious population groups, to scientifically measure something that had not previously belonged to the realm of computable phenomena. Detailed statistics enumerating Jewish households became a staple part of Prussian census efforts from 1769 onwards.[30] Berlin, 1879–80, marks a significant time and place for thinking about the relationship of census and statistics to anti-Semitism. It was during this time that modern statistical arguments were for the first time used and disseminated to project the Jewish population as growing due to immigration, more fertile families, and a lower mortality rate and as inherently more talented yet prone to mental illness and asociality.[31] Statistics became 'a fuel for antisemitism'.[32] While these claims appear absurd today, and many were disproven by cooler heads at the time, what is of special import to our study of the technics of politics is that this grafting of 'scientific' statistical practices onto the 'Jewish question' required even more penetrating statistical inspection of the Jewish population to disprove the bizarre allegations.[33] In a tragic reversal many of these statistics would then be used in the 1930s both as arguments against the Jewish population and means for identifying 'Jews'. Knowledge generated by statistics and censuses, even if for distinct emancipatory political purposes, can always be used as intelligence for exploitation, in the sense of Cortés and Petty.

Passports

If maps help to legitimate territorial authority and a binary model of land ownership, and censuses and statistics provide 'intelligence' of foreign lands as well as measure and evaluate 'suspicious' parts of the population, then passports enable states to control the migration of humans and identify individuals to an unprecedented degree. Passports standardise political subjectivity into a global ontopological system. Out of all of the archival forms discussed here the passport, and the border sites it is evaluated at, are the most frequent manifestations of state power in a modern individual's life. Just as time and space were standardised, and territorial authority and simple land ownership were legitimated, the passport contributes to a specific construction of the world and self. Two effects of it, which I consider below, are individualisation and the establishment of state authority to control human migration.

Before the late eighteenth century passports granted by the state had primarily been used to regulate internal migration, and it was relatively easy to get a passport under a false name. Fearing a reactionary émigré invasion, the French revolutionary government began to change the administrative practices, legislation, and archival form of the passport:

> All passports are to contain the number of persons to whom they are given, their names, their age, their description, and the parish inhabited by those who have obtained them, who are obliged to sign both the register of passports and the passports themselves.[34]

A year later a further crucial addition was made to the production of passports: 'henceforth, they should all be issued to *individuals*'.[35] I want to draw attention to two different processes at work here. The first is that the emergency circumstances of war, either civil or international, leads states to create more exacting migration controls. Consider the quote below about World War I as a further indication of this trend:

> I am positive that the Great War was fought, not for democracy and justice, but for no other reason then that a cop, or an immigration officer, may have the legal right to ask you, and be well paid for asking you, to show him your sailor's card, or what have you. Before the war nobody asked you for a passport.[36]

The second thing I wish to draw attention to is the state appropriation of the means of identification and legitimate circulation. John Torpey, who I have already drawn on strongly in this section, has a wonderful way of putting this that places it within a Marxist and Weberian history of political thought:

> ... modern states, and the international state system of which they are a part, have expropriated from individuals and private entities the legitimate "means of movement," particularly though by no means exclusively across international borders.[37]

After the First World War this monopolisation of the legitimate means of movement and migration was so widely standardised that 'national borders had even replaced other impediments such as distance, cost, and local institutions as the main obstacles to mobility'.[38] A qualitatively new migration regime was put into place. A number of bureaucratic innovations were necessary for states to implement passports for the whole population. This is a case where such archival administrative 'power can only become established if the coding of information is actually applied in a direct way to the supervision of human activities'.[39] Perhaps the most important archival technics for these purposes, and a force multiplier for the bureaucratic state in the twentieth century, was a card registry or card index filing system.

The Card Registry

Systems developed for the organisation of printed information in libraries have been vastly influential in other realms requiring information management, such as accounting, collaborative research, and the surveillance of suspicious populations. One could go so far as to say that rational bureaucratic governance is only enabled through such information technology. Yet these information systems are seldom identified as key components in any modern bio-political enterprise, and this despite the fact that such practices—and the rationalisation of the modern state—owe much to the humble library card catalogue.[40] The card catalogue was a significant breakthrough in information technology for all of the important institutions of modernity: prison, police, hospital, university, government, military, and the border. Yet today such catalogues appear as historical relics, thereby obscuring the revolutionary forms of retention and retrieval they enabled.

To grasp the extent of their importance and utility we can consider what life was like without them. To find a particular papyrus scroll housed in the hallowed library of Alexandria one would have literally had to know where it was. The greatest collection of texts in antiquity had no 'classmarks', no addresses. Storage cases were described by field, medicine, philosophy, etc., but texts themselves were not marked. The organisation was not thoroughly legible and the physical library could act as its own map. In most medieval libraries the situation was not much different. As the amount of written material increased lists were made;

their obvious drawback being that adding material always requires either placing it at the end—in effect sorting according to acquisition date—or laboriously reconstituting the list *in toto*.

When large collections of books were amassed in a locality during the middle ages, such as in Leipzig, Paris, and Avignon, entire stacks were often forgotten, and recurring clean-up and listing exercises had to be undertaken. With no stable system of organisation or uniform means of legibility existing, an intimate local knowledge of book collections was essential for their utility. In this time library management was a feat of familiarisation, memorisation, and situated local knowledge, what others have called *mētis*,[41] and not procedural classification and organisation, *tekhne*, as it is today. The paradigmatic figures that come to mind are the wizened old librarian who finds hidden books by knowing and remembering them, contrasted to the rigorous bureaucrat who can rely on his system and apparatus to locate the required text.

Simple lists and their accompanying anarchy did not pose a large problem for library management before the invention of movable type technology (1439) and the groundswell of books that followed it. 'In western Europe', prior to Gutenberg and 1439, 'the only library to exceed two thousand volumes was the Papal library at Avignon.'[42] The novel, relatively cheap, reproduction of books created a data surfeit that would prove to be insurmountable for the old system of information management. There was simply too much unorganised data constantly being produced for a librarian's *mētis* to handle it. This spread of print technology also coincided with an explosion of political correspondence. Bern, for instance, 'averaged an output of fifty letters per night during the war against the Burgundian duke Charles the Bold (1474–7), a figure that only a generation earlier would have been reached in a month'.[43] Of significance for the politics of knowledge production is that individual's collections began to grow. By the late sixteenth century a retired Michel de Montaigne's personal library held 1,000 texts.[44] In this way the invention of movable type also led to a decentralisation and reconfiguration of sites of power and knowledge.

Academics have always sought to find ways to deal with large amounts of written information. Leibniz's personal data storage system is worth considering as a precursor of the index card:

> That which came to mind, in part while reading many books, in part while meditating, during travels, while walking, he wrote on notes, which he thought

(especially the quotations) did not leave in disorder, but would from time to time place into order. … Later he also procured a special closet to store his quotations. Leibniz would write his quotations on special notes and papers.[45]

Considering this practice, as well as his concern for Prussian statistics, it is no surprise that Leibniz wrote a proposal in 1680 for the construction of a universal library. This motif of the universal storage of information reoccurs in different technics of politics.

The card index was produced in the race to maintain order in such a mass of information. There was always already 'too much to know'.[46] Invented at least twice—once in sixteenth-century Europe and once at Harvard in the nineteenth century[47]—this data-management technology enabled new forms of legibility and knowledge. Its essential components are only standardised cards, a container, and a stable set of sorting rules. Yet the labour of information management radically changes with the advent of this apparatus. Were one to punch holes in the cards and build

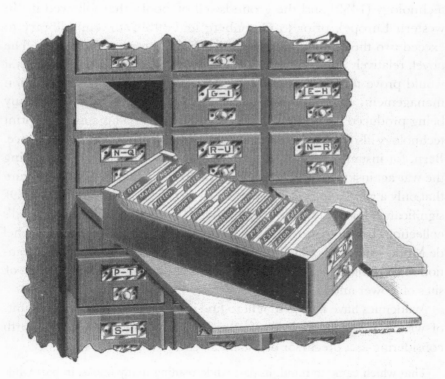

Figure 9: Library Bureau Tray Cases

a machine which sorts on the basis of these holes, one would have already constructed a rudimentary computer/search machine.[48] With the card registry, suddenly the representation of texts can be disassociated from the physical organisation of the library; all of the work required for a new addition is the production of a new card, and one can begin to sort according to any of the criteria on the card. Use no longer requires thick local knowledge. In short, the card catalogue acts as a proto-database permitting different search functions. Like the *khipu* it represents a type of the class which Bruno Latour calls 'immutable and combinable mobiles', things that can be moved around, are stable and can be combined, such as surveys.[49] Latour identifies these artefacts as constituting a crucial technological basis of scientific practices from the sixteenth century onwards.

What is different about the card index from many other immutable and combinable mobiles, such as standardised questionnaires and forms sent throughout the country, is that its primary mobility occurs within a constrained space, the index card drawer. It is the fact that the card is fixed, standardised, immutable, and mobile with relation to other standardised cards that make it so powerful. Walter Benjamin recognised in this mobility 'the conquest of three dimensional writing'.[50] In a similar vein Wilhelm Dux claimed that the 'card registry is the overcome book'.[51] For it to reach its maximum potential it would have to deal with objects that also have a stable name and address. This is where smart numbers enter the picture.

At its most fundamental a smart number is a number combination that acts as a signifier for an object, not as a quantity—as a name, not as an amount. A famous example of a smart number is the decimal classification system developed by the American librarian Melvil Dewey in 1876; Dewey is sometimes falsely identified as also being the progenitor of the card catalogue, while he was only its main distributor. An example of a Dewey Decimal smart number would be:

973.931

B62

In his system the number holds information about where in the organisation of knowledge the book is located. There are ten main classes of human knowledge, each further subdivided into ten divisions, and each division further divided into ten sections. The intellectual tyranny of the decimal system is made apparent at this stage. Coupled with the smart number the card catalogue became a powerful tool for producing legibility and finding individual texts in individual libraries by creating a systemic order for all libraries. For the system to work, cards need to be rigorously standardised and identical in form and layout. 'The cards have to be as precise as munitions … cards delivered today must in every quality, thickness, and size be identical to those delivered in decades.'[52]

The late nineteenth and early twentieth centuries saw a spread of this technological apparatus to many areas. In 1891 Mr Davidson and Mr Parker, business associates of Melvil Dewey at the Library Bureau, described the situation as follows:

> From an author's catalog it has spread to an almost infinite application. Every list, record, index, etc., that is in a state of growth can be thus kept with great saving labor. Business houses find it invaluable for lists of goods, customers, discounts, and the 1,000 growing records of commerce. Science adopts it even more widely, and its use is spreading with growing rapidity.[53]

At the end of the nineteenth century libraries, police, and armed forces applied the smart number card registry apparatus to a great variety of objects, subjects, suspects, and patients. What had previously been an anarchic, illegible, and unrelated amount of data was disciplined and made safe for searching, retention, retrieval, and cross-referencing. The world became a reservoir of data.

Structurally identical to the problem of finding a text in an unorganised library is the problem of the recidivist—the repeat offender. How and why to punish recidivists was known and generally accepted, how to reliably identify them posed a real difficulty. Uniform discipline and punishment could not be administered without reliable means of identification and classification. The state of the art was to measure people. In 1897 Dewey's Library Bureau received a contract from the Orwellian-sounding U.S. National Bureau of Identification to create a nation-wide card registry based on Bertillonage for the identification of criminals.[54] Bertillonage, introduced in France by Alphonse Bertillon in 1883, was a popular anthropometric system that took eleven measurements of the human body for the purpose of establishing a set of identifying numbers that were individual to each person.[55] Designed for the precise purpose of identifying recidivists it functioned as a formula for producing an individual's 'smart number'. It was recognised that 'the usefulness of criminal records depends upon the ability of the police to *fasten upon each human being an identity from which he cannot escape*'.[56] Coupled with the card catalogue this type of smart number invested the early national security state with an unprecedented capacity for mass surveillance. The technological apparatus became indispensable to modern statecraft: it allowed 'for the first time an advance beyond punishment of the few to control over the many—a critical, defining attribute of the modern state'.[57] This shift in state capacity from spectacular punishment to surveillance and identification is as momentous as that from tribute to taxation; advances in information technology fundamentally enable both.[58]

Suspected subversives could now more easily be tracked across geographical distances and whole new forms of policing became possible. This system also permitted and enabled a centralised, national documentation of individual identity. Such technical ability made a national passport system feasible. It is no coincidence that it corresponded with the legal invention of the passport and the nationalisation of migration control in the late nineteenth century.[59] Without a card registry and a smart number it would not have been possible for a state to achieve the centralised registration and documentation of all of its citizens or subjects. Today these practices have been normalised; they appear as natural and neutral. Registration by a state at birth is treated as a universal human right and states which fail to register are seen as weak or failed. The global spread of the migration regime and means used to identify and document individuals appears to not have followed a pattern of functional adaptation due to necessity, but rather of mimicry of practices of power.

The card index entailed as much a practice as it did a technical artefact, as it did a world-view. At the dawn of the mechanisation of information it reanimated old sovereign dreams of a total and complete knowledge of all their human subjects. Up to this point in the chapter I have sought to argue that the modern state system is intricately connected to a number of archival forms that helped homogenise political power in important ways. But how do these practices connect to rationalisation, bureaucracy, and reproduction? A short excursion into Max Weber and Walter Benjamin's writings offer some possible responses to this question.

THEORISING THE ARCHIVAL MODE

Weber

For our purposes, reflection about the rationalisation of the archival mode begins in earnest with the work of Max Weber (1864–1920). Weber understood himself as living in a period featuring the advent of great impersonal bureaucratisation that depended on the establishment of individual identity and was closely connected to the means of modern administration.

When listing the actual benefits of the kind of knowledge social science can produce in his famous lecture on 'Science as Vocation' (1919), Weber begins by saying that '[f]irst of all, of course, there is knowledge of the techniques by which life—both external things and the behaviour of people—can be ruled through calculation.'[60] These kinds of techniques form a prominent bridge between academic activity and the process of rationalisation as a whole and are a part of what we call technics. In the same lecture Weber points out that rationalisation does not imply that his audience suddenly has a deeper knowledge of how their world works, much rather that it is marked by the belief that there are principally no mysterious forces which cannot be known and calculated. This leads to a demystification of the world.[61] In this sense, rationalisation is a fundamental attitude to knowledge and the world that maintains that the latter can be understood and dominated; hence it has its own implicit cosmology, epistemology, ontology and power relations. At the same time though, 'rational technics' and 'economic rationalism' are not simply inventions, but are dependent on the 'ability and disposition of humans for particular types of practical-rational lifestyles'.[62] For Weber, the very birth of rationalisation, and techniques of calculation, can be traced to a human disposition for an ordered and regulated, perhaps even ritualised, lifestyle. A similar argument can also be discovered in the thought of advocates of rationalisation. For instance, Erwin Cuntz (see Chapters 4 and 7), exclaims that '[o]ne need only proceed with the knowledge that man is a versatile and self-directing being'.[63] In other words, the foundations of rationalisation can be found in the pattern-like nature of human existence; the rationalised archival mode thereby proceeds from assumptions about human behaviour not anchored in ritual or spirituality.

A wider look at Weber's oeuvre permits other characteristics of rationalisation to come into focus. For Weber a prominent aspect of rationalisation is its pervasive tendency to spread. This stems in part from the fact that rationalisation 'always' results in a selection process—those 'who did not succeed, must fail'[64]—and that:

[e]very bureaucracy has the tendency to achieve the same effect through escalation. Even ours. And while in antiquity politics of the polis had to form

the 'pacemaker' for capitalism, today capitalism has become the 'pacemaker' for the bureaucratisation of the economy.[65]

Hence, we can see that while bureaucracy—which Weber regards as the purest technical form of legal rule[66]—is a type of political organisation, it is radicalised and advanced through the spread of capitalism. It is important not to lose sight of the fact that rationalisation also exists and persists at the level of ideology within capitalism: 'labour in the service of a rational formation of the material provision of goods for humanity has without a doubt been envisioned by the representatives of the "capitalist spirit" as a formative purpose in their lives' work'.[67] Returning to our focus on technics, an appropriate place to look for the factors and drivers of modern techniques of governance would then be in the concrete practices and ideologies of capitalism. This should include Frederick Taylor's *The Principles of Scientific Management*,[68] Henry Ford's assembly lines, the organisation of Toyota (1990s), the use of automatic resupply in Walmart (2000s), and the data-mining techniques of large supermarkets and marketing companies.

One of the most well known characteristics of modernity and capitalism for Weber is that the concern for external goods was supposed to just be a 'light cloak', but had been empowered and become 'a steel-hard housing'.[69] Co-constitutive tendencies of these spheres come into focus when we observe that modern capitalism is itself obviously strongly determined by the development of technical options: 'Its rationality is contingent upon the *calculation* of the technically crucial factors: the documentation of exact calculation'.[70] This is a further point where the academic techniques by which 'life can be controlled through calculation' provide a foundation for modern rationalisation and technics.

The principles that lie at the heart of these calculating practices are efficiency and increasing profits. Most importantly, these 'real', easily quantified categories of rationalisation manage to shroud the strange assumptions at the foundations of a discipline such as economics. In a passage from 1904, which is worth quoting at length, Weber states that:

> Macroeconomics was ... originally, at least in the emphasis of its inquiries, 'technic'. This means that it regarded the appearances of reality from an, at least seemingly, obvious and fixed practical point of view: the increase of the wealth of its citizens. ... But the peculiarity of this worldview, with its optimistic belief in the theoretical practical rationalisation of the real was significant, in so far that it hindered the discovery of the problematic character of these 'self-evident' assumed points of view.[71]

In other words, economics—and this is characteristic of rationalisation as a whole—by taking on a technical mantle, makes it difficult to analyse the originary assumptions at the heart of it. A demystification of the world, its relationship to capitalism, and the shrouding of its own, possibly absurd, metaphysical assumptions mark Weber's understanding of rationalisation. The critical reader might reply that a simplistic review of the twentieth century contradicts the first characteristic (demystification of the world), while it can support the second and third. Furthermore, if, as Weber writes elsewhere, 'all theology is intellectual rationalisation',[72] then why should rationalisation necessarily lead to a demystification? Theology is after all quite mystifying. My response to this is that rationalisation in the sphere of politics only leads to demystification for some, the rationalisers. This is a recurring motif in the technics of politics: the experience of legibility and rationality for some, and of illegibility and apparent irrationality for others. Of course Weber is quite aware of this when he writes that 'what appears "rational" from one point, can, observed from another point, be "irrational"'.[73]

An example might help here. Thinking through rationalisation as a force in a field of power relations, one can imagine a scenario in which a university, city, or country is being restructured along *rationalising lines* when surveilled from the space of power, the centre of the Panopticon,[74] but that this new social reality is experienced as highly *irrational* by the students or citizens. A case that illustrates this unexpected relationship of rational plan to irrational experience is the planned city of Brasília.[75] Designed by Oscar Niemeyer and Lucio Costa, architects who followed the Le Corbusier[76] (1887–1965) school, Brasília was imagined and constructed as a giant axis at the centre of which lay the huge Plaza of the Three Powers and the Esplanade of the Ministries. The city features identical superquadra apartment blocks organised in a grid. It is interesting to note that Cuzco, the Inca capital, was also arranged into clearly legible quarters with three *ayllus* (families claiming a shared ancestor) in each quarter.[77] While this organisation of Brasília is highly rational when overlooked from a seat of power in the centre (there are no hidden alleyways or illegible slums), it is alienating and irrational for the people living in it. Every building looks the same, there are no corners, the city lacks 'the complex intersections of dense neighbourhoods comprising residences and public cafés with places for leisure work and shopping'.[78] In this case the rational construction of the city ended up erasing all the markers that a subjectivity within the city requires to navigate and make sense of its surroundings.

Radical rationalisation can thus be experienced as its opposite, which using Weber's terms would lead to a renewed mystification of the world for those being rationalised. Furthermore, the techniques by which 'life can be controlled through calculation' need to be understood not just as neutral procedures, but as abstractions which transform our epistemologies, ontologies and politics. For practices of calculation to be enabled, reality has to be quantified and represented by numbers. This has two obvious results: (a) objects and aspects which cannot be converted into a number are necessarily excluded from this analysis, and (b) knowledges which do not feature these characteristics are devalued.[79] While the methodology through which this can be done may vary, this principle must be an inherent element to any description of rationalisation and attempt at a theory of technics of politics. Furthermore, the procedures of calculation need to be reproducible for a technic to be regarded as legitimate and take hold. The problem of reproduction and calculation mark the archival mode in a manner distinct from the ritual mode.

Benjamin

Contrasted to Max Weber's systematic analysis, the intellectual excursions of Walter Benjamin (1892–1940) take on a more fragmentary and aphoristic character. Significant for our understanding of technics is a popular essay Benjamin wrote, titled 'Art in the Age of Mechanical Reproduction', which was first published in French in 1936. It was at this unsure political time in Germany that he already observed the significance of mechanically reproduced art, in particular film, for politics. For Benjamin, 'art was principally always reproducible'[80] yet the modern sophisticated mass production of art has a new effect: it erases the 'here and now of the piece of art—its singular being at a place'.[81] This means that 'the entire sphere of realness [*Echtheit*] removes itself from technical … reproducibility'.[82] By reproducing objects their singularity is lost, and thereby also the comprehension of their immediate local effects. This is a crucial characteristic of the normalisation that occurs through reproducing a technics of politics. Or, to put it differently, if only one passport existed in the world it would be easier to recognise its political effects. In a remarkable passage Benjamin declares that the 'singular value of a unique piece of art has its foundation in ritual',[83] but through reproduction where our understanding of the 'measures of realness fail' there has also been a change in the essence of art: 'its foundation [is now] on politics'.[84] A section combining these thoughts with an analysis of the political times he lived in is worth quoting at length:

> The increasing proletarisation of today's person and the increasing formation of masses are two sides of one and the same event. Fascism attempts to organise the newly created proletarised masses, without touching the property relations, which [the masses] strive to change. It sees its salvation in permitting the masses to come to their expression (but not their right). The masses have a right to change the ownership relations; fascism seeks to give them expression in their conservation. Fascism subsequently leads to an aestheticisation of political life. The rape of the masses, which are forced to the ground in the cult of a Führer, equates to the rape of an apparatus, which is placed in the service of producing cult values. All attempts concerning the aestheticisation of politics lead to one point. This point is war. War, and only war, makes it possible to provide mass movements of the largest order a goal while maintaining the inherited property relations.[85]

This quote deserves to be dwelled on. From what at first appears as an exposition of the essence of art in an age of reproducibility we are led to an argument that ineluctably grafts art with property relations, political mass movements, and war. What we are shown here is a world in which the reproducibility of art, in particular the moving image (film), is a necessary foundation for fascism, which Benjamin understands in this passage as primarily a mass movement that maintains property relations. For our discussion of technics, it could therefore be said that 'only war enables the mobilisation of the entire technical means of the present age while property relations are maintained'.[86] Two strands of thought follow from this: (a) contemplation of the consequences of reproducibility, which achieves a radical new quality with the invention and ubiquity of the digital computer. Mechanical reproducibility characterises our contemporary age to an extent that Benjamin could probably not have foreseen. (b) Recognition that new technologies need to be embedded into and appropriated by existing property and power relations. To do this without radically changing the existing property and power relations requires determining the meaning of a machine to serve existing relations.

As we will see further below, reproducibility of technics of politics is a key component of depoliticising their application, but also an inherent property of mass-produced technical artefacts *and* proto-scientific academic discourses. In our contemporary age, the condition of reproducibility opens up the question of determining legitimate and illegitimate copies to an unprecedented degree.[87] For a technics of politics, this means that by always instantiating a practice or a copy that is widespread, responsibility and a focus on local effects can be erased while these same effects are multiplied. Politics is effaced. Benjamin ends his essay on a grim poetic note. He claims that 'imperialistic war is' actually 'a revolt of technic' which has now come to collect the same demands of 'human-material', which 'society has extracted from its natural materials'.[88] World War was indeed the coming future that extracted horrific demands from the 'human-material'.

Up to now I have sought to provide an empirical description of different archival forms as well as a theoretical discussion of rationalisation and reproduction to understand the homogenisation of political power and subjectivity that occurs. But how can we think about the political power that is homogenised by these technologies and forms? Is a different kind of political power being projected with archival technics, and if so, how are we to understand it?

7

THE DATABASE

The digital mode is prevalent in societies in which political legibility is primarily achieved through recourse to systems of networked computers. The ideal of such a kind of governance is the paper-less office, in which the work of information production, management and communication takes place outside of the physically printed form so fundamental to the archival mode. Writing is still predominant here, but it is now writing with a computer that produces a searchable and clickable 'hyper-text',[1] the computer, in turn, leads to a new set of 'human-machine' relations.[2] For now, the different strands of the history I have been sketching out and gesturing towards have led to the networked relational database which features an unprecedented ability to combine both variety and quantity of information into a system productive of novel forms of legibility of populations by identifying and sorting of individuals.

A database is commonly defined as a structured organisation of data stored on a computer system that produces information.[3] Information is measured in 'bits'.[4] In a database bits of data are arranged according to a model that logically relates them to each other. Databases therefore have architectures ranging from the hierarchic to the rhizomatic, even anarchic. As the material basis for—and expression of—what Edmund Husserl referred to as 'an arithmetisation of reality' databases entail calculation.[5] They are the modern apparatus of a particular form of knowledge about the human and the international that collects and weighs massive quantities of data exceeding personal experience and recollection, to be organised into attributes and objects, presented in rows and columns. The information produced by these means is inherently instrumental; it is part of what Max Weber referred to as 'knowledge of the techniques by which life—both external things and the behaviour of people—can be ruled through calculation'.[6] It is difficult to exaggerate the need for developing a mode of political thought appropriate for analysing the power and functions of the database. Databases are pervasive and proliferating, practically ubiquitous in global politics, while there is a lack and lag of thought dealing with the fundamental political implications of the retention, manipulation, and mining of data. How is this new tool of governance best conceptualised? It exists somewhere between ideal and material, theory and practice, structure and agency. It is wholly political yet emerges removed from politics through grounding in utility, thus maintaining an apodictic, factual appearance.

Once a database is assembled it is acted upon with a range of data-mining practices that segment, aggregate and present the data to make it meaningful, to turn it into information. The most dominant data-mining practice we consider can be analytically disassembled into the following, repeatable, steps:

- assemble a large amount of differently sourced properties of entities or groups of entities;
- quantify these properties by turning them into calculable values;
- aggregate these values into a score, such as a risk, support, credit, or merit score;
- categorise the initial entities or groups, on the basis of that score, into new entities or groups; and
- act and differentiate your strategy on the basis of the newly created groups.

The application of this method to large population sets, pioneered by the Stanford Research Institute in 1978, primarily for marketing research, led to the development of new categories of consumers, the VALS (values, attitudes, and lifestyle) consumer segment descriptions: 'innovators', 'thinkers', 'believers', 'achievers', 'strivers', 'experiencers', 'makers', and 'survivors'.[7] Other demographic artefacts which were constructed later in the same fashion consisted of categories such as 'pools and patios', 'shotguns and pickups', 'young digerati', 'urban achievers', 'blue blood estates', 'big city blues'.[8] These *'limit-shapes'*—more on that term below—were the first in a new technology of segmentation that would be applied to many different aspects of domestic and world politics.

A central problem when working with a mass of data is how to exclude all of the irrelevant parts when searching for something. With the total registration of a population, a new—inverse—practice is enabled and occasionally required. When searching for single, hard to find individuals, it now becomes possible to begin with everybody and proceed by excluding people one isn't interested in. This data-management practice was called 'negative *Rasterfahndung*' in Germany and was very publicly deployed during the 1970s hunt for the Rote Armee Fraktion (RAF) terrorists. In the case of searching for German terrorists, it took on the following form, seeking to exclude all the elements that were not suspicious:

- exclude all rented apartments that are paid for by bank transfer and that pay their electricity bill by bank transfer;
- out of those rented apartments remaining, exclude all that are rented by locally registered individuals;
- out of those remaining, exclude all that are rented by individuals with driver licences;
- out of those remaining, exclude all that are recipients of state subsidies; and
- take the greatly reduced mass of rented apartments remaining and begin to cross-reference them with the criminal files.[9]

That this technic of politics has much wider implications than its initial purpose can be seen in how comprehensive a data-management worldview is. The glossary of the U.S. Biometric Identity Management Agency (BIMA) provides a taste of such a worldview. They define analyse as meaning to 'convert data to actionable information', to collect is to 'capture biometric sample(s)', identity 'is a set of characteristics by which an entity … is recognizable', and submission is 'the process whereby a subject provides a biometric sample to a biometric system'.[10] Through data-management technique the technical artefact of the database is manipulated to produce novel orders and visions of information. At the same time the biometric vision enframes the human subject in a new and different way: identity is now a set of characteristics by which an entity is recognisable and can be indexed.

The International and Digital Power

Databases and data practices are relevant to world politics for a variety of interrelated reasons, at a number of different levels of analysis and abstraction. First, and most apparently, they are heavily used and developed in and by the United States, therefore affecting the conduct of the major superpower. As was visible in the case of Dewey's Library Bureau and the development of the card registry, great innovations of information and communication technology occurred in the United States before spreading throughout the world. This has occasionally led to an inflated sense of control—in the words of Arthur Schlesinger Jr.: 'No people in the world approach the Americans in mastery of the new magic of science and technology.'[11] Today the powerful industries of Silicon Valley continue this tradition. Secondly, specific technical information management practices have spread to the point where they are increasingly used or aspired to by all states, leading to a progressively homogenous set of political tools and techniques in the international system.[12] Third, certain information technologies are also used to produce knowledge of the 'international'—states operating in the world today are measured, sorted, and known through indexes, compiled with databases. Democracy indexes, prosperity indexes, freedom indexes, peace indexes, development indexes, health indexes, all vie for position, using similar methods but advocating different ways of framing and sorting global human life. Fourth, these modern tools are used to maintain a complex international migration regime in which certain classes (*the mobility*) circulate easily while others face a huge barrier to entry, both literal and metaphorical.

Mastering databases is a part of practices which make 'states' into modern stable states; which constitute the difference between formal-legal sovereignty and technical-actual sovereignty. In this way databases are means for reproducing individual societies and the international system. They are both a way of knowing and devices of order—epistemologies and disciplinary apparatuses. Accepting the premise that '[power is the production, in and through social relations, of effects that shape the capacities of actors to determine their circumstances and fate' impels a recognition and close study of the particular type of political power exercised through this information technology.[13] This forces the question: What is 'seeing like a state' when the state sees through databases? My answer is that this technical force multiplication constitutes a new form of radicalised bio-power that is sufficiently distinct to warrant its own signifier, *digital power*.

This form of power has the following characteristics: digital power is primarily organised around the problem of identifying individuals and then of sorting and organising them into new categories. It does this predominantly by making massive reams of data meaningful. What is special about digital power is that visual characteristics, which have always served as an index of identity—the badge, the uniform, skin colour, the robber's severed hand—can now be abstracted to the point where they are only visible, legible, and meaningful to the operator with a database and a screen. This is the novel response of digital power to the problem of identification shared by all technics of politics: the labour of labelling is internal to a network and a machine. A new world of conspicuous identity is created on a screen, abstracted from an observed reality that is not legible to the same degree when viewed with a naked eye.

To achieve such tasks digital power requires a mechanism, as well as the technical competence and capacity, to retain and manipulate vast amounts of data about human subjects. Through this apparatus the individual is made legible to a centralised authority to an unprecedented degree. Digital power is not distributed equally in the world. Some countries are more adept at wielding it—the United States, China, Germany— while others such as Egypt, Liberia or Ghana are not. But digital power is not only an aspect of the modern territorial state; companies and private actors can also have it. Because I define digital power as the ability to retain and manipulate a massive amount of information about human subjects, in our contemporary technological configuration it always requires something resembling a database.

With this groundwork in mind the next section considers the technologies of the 2008 Obama U.S. presidential campaign, a campaign and subsequent administration that have had especially close ties to Silicon Valley.

Barack Obama's Campaign Machine

'We tend to think of organizing as a mechanical, instrumental thing [but it is really about] building up stories and getting people to reflect on what their lives mean and how people in the neighbourhood can be heroes, and how they are part of a larger force.'[14]

Barack Obama, 1988

Jeffrey Alexander convincingly argues in his sociological analysis of the 2008 U.S. presidential election, *The Performance of Politics*, that democratic electoral campaigns are competitions in which the candidate seeks to become a collective representation, a superman of the civil sphere. A successful presidential performance therefore requires establishing heroic scripts and images that are more salient and powerful than that of the opponents. Such an endeavour is always threatened, and in danger of being undermined, through narratives that emphasise the mundane material basis of a campaign: the money, staff, or organisation that go into 'selling the president'.[15] Discourse about the Obama campaign featured all of these polluting material elements, but it also drew particular attention to a new object of public discussion, the campaign's means to represent and engage with the population whose votes they were seeking—their information and communication technologies. Asking the questions of Cuntz's Tower—where is the data stored, how is it stored, and what is done with it—has the potential to ground and destabilise the heroic myths that campaigns seek to construct about their candidate. What occurred to draw special attention to the technological basis of campaigns? A short answer is that the internet boom of the late 1990s exploded into the bureaucratic life of government, opening up new means of organising. Two different metrics of White House emails provide a rough indication of this trend. During his time in office, 1993–2001, Bill Clinton sent two emails; eight years later, at the end of George W. Bush's presidency, 2001–9, it was discovered that the Bush administration had lost 22 million White House emails.[16] This new reality, in which information and communication were digital, inevitably had an impact on presidential campaigns.

A presidential campaign can be understood as a complex combination of different hurdles and challenges, financial, logistical, and political. Yet a modern electoral campaign also poses significant intellectual and technical problems requiring epistemological commitments as well as ontological assumptions. How is the campaign to know the population? Who are the supporters? What does a likely supporter look like? How do you get out the vote? These challenges are responded to by registering voters and supporters, a practice in close vicinity to census operations and passport requirements.[17] Here the issue of identification arises anew but in a different light. It is no longer sufficient to just take down some biographic information and to document the identity of an individual; rather it is now necessary to construct a field of shifting indicators that produce probabilities of individuals being supporters. For the Obama campaign much of this process centred on working with large amounts of data:

> It involves ... keeping track of those who are on their side; staying in touch throughout the campaign; checking on Election Day to see whether they have voted and, if not, making sure they get to the polls before closing time. ... The results from canvassing and calling must be entered into the office computer, separating the 'maybe' Obama voters from the definite 'nos' and 'yeses'—so that the maybes can be revisited and all registered voters who are potential Obama supporters can be tracked to make sure they get to the polls.[18]

Modern Customer Relationship Management databases thereby open up a novel range of technical opportunities and strategies: for political parties sophisticated new lists, correlations, and representations of populations lend themselves to different allocations of resources in campaigns and long-term policies. More targeted canvassing of supporters and undecided voters through an effective database can make the difference between winning and losing an election. A characteristic that makes it difficult to research these kinds of technologies is that many of them are currently being created as proprietary tools.[19] Ethan Roeder, Data Manager for the Obama Campaign, states that he 'can't think of a single document that informs the work [he] ha[s] done'.[20] Practice precedes theory here.[21]

In the case of Barack Obama's successful 2008 presidential bid we now know that a database of supporters was constantly updated and coupled with a networking platform for volunteers on www.myBarackObama.com, also referred to as 'my BO'. Many observers have commented that it was this combination of centralised data with a networking facility that made the Obama campaign's organisational capacity so superior to that of the McCain campaign, as well as, and perhaps even more importantly, to that of Hillary Clinton.[22] Obama was seen as especially 'tech-friendly'. During the campaign new media was used in novel ways: there was a campaign 'app' for mobile devices and, for the first time in history, campaign posters were placed in video games. The Obama campaign also had one of the most sophisticated voter databases ever constructed.[23] A key strength was that it collected data on voters and supporters at various stages—when donating, volunteering, etc.—while also combining it with data from marketing databases and voter records:

> A sophisticated battery of databases has been tapped to find voters [who are] culled from a variety of sources, including magazine subscriptions, the types

of cars people drive, where voters shop and how much they earn. Commuting patterns are analysed. Voting history in local races is factored in. The data, after it is studied and sorted at campaign headquarters in Chicago, is sent to every battle ground state. The names are bar-coded and ultimately show up on the lists given to volunteers. And the theory is verified, or disproved, through conversations at doorsteps or in telephone calls where voters are identified on a scale from a No. 1 (strongly for Mr. Obama) to a No. 5 (strongly for Mr. McCain).[24]

A company called Catalyst Data Services provided much of the data, primarily consumer history, from which the Obama Campaign voters database was constructed. Catalyst Data Services describes itself as a 'licensed Private Investigations Corporation providing pre-employment background screening services to businesses nationwide utilizing a state of the art online ordering system'.[25] Practices generated at this conjuncture of capitalism, the penal system and information technology were used by the Obama campaign to construct the probability of an individual voting for or supporting Obama. Data points (up to 100 different ones) about individuals were added up and weighted (geography was more weighted than education) to construct *support scores*. The 'veracity' of these scores was then monitored daily, with the model being revised on a weekly basis.[26] While all of these tools no doubt assisted in the ultimate victory of the campaign, the list of established Obama supporters and potential volunteers appears to be one of the most valued assets:

> [It] is an e-mail database of more than 10 million supporters. The list is considered so valuable that the Obama camp briefly offered it as collateral during a cash-flow crunch late in the campaign, though it wound up never needing the loan, senior aides said. At least 3.1 million people on the list donated money to Obama.[27]

One of the indications that this type of political technology is far from neutral is the fact that vendors and companies offering data services and tools to campaigns are openly partisan. On the democratic side, for instance, there is Blue State Digital, which designed the web platform that the Obama campaign ran all of its sites from and has subsequently done work with the U.S. State Department.[28] With a different company using different tools employed by the Republican Party, the construction of separate models and images of society appears guaranteed.

At this point it can already be concluded that campaign organising is about telling stories and building a common identity, as well as an heroic image, but also that there is a profound material-technological basis to it that determines a campaign's capacity to do these things. Within a large electoral campaign's database, such as that of the Obama campaign, one can observe the uneasy articulation of techniques and industries origi-nally developed for more sophisticated targeting of consumers and effi-cient execution of background checks for criminal histories. At this juncture of capitalist processes and a disciplining prison apparatus a new form of political gaze was manufactured, characterised by what could be termed 'radical individuation': a focus on the individual as the most rel-evant political unit, and not any particular demographic, class, or geo-graphic group. After such a disaggregation occurs a new aggregation is undertaken. This second step is a typical actuarial practice which the legal academic Jonathan Simon describes in the following manner: the 'individuals, once understood as moral or rational actors, are' placed into new groups and 'increasingly understood as locations in actuarial tables of variations'.[29] Individualisation in the Obama campaign's database was followed by an aggregation into groups according to the likelihood by which individuals supported Obama. While modernity and capitalism have often been identified as forces that inherently individualise, the present state of the technology of the database, for the first time, permits the entire population to be tactically acted upon as individuals in national election campaigns through disaggregating salient groups and then re-aggregating them into new groups that are useful for sovereign power.

A prominent question for both the supporter list and the voter data is: Who owns it and what will become of it? Today, the database belongs to the legal entity Organizing for America (OFA)—not the Democratic Party. OFA morphed from a vehicle to get Obama re-elected into an advocacy group for Obama's policies (such as using the database to encourage Americans to sign-up for healthcare). As permanent cam-paigns become more widespread these kinds of digitally enhanced and enabled civic engagements become more prevalent. With electoral cam-paigns and government practices increasingly turning to data-mining as a technique to manipulate the technological artefact of the database, new practices of the social sciences and modern marketing are finding their way into politics.[30]

Apart from focusing on issues and images, future campaigns will need to place their models of society in competition with each other: the side with the more complete, specific, and private data combined with the more sophisticated data-mining algorithms will have a strong advantage—leading to a tendency for the repeated escalation of the collection of private and effective information and the development of novel mathematical tools to act on it. While much of the use of digital technics in the campaign was applauded for the political power it has given to 'average citizens', a few obvious anti-liberal tendencies are also at play. Firstly, a majority of the population believes that much of their lives are private (where they shop, what they buy, who they voted for), when the reality is that this information can be accessed and purchased by parties attempting to gain power. The strategic significance of this information of course lies in the fact that it is regarded as private; the 2008 economic crisis once again demonstrated that the distinction of what counts as private and public must be recognised as a function of sovereign power and not a condition it is embedded in. Furthermore, this technical configuration can only lead to a digital Ohio, a scenario in which voters judged to be more swayable or influential receive far greater tailor-made attention than those who are more predictable in their voting pattern and have less impact on others. In this way, there is also an anti-egalitarian tendency present in these data-mining practices. This is a case where a lack of willingness on the part of social scientists to reflexively analyse their own methods may become an inability to comprehend the effects of similar tools being deployed by political campaigns. When academic tools are used in different settings an approach that considers how knowledge is situated in the power relations of society is especially called for.

Most important though, is the fact that within these models the United States is imagined and acted upon as a land of single persons. With the digital power at hand to calculate individual support scores for such a large population this practice erodes earlier political strategies focused on winning over classes and organisations; it acts on a country that is assumed to be 'bowling alone' and must therefore be organised.[31] It imagines the social ontology of the United States not as consisting of groups and classical hierarchies—unions, churches, and clubs—but rather as individuals arranged in a new hierarchy according to their support scores. While this poses a great innovation in the practices of campaigns, having the best database does not automatically mean that a campaign is guaranteed to win; it simply means that the arena of political conflict has spread into a different, technical, field:

> [C]ontrolling 'the means of symbolic production' has little to do with whether the ends, the symbols themselves, are compelling. Controlling the symbolic

means allows a campaign to buy access to symbolic production and distribution but cannot guarantee performative success. In the private sector, as both empirical studies and practical experience continually demonstrate, even the most expensive advertising campaigns largely fail.[32]

What characterises this technical field and these kinds of databases is that they are post-visual in that they observe and produce phenomena that cannot be seen in a normal social space by a single human eye; this recalls the ocular-centric limitation of the Panopticon discussed in the second chapter. Support scores—as well as the merit scores and risk scores I discuss further below—have no existence in and of themselves; they are statistical artefacts that can only be created, manipulated, and deciphered with a machine. Once they are manufactured and applied to the social sphere, however, they do begin to produce visible phenomena: organised Obama supporters, bumper stickers, posters on front lawns, and most importantly, votes.

Migration, Terrorism, Data

When Umar Farouk Abdulmutallab bought a ticket with cash and boarded a plane from Amsterdam to Detroit with no bags or winter coat on 25 December 2009, he was already on the main U.S. terrorist watch list. Called TIDE—Terrorist Identities Datamart Environment—the database was established by the Intelligence Reform and Terrorism Prevention Act of 2004.[33] To warrant inclusion data must fulfil two requirements: identify individuals 'so that a person being screened can be matched to or disassociated from a watchlisted terrorist' and 'meet the "reasonable suspicion" standard of review'.[34] At the time of Abdulmutallab's Detroit flight the requirements of 'reasonable suspicion' were sufficiently lax for there to be around 500,000 names on the list, with an average of 1,200 additions or modifications undertaken daily. Abdulmutallab was not hindered from boarding the plane for two reasons. Firstly, inclusion on TIDE does not mean that one is on the no-fly list, which has about 3,400 individuals on it. Secondly, the software used could not compensate for a misspelling of Abdulmutallab's name—something the popular search engine Google is capable of—leading agents to believe that he did not possess a valid U.S. Visa. It is estimated that there are close to 50,000 duplicate entries in TIDE due to misspellings.[35] During the flight, somewhere over the continental USA, Abdullmutallab lit an explosive contraption hidden in his underpants.

This case says much about the capacity and limitations of information technology in the service of a state today. It immediately brings into clear relief the material and technological basis of a Global War on Terror against illegible others and shows how prone to errors—with 10 per cent duplicates—this basis is. A familiar feedback pattern of the technics of politics also becomes visible at this stage. When the various databases and watch-lists fail to identify and detect a known suspect on his suicide bomb trip, as they did in the case of Abdulmutallab's exploding under-wear, then more inclusive lists, more data, and biometric markers must be required. Failure, despite being systemic, only spurs a renewal of more extreme attempts at data gathering. This impulse was also visible, and especially pronounced, after 9/11, when a consensus emerged that the novel threat of international terrorism demanded new legal and tech-nical responses. After such moments of 'system failure' more support can always be garnered for previously disputed *dataveillance* practices.[36] Larger databases began to be constructed on national security grounds; some plans even called for the creation of databases of *all* phone calls and emails.[37] This embodied a strange fantasy of total data capture, conjur-ing up images of a Borgesian map, useless because it is so detailed as to be equal in size to the country it is representing.

One of the central sites at which new technical fixes were sought was in the documentation of air travel and migration. Passenger Name Record (PNR) data were aggressively sought by both airlines and federal agencies and became the focus of some media attention.[38] For obvious reasons PNR data needs to be standardised, despite being subject to different countries' privacy laws. While all travel agencies compile PNR data, the data is centrally stored in one of three 'global distribution sys-tems': Amadeus, Sabre, and Galileo.[39] What is important to note is that information is continually added to a traveller's profile that is associated with every PNR that might later be generated for that traveller—a simi-lar reiterative process of data collection that was used by the Obama campaign. In the case of the PNRs, for a regular traveller they can:

> ...show where you went, who went, when, with whom, for how long, and at whose expense. Behind the closed doors of your hotel room, with a particular other person, they show whether you asked for one bed or two. Through departmental and project billing codes, business travel PNR's reveal confiden-tial internal corporate and other organization structures and lines of authority and show which people were involved in work together, even if they travelled

separately. Particularly in the aggregate, they reveal trade secrets, insider financial information, and information protected by attorney-client, journalistic, and other privileges.

Through meeting codes used for convention and other discounts, PNR's reveal affiliations—even with organizations whose membership lists are closely-held secrets not required to be divulged to the government. Through special service codes, they reveal details of travellers' physical and medical conditions. Through special meal requests, they contain indications of travellers' religious practices—a category of information specially protected by many countries.[40]

In the United States, the Defense Advanced Research Projects Agency (DARPA)—which handles the research and development of promising new security technologies—created the Total Information Awareness Office under the leadership of John Poindexter, National Security Advisor to Ronald Reagan during the Iran–Contra scandal. The purpose of the office was to bring various databases and data-mining techniques under one umbrella, with the hope that the unification of data could *predict* future terrorist attacks.[41] After strong complaints that this programme violated privacy laws, the U.S. Congress shut it down and Poindexter was forced to resign.[42] Recently, there has been some indication that the programme was never really closed, but rather renamed and moved to the National Security Agency (NSA).[43] A facility is currently being constructed in Utah by the NSA, which is expected to be able to hold Yottabytes of data by 2015—equivalent to around 'a septillion (1,000,000,000,000,000,000,000,000) pages of text'.[44] The key difference from previous known state attempts to collect vast quantities of information, such as the Stasi in the German Democratic Republic, is that digitalisation permits the automated trawling of this data, thereby overcoming previous friction and system-limits. A further important difference is that there is no single database, but rather a combination of databases; multiple databases are drawn on for the construction of one image. It is by circulating data and bringing it into different fields of relations that it becomes useful and meaningful. Consider the example of U.S. immigration control:

The "weeding out" of criminals and terrorists from legitimate travellers is undertaken through the interfacing and integration of over 20 existing databases. Among the most significant are: IDENT, an automatic fingerprint identification system storing biometric data on all foreign visitors, immigrants and asylum seekers; ADIS, storing travellers' entry and exit data; APIS, containing passenger manifest information; SEVIS, containing data on all foreign and exchange students in the US; IBIS, a "lookout" watch list interfaced with Interpol and national crime data; CLAIMS 3, holding information on foreign nationals claiming benefits; and an array of links to local law enforcement, financial systems and educational records. The integration of these searchable databases allows the authorities to profile and encode people according to degrees of riskiness.[45]

Risk and support scores draw on the same technologies and share many characteristics; they are two different manifestations of the same kind of digital power. One of the sophisticated ways in which new computer technologies are supposed to hinder terrorist attacks is by controlling the international circulation of capital, and creating images of what 'normal' economic footprints and transactions look like for the *average* baker, butcher, etc.[46] With the strategic imperative shifting towards prevention, the crucial question for these practices then is what constitutes a risk or a threat? The impetus for prevention opens up space for an apotropaic[47] logic that was especially visible in the ritual mode: since the practices are undertaken to prevent something extreme but infrequent (apocalypse, mass terrorism, etc.) from occurring, when it does not happen they are seen to be successful. If the system fails and something terrible does occur then the call is made for more intrusive and extensive data gathering.

The technologies that are used to quantify and analyse threats are not only significant in the kind of policies they engender, but also in the very 'ontology of the enemy' they construct.[48] The enemy in the database is not a Cold War superpower or a soldier in a tank, nor a foreign city or a group of rag-tag rebels, but rather an individual hiding in plain sight— an individual whose real threatening essence can only be recognised when different data points about them are connected and accrue. While phrenology, finger-prints, and studies of blood type are no longer legitimate forms of expertise to identify habitual criminals and the like, multiple acts of measurement now seek to get to the essence of the threat an individual poses.[49] I return to this question of the social ontology of the enemy in more detail in the fourth chapter.

At a mundane level, bigger databases used by government agencies also mean a larger risk that peoples' personal information will be lost or abused; this has led to the creation of various citizen groups and 'watchdogs', such as Privacy International and the Information Commissioner's

Office (ICO) in the United Kingdom.[50] It is often underestimated how many significant roles modern databases already play in the functions of state. In the United Kingdom, for instance, communication data (which means information about the identity and location of the communicator but not the content of the message) have been used as 'important evidence in 95 per cent of serious crime cases and almost all security service operations since 2004'.[51] A further way in which databases are being employed is in the regulation of the circulation of vehicles through Automatic Number Plate Recognition (ANPR) assemblages, which can pick up a vehicle's number plate, write the owner a ticket if they have been speeding, charge them a congestion fine, or track suspicious vehicles travelling to airports and other potential terrorist targets. This technology enables a kind of automated justice system; where the cameras pick up offences and a system writes out tickets without having to rely on the ocular observations and judgements of a police official. In 2008 the Federal Constitutional Court of Germany ruled that the automated blanket plate recognition systems in Germany violated an individual's right to privacy.[52]

All of these examples of applications of the database—in changing political campaigns, the practices of travel agencies, as a means of security—are not just technologies and techniques but also profitable industries. There is a political economy of digital power. Many of the data-mining tools—the means of information production—are in the hands of corporations and therefore proprietary. In the United States the Diebolt Corporation owns the code that the majority of election machines are run on.[53] In the United Kingdom there has been some talk of a private corporation being awarded a contract to 'keep track of everyone's calls, emails, texts and internet use'.[54] The implications of this potential privatisation of surveillance and retention of data are significant for any democracy, let alone an aspiring social democracy. Yet the technological artefact of the database has even deeper transformative tendencies than the ones listed above. Marked by rationalising impulses—stemming from proto-scientific capitalist practices—it depoliticises social and political issues and privileges a centralised, uniform, and standardised sovereign knowledge that marginalises other habits of thought. Furthermore, the production of a society legible through the database can manufacture a social order which is rational from the vantage point of the sovereign (or researcher) who casts their gaze upon the streams of data; but irrational from the view of the subjects who experience this new order. An order made legible through indexing and categorisation on the screens of select officials and operators will be experienced as chaotic and illegible without such an apparatus. Finally, databases produce a particular form of knowledge that struggles with dynamic unquantifiable information; it is a type of ordered knowledge that can end up producing disorder due to its stratification.

THEORISING THE DIGITAL MODE

While Max Weber was charting the developments and implications of modern capitalism and rationalisation and Walter Benjamin thought hard about the political effects of mechanical reproducibility and aestheticisation, Edmund Husserl (1859–1938) took philosophical aim at some of the very foundations of the mathematical practices of calculation that play such an important role in all of these areas. Husserl and Martin Heidegger (1889–1976) had a very complicated relationship. Despite being relatively close philosophically, with both regarded as founders of phenomenology, they were in radically different political and social positions in Nazi Germany.[55] While the former mentor (Husserl) was denied the right to use the Freiburg University library from 14 April 1933 onwards, the former student (Heidegger) was made Rector of the University barely a week later, on 22 April 1933.

Husserl

A selective reading of Husserl's writings forms a useful bridge to understanding the categories in Cuntz's tower and the digital mode of the technics of politics; it illuminates aspects of the Obama campaign's database as well as other global data-centric attempts to regulate migration. In one of his last, unfinished and most unusual works, *The Crisis of the European Sciences* (1936), Husserl developed a sophisticated critique of the practices of abstraction and calculation.[56] For Husserl, modern science was imagined as a 'single group of theoretically connected truths, which grew from generation to generation and were supposed to solve all imaginable problems: factual problems and problems of reason'.[57] This attitude and approach, which was initially just about the external world, begins to hold important implications for the very idea of philosophy and humanity. According to Husserl, the most important aspect of the modern age of science then is the new formulation of its central idea, which comes from mathematics. The transformation of this idea—of the very purpose of science—is characterised by the ascendancy of idealised abstractions (such as standardised measurement units), a singular reality, and the establishment of empirical measurement as the epistemological cornerstone. It represents an arithmetisation of reality. For Husserl, this transformation takes place first in the sphere of geometry, where the asking of universal questions in formally abstract terms represents a 'violent change of perception' to the knowledge practices of antiquity. This rationality then 'springs over to the sciences and produces for it the wholly novel idea of a mathematical science'.[58] The practical skill and activity of measurement has a central place in this new configuration, making way for a novel class of expertise and operators:

> The art of measuring discovers practically the possibility of relating particular forms ... to universally accessible empirically fixed terms. [It measures] first within narrow spheres (as in the art of *surveying land*), then in a new sphere where shape is involved. Following the desire for a knowledge which can objectively know the world ... the empirical art of measuring and its empirical-practical objectivating [*objektivierende*] function, in a change from practical to theoretical interests ... was idealised and became a part of the pure geometric thought processes. The art of measuring thereby becomes a precursor of the universal geometry and its world of pure limit-shapes [*Limes-Gestalten*].[59]

To this evolution of measurement, from 'surveying land' to measuring 'shapes', we can add the measurement of social phenomena which cannot be observed: support, risk, and merit scores.

For Husserl 'limit-shapes', a term that refers to the limit concept in mathematics, are the idealised objects produced at the boundaries of our knowledge from a desire to complete that very knowledge system.[60] Examples of limit-shapes are ideal geometric forms, such as the perfect circle. Limit-shapes are a central characteristic of the digital mode, where they are also produced of types of individuals and segments of populations: the ideal supporter, the average terrorist, and the risky subject. Such limit-shapes are a necessary building block to making data legible. They can be both arbitrary, as in Cuntz's Tower where they are generational classes twenty-five years apart, as well as highly salient, such as the Obama supporter. The most important aspect of limit-shapes for our own analysis is that they stem from a desire to complete *incomplete* knowledge and become the precise but simultaneously abstract building blocks for ideas, policies, and knowledge-systems. Limit-shapes offer a precision which reality cannot and thereby begin to serve a practical function, to act on that which they approximate:

> If the empirical and very limited requirements of technical praxis had origi-
> nally motivated those of pure geometry, so now, conversely, geometry had
> long since become, as 'applied' geometry, a means for technology, a guide in
> conceiving and carrying out the task: to systematically construct a methodol-
> ogy of measurement for objectively determining shapes in constantly increas-
> ing "approximation" to the geometrical ideals, the limit-shapes.[61]

Due to this pure and abstract mathematics being combined with the practical art of measurement an entirely novel inductive type of predic-tion is produced. This type of thought enables the calculation of various phenomena that cannot be observed;[62] aspects of reality that could never be calculated previously become calculable indirectly. These self-same practices lie at the heart of modern data-mining techniques where population groups that cannot be observed are abstracted, represented, and calculated: How risky is this part of the population, how likely are they to support this candidate, how likely are they to pay back a loan? This practice produces new groups. As I sought to argue with the image of Cuntz's Tower, whether such groups have any group consciousness depends on how the sovereign acts upon them. In this manner the abstract and removed practices of ideal geometry are applied and become the general method, and accepted form of expertise, for the knowledge of reality.[63] This epistemology forms the bedrock of much of the digital mode of the technics of politics. Within the database these types of measurements achieve a kind of 'obvious', apodictic, matter-of-factness that shrouds their reliance on idealised units and limit-shapes. When we speak of 'measurements, of units, and methods' we are always already speaking of 'those that are related to idealities' and that are 'exact'.[64]

That we speak of kilometres but forget the invention of the kilometre may have no great consequences. However, that we speak of the threat score of an individual but forget the invention of the threat score is of great significance, not the least for that individual. For Husserl a further common characteristic of this type of knowledge is that everything is observed as an example of a concrete and universal nature: What is observed is not the falling of one object, but the falling of one object as the example for the falling of all objects, and thus of the general laws of gravity.[65] What is observed are not the actions of a militant terrorist, but the actions of a militant terrorist as an example for the actions of all militant terrorists, and thus of the general principles of 'radicalisation'. This drive for the universal principle behind the particular manifestation is a key assumption for the manipulation of a database.

The 'arithmetisation of geometry', Husserl goes on to write, leads to an 'emptying of its meaning', this process produces results but negates original thinking.[66] The main goal of this type of thinking is to generate formulas that permit prediction.[67] Through databases one can create measures of likely futures. In what sounds awfully close to how Heidegger would describe technology decades later, Husserl writes that 'Galileo, the discoverer ... of Physics, the physical nature, is simultaneously uncovering [*entdeckender*] and covering [*verdeckender*] genius'.[68] Here lies the crisis Husserl refers to. The successes of the disciplines that measure and calculate 'cover' aspects that lead to stagnation in the philosophical contemplation of knowledge and being. Whereas the latter type of knowledge can contemplate ethics, the former cannot; whereas the latter can make space for the political, the former negates it.

One of the most important aspects of Husserl's analysis is the hegemony of the former kind of knowledge, the fact that there are not 'two geometries, but only one'.[69] Within this world of 'one geometry' contemplation is removed from reality—a disconnected type of systematic thought about numbers takes place.[70] This kind of abstraction Husserl identifies can also be found in databases and data-mining practices, where it is automated, where it legitimates and depoliticises knowledge practices which in turn legitimate and depoliticise policy options. As we saw above, geometry itself draws some of its roots and practices from land surveillance. The message here is that practice again precedes theory. Just like the invention of the steam engine led to the development of the laws of thermodynamics, the invention of massive databases appears to be leading to the formalisation of new notions of human ontology and new ways of understanding social and political orders. Comprehended as digital power, modern data-mining techniques abstract, represent, and calculate population groups that cannot be observed directly. Drawing on Husserl's work on geometry one can see that this has significant implications for knowledge itself (precision and measurement are established as important forms of expertise), as well as on the object of knowledge (digital power both reveals and obscures the human). Martin Heidegger's work contributes to grasping the intellectual effects of different technologies, as well as continuing a strand from the previous chapter about anti-Semitism, Germany, and technology.

Heidegger

Shortly after his election as Rector, Heidegger gave an infamous *Rektoratsrede* extolling the necessity for a German University and essence, which he concluded with 'Heil Hitler'.[71] In private, Heidegger later spoke of his Nazi political commitment as the 'greatest act of stupidity of his life'.[72] In a 1945 testament he goes on to describe the 'case of the rectorate' as 'a sign of the metaphysical state of the essence of science [*Wissenschaft*]' which can 'no longer be ... delayed in its essential *transformation into pure technic [Technik]*'.[73] In that sense, one of the reasons later offered by Heidegger for his Nazi involvement is a Husserlian concern for the development of our knowledge practices into technics; he seemed to believe that the Nazi movement held within it the potential for a turn to a German essence that is liberated from such homogenising tendencies. From 1933 onwards the theme of technics begins to play an ever more prominent role in Heidegger's thinking.

In 1954 Heidegger published a famous essay called 'Die Frage nach der Technik', which is typically translated as 'The Question Concerning Technology'—while a further possible translation would be 'The Question of the Technic'. In this essay, which is surprisingly legible compared to some of his other works, he makes a number of observations that are significant for our understanding of technics.[74] First, Heidegger points out that 'where ends are followed, means are used, where the instrumental rules, there causality rules'.[75] Here he provides us with a connection of epistemology to instrumentality; a link of political dominance to our knowledge practices, in particular causality. Heidegger goes on to write:

> Hence the technic is not just a means. The technic is a manner of revealing. When we pay attention to this an entirely different area for the essence of technic opens itself to us. It is the area of the revealing, which means, the truth.[76]

According to Heidegger, one of the aspects that is revealed in our modern planetary technics is the stringent (unrealistic) demand we place on nature. A very significant shift has taken place in our thinking: the world has become reduced to the dimension of a resource; its meaning is given to us primarily through the industries that exploit it. It has become a 'standing-reserve'. A forest is given to us only as a producer of timber, the sea only as a tank of fish, a population as a reserve of supporters, or as a hiding place for terrorists. In a famous example Heidegger explains further:

> The hydraulic plant is not built into the Rhein-stream like the old wooden bridge, which for centuries connects bank to bank. Rather the stream is built into the plant. It is, what it now is as a stream, which means a deliverer of water pressure, due to the essence of the plant. But the Rhein remains, one will respond, stream of the scenery. ... But only as an orderable/harvestable [*bestellbares*] object for a tourism company.[77]

This is the stage at which Heidegger introduces his concept of *Ge-stell*, which is often left in the original but can be translated as frame or en-framing. While frame is commonly thought of as a picture frame, and this is also a useful image, the frame Heidegger is invoking here is more akin to the structural framework of a house. *Ge-stell* is what lies at the essence of modern technics. It is the 'gathering together of that setting-upon which sets man, i.e., challenges him, to reveal the real, in the mode of ordering, as standing-reserve'. What he means here is that technic en-frames all of reality as a resource, it orders it for its own purposes. A similar effect and way of seeing the world—Heidegger would say 'of revealing the world'—can be found in the essence of technics of politics. And just like '[e]n-framing means that way of revealing which holds sway in the essence of modern technology and which *is itself nothing technological*',[78] the en-framing in our technics of politics is nothing technological, but rather something deeply political which appears technical through its assumptions and processes. In a later work Heidegger makes a related point about mathematics. 'The mathematical is a fundamental position towards, things,' Heidegger writes 'one in which our apprehension pro-poses things with regard to the way in which they are already given to us and must be so given. The mathematical constitutes therefore the fundamental presupposition of the knowledge of things.'[79]

What is important to note in the 'Question of the Technic' is that for Heidegger the very condition of human freedom is established by the fact that we have the ability to reveal.[80] Continuing from this position, it would appear that when our practices of 'revealing' and 'en-framing' are standardised and given to us by our technics (such as the cadastre, census, or database), this condition of freedom is curtailed and endangered. It is perhaps because 'revealing' is the condition of human freedom and the essence of technics that 'the human does not encounter his own *Wesen*' anywhere as much as (s)he does in technics.[81] A complicated methodological point arises from this relationship. Because the *Wesen* of technic is 'nothing technological' an intellectual engagement with technics must take place in an area that is 'on the one hand related to technics and on the other completely different from it'.[82] This is one of the reasons why this book begins with ritual—something that appears to be technical as well as completely non-technical.

Heidegger is often cast as a critic of technology. While much that he writes is indeed a critique he offers an almost religious hope of alternatives and attempts to move beyond a merely normative discussion of technics. Much of Heidegger's response to the question of 'technics' is to remind the reader that τέχνη (*tekhne*) once, in ancient Greece, also meant art and the 'revealing of truth'.[83] It is therefore fitting that he turns to art at the end of the 'Question of the Technic' where he invokes the German poet Hölderlin who begins his ballad 'Patmos' with the following lines:

> The God,
> Is near and hard to grasp,
> But where there is danger,
> That which rescues also grows.[84]

In the final instance, technics for Heidegger holds a hidden potential for salvation. Where danger grows, that which rescues also grows. Furthermore, much of his philosophy strives to move beyond a simplistic normative critique, which means that it would be a mistake to read Heidegger as stating that technics was categorically 'bad'. For instance in *Sein und Zeit* (1926) Heidegger makes the important point that one would:

> misunderstand the ontologico-existential structure of falling if we were to ascribe to it the sense of a bad and deplorable ontical property of which, perhaps, more advanced stages of human culture might be able to rid themselves.[85]

Following Heidegger when attempting a theory of technics of politics would mean to engage in a form of understanding which emphasises the en-framing and 'revealing' aspects of technics, a methodology that draws on non-technical and non-political essences within technics of politics, and an attitude which expects 'that which rescues' to be hidden in the very technics being analysed. After this drilling down into specific practices and readings of Husserl and Heidegger it is helpful to come up for air, to return to our empirical object of analysis, a world of standardised technical practices, and to ask why and how these technical standards might have spread.

The Panopticon works because subjects assume the gaze and guess the desire of the sovereign; despite the negative image a prison conjures up, there is something transparent about this relationship. Everybody knows where he or she stands and who they are in relation to the other. In the world of Cuntz's Tower, however, all of the sovereign's desires are opaque, dynamic, not expressed in salient political categories. They can change from one instance to the next. In Cuntz's Tower state behaviour does not have to appear as rational to the subjects. Indeed as Max Weber tells us, 'what appears "rational" from one point, can, observed from another point, be "irrational"'[86] and especially so in this power relation. This is because with Cuntz's Tower society can be deracinated of the public markers previously necessary for states to effectively understand and interact with their population: clear lines of classes and races are no longer necessary. It is a new 'polite' order in which scarlet letters, poor masks, yellow stars or black triangles are no longer needed. Put in more Marxian terms, groups identified in Cuntz's Tower constitute classes *in* themselves but not *for* themselves, and is it not apparent how they could ever achieve group consciousness unless the sovereign wishes them to. The groupings of people born twenty-five years apart are the most direct example of a class in itself, but not for itself. It is entirely arbitrary, yet necessary for the population to be divided into manageable chunks, and the files to grow without having to reorganise the entire system. This dynamic system is also more appropriate for a new economy of changing relations. Instead of being placed into one of nine social categories, like earlier Prussian systems did, each individual now stands on their own.

The switch from the Panopticon's sovereign to the sovereign in Cuntz's Tower can be summarised as the following: instead of attempting to control the individuals by having them control themselves, a representation of the individuals is produced permitting the state to sort and intervene with an unprecedented specificity. By virtue of this system state interventions can be deracinated, thereby depoliticising earlier salient political categories, such as class or race. To translate this into modern terms, walking through a world of CCTV cameras is akin to being in a Panopticon. Having one's identity sorted, labelled, categorised, manipulated by data-management practices *without one's knowledge*—without the sense that one is being observed and must integrate the desires of the observer—is akin to being connected to a name card in Cuntz's Tower. The first leaves an obvious space for political resistance and consciousness. The second does not. The key difference between the two powers is that of surveillance and identification. While observation and the Panopticon entail humans looking at other humans, identification and the manipulation of a card registry in Cuntz's Tower is further abstracted and removed from that constraint. It is only a short step from Cuntz's Tower to our current reality of a data-centric surveillant and actuarial order in which individuals can be sorted and ranked according to 'risk', 'support', or 'merit' scores.

I have sought to undertake three moves in this chapter to help illustrate and advance our understanding of the digital mode of the technics of politics. The first was empirical, a study of the use of databases in an electoral campaign as well as in the regulation and documentation of the movement of individuals. In this part I emphasised the type of human ontology that was being imagined by the Obama campaign, as well as the post-ocular nature of statistical actuarial artefacts, such as support scores. The second section offered readings of Edmund Husserl and Martin Heidegger to help furnish a vocabulary for thinking through and understanding different dynamics of the digital mode. The concepts I wish to retain from this discussion are 'limit-shapes' and 'enframing'. With the former one can capture the scientific, yet constructed nature of categories in databases, with the latter one can begin to grasp the wider pervasive effects a technics can have, effects that often exceed the narrow function they were designed to fulfil. The third move was to undertake an inter-disciplinary survey of useful ideas that would help to describe and account for the globalising dynamics of the technics of politics. Instead of settling on one account and declaring it to be the correct one, I undertook a methodologically and disciplinarily heterodox approach and read them all in conjunction. Together they provide an array of traditions that offer valuable intellectual resources to help narrativise the homogenisation of political technologies and techniques on our planet.

8

THE NETWORK

ONTOLOGY IN THE DIGITAL AGE

When an enemy is not immediately apparent or obvious, different ways of imagining and representing them need to be developed. In 1622 Francis Bacon coined a theory of monstrosity that justified and called for the extermination of various groups of society, as diverse as Canaanites, Anabaptists, and Amazons.[1] The metaphor he used to other and give form to this shapeless mass was that of a many-headed hydra, the mythological beast Hercules slew as his second labour. What is fascinating about this obscure historical fact is that the very same metaphor is commonly used in descriptions of Al-Qaeda and even Islam. The metaphor is both widespread—a Google search for 'Islam' and 'Hydra' returns 218,000 hits[2]—and present in select U.S. government publications, most prominently in the 9/11 Commission Report, which speaks of the (false) image of Al-Qaeda as 'an omnipotent, unslayable hydra of destruction'.[3]

Whatever its applicability, the use of this metaphor has the same implications in Bacon's time as it does in ours. The enemy is represented as a dehumanised, decentralised mass. Things are not as they look: forces appearing as separate individual components are identified as sharing a purpose and belonging to one being that requires utter destruction. The choice of words to describe a foe always has far-reaching consequences; for instance terms that represent the foe as an animal or a machine inevitably dehumanise. An implication of this particular metaphor is that to

117

insure that the heads of the Hydra do not reproduce, it is necessary to turn to extraordinary means. Hercules decided to burn the neck. But most importantly, the basis for the conflict is produced as ontological. The Hydra, like Al-Qaeda, does not need to be battled because of political grievance but due to its very being. This conceptualisation of the difference of the other to the self as the very cause of conflict produces difference *as* a problem and a threat. Under these circumstances special intellectual (anthropological) and technical (primarily visual) resources are mobilised to understand the other's culture. Of course such mechanisms of othering are not particular to the Global War on Terror, but have many historical precedents.[4]

A term that plays a similar role to 'hydra' in modern military discourses is 'network',[5] where it is often used to refer to terrorist actors or insurgents. 'Network' has veritably exploded into the intellectual life and discourse of the military. In a 1940 military handbook on illegible military circumstances approximating counter-insurgency campaigns, the Small Wars Manual (SWM), there is only one reference to network: 'connected with other towns in a large *network*',[6] while in the Stability Operations Field Manual (FM 3–07) of 2008 there are fifteen, and in the Counterinsurgency Field Manual (FM 3–24) of 2007 there are 193 instances of 'network'. FM 3–24 provides the following definition of network:

> … a series of direct and indirect ties from one actor to a collection of others. Insurgents use technological, economic, and social means to recruit partners into their networks. Networking is a tool available to territorially rooted insurgencies....[7]

Network is deployed as a very versatile concept in modern military discourses. It is described as a noun ('a series of direct and indirect ties from one actor to a collection of others'), as a verb ('networking is a tool'/to network), and as an adjective ('networked organization').[8] Instead of referring to a technical distribution network—as it does in SWM—it has been redefined to mean a form of social organisation which is characterised by being relatively non-hierarchical, diffuse, and often secret in character. In a network clear lines of authority and responsibility, and thereby accountability, do not exist. In contemporary military discourses, networks are typically described as organisational forms that the enemy successfully assumes and U.S. forces need to emulate.[9] Returning to the metaphor of the ship of state, networks do not require captains to operate; they self-organise, swarm, and emerge.[10] A network is primarily characterised by its density, as well as the number of 'edges' or 'nodes' each entity in the network has. The idea of self-organisation and a return to stasis can be traced to cybernetic and systems theory, as well as ecology. As such, the notion of the network is closely related to the computer. This is an example of models initially developed to understand nature and technical systems being applied to the social sphere and used for developing public policies.[11]

One reason why the signifier of 'network' is becoming more widespread is that operators in the U.S. military are finding that to receive the kind of logistical support they want it helps to refer to whatever opponent they are encountering as a network. Consider this email from an Intelligence Officer returning from a tour of duty in Afghanistan at the beginning of 2010:

> The 'Network' thing is just an example of how using certain buzz words will better get your asset requests approved over the other guy. The shrewd intel or operations officer identifies those buzz words quickly and peppers his asset requests with them. 'Network' made Haqqani sound like something extra special, and not just the Taliban in that particular area. Whereas I don't think Haqqani represents a Network as is traditionally thought of in intel work.[12]

Beyond these feedback dynamics, why does the notion of the 'network' take off precisely during the illegible wars of Iraq, Afghanistan, and the Global War on Terror?

A paradigmatic moment that occurs in Gillo Pontecorvo's *The Battle of Algiers* (1966), which was watched with great interest at the Pentagon after the 9/11 attacks, may provide a clue.[13] In the middle of the movie, Lieutenant-Colonel Mathieu is showing a video to a class of soldiers. The video shows soldiers searching people at checkpoints.

MATHIEU

Here is some film taken by the police.
The cameras were hidden at the Casbah
exits. They thought these films might be
useful, and in fact they are useful in
demonstrating the usefulness of certain
methods. Or, at least, their inadequacy.

The soldiers are searching ordinary civilians to find FLN terrorists. The displayed action at the checkpoint does not go well. There is chaos and the terrorist bombings still occur. Clearly, something is not working; the terrorists must have walked right by the checkpoint. The videos set up to see the foe have demonstrated the French military's blindness. The machine placed to record the terrorist has only demonstrated that he or she, and in this particular case it is a she, cannot easily be recognised and picked out of a crowd. When the video cuts out Mathieu draws the image of a network on the blackboard.

MATHIEU

> We must start again from scratch. The only information that we have concerns the structure of the organisation. And we shall begin from that ...

The network is drawn when vision is not up to the task of finding the foe. Contrasted to the video camera which surveilles what is seen, the diagram of a network acts as the objectified and constructed image of a social reality that cannot be observed directly; it both complements visual reality, and undermines its positivist basis. The network functions as representation and simulation of the social ontology of the foe. Said provides a nice description of this when he writes that '[n]arrative is the specific form taken', in this case the narrative of a network, 'to counter the permanence of vision'.[14]

The fundamental difficulty of coupling a data-centric approach with the ontology of the network is that terrorism is a profoundly non-predictable type of warfare. But, of course, it is precisely the illegible nature of future terrorism that drives the development of statistical tools to attempt to data-manage it. In one way this type of ontology, where the enemy is understood as the risky part of an actuarial table, seems to be far removed from a racialist or orientalist conception of the other. In an article on a cybernetic vision of the enemy Peter Galison argues precisely this point: 'The cybernetic Enemy Other has little to do with the racialised Other ... examined, for example, by Edward Said in Orientalism.'[15] Yet the network coupled with digital power goes beyond a cybernetic vision that views both self and other as a proprioceptive process. By modelling culture and adding it to constructions of the other, both race and Orientalism find their way back into visualisations of the foe; but now they are legitimated through statistics and massive data-sets, and not the discredited discourses of biological racism or phrenology.

The ontological shift from territory, to individuals, to network moves away from observed reality, as well as politicised categories with established rights discourses. In this way, the emphasis on network can also be read as a depoliticising practice, avoiding the more salient categories of race, individual, class or country.

9

DIGITAL POWER GOES TO WAR

Digital power sets the table for a new kind of warfare. Two trajectories exist. First, drones enable a kind of unmanned occupation of foreign territories. Secondly, warfighters can target their enemies as individuals—just like an electoral campaign. Night-time raids are not only undertaken on groups of fighters assembled in a particular location, but much rather are individual raids on houses, selecting single persons—this is the equivalent of a campaign machinery that focuses on individuals and not classes. It is fair to say that the intellectual history of military strategy and the laws of war are wholly unprepared for this moment.

In this chapter I consider applications and manifestations of digital power in modern warfare. As we will see, the individualising trajectory present in identifying and sorting for domestic political campaigns and marketing strategies also flourishes in the military domain. It culminates in an ontology of the enemy as a set of individuals organised into a network. Military conflict is always fundamentally characterised by a requirement to 'know the enemy', which demands the ability to identify and see the foe, to, in General Stanley McChrystal's words, 'estimate its tactical strength and intuit its planned strategy'.[1] The primary way of doing this is to rigorously document the identity of individuals in and around warzones. David Galula, the small war sage, went so far as to elevate identifying practices and identity cards to essential warfighting tools in *Counterinsurgency Warfare: Theory and Practice* (1964). 'Control of the population begins obviously with a thorough census. Every inhabitant

123

must be registered and given a foolproof identity card.'[2] The conjunction of this knowledge requirement with the exploding capacity of the computer revolution leads to fantasies of an automated, fully surveilled, and totally controlled martial environment. General William Westmoreland's vision of 'the battlefield of the future', which he believed in 1969 would be in full effect ten years later, is an exemplar of such a fantasy:

> [E]nemy forces will be located, tracked, and targeted almost instantaneously through the use of data links, computer assisted intelligence evaluation, and automated fire control. With first round kill probabilities approaching certainty, and with surveillance devices that can continually track the enemy, the need for large forces to fix the opponent becomes less important. I see battlefields that are under 24-hour real or near-real time surveillance of all types.[3]

In some ways Westmoreland's vision was eerily prescient. Today the means he imagined exist, as drones can and do place a battlefield under complete surveillance, yet they have not delivered the desired ends: 'tracking' the enemy and 'fixing' the opponent have proven to be more difficult than anticipated. In circumstances of 'small war', Counter-Insurgency (COIN) Campaigns, or overseas contingency operations, the capacity to clearly see the movement, intent and capability of the foe is inhibited to a remarkable degree. In such conditions of war, where one fights in and among 'the people', the foe does not wear a uniform or march in formation; the foe may look like the civilian population during the day only to undertake martial operations at night. This problem of visuality creates potential pathologies of decision-making for military organisations. 'In warfare, you make decisions based on indicators', McChrystal explains:

> This is much simpler when the enemy is a column advancing toward you in plain sight. Our problem in both the Iraq of 2003 and the Afghanistan of today is that indicators popped up everywhere, unevenly and unexpectedly, and often disappeared as quickly as they emerged, flickering in view for only a moment.[4]

Under such challenging conditions of illegibility and disfluency—where 'indicators pop … up everywhere, unevenly and unexpectedly'—data is sought to an unprecedented degree, in part to achieve 'identity dominance'. According to the Biometrics Identity Management Agency in the US, 'Identity Dominance is defined as the operational capability to achieve an advantage over an adversary by denying him the ability to mask his identity and/or to counter our biometric technologies and processes.'[5] Novel technical and conceptual resources are developed to reliably hear, read, and especially *see* the foe. '[F]or men at war, the function of the weapon is the function of the eye.'[6] This chapter is concerned with the material basis of this function of the eye, what Paul Virilio called the 'logistics of perception'. As in preceding chapters, I seek to make visible the technological machinery and intellectual edifice that present and en-frame human subjectivity. In any discussion of contemporary warfare, in an age of a Global War on Terror, these subjectivities are primarily and necessarily the oriental other and the terrorist foe. A central question then is what kinds of visions of the enemy and the oriental other are being generated through and within databases.

This particular constellation of 'small war', problems of seeing, and conflicts in non-Western environs places the contemporary 'logistics of perception' into a colonial tradition, or, as some have called it, a 'colonial present'.[7] Arriving at a colonial present means that writings grappling with questions of knowledge, power, and vision in the colonial encounter are especially pertinent, perhaps even policy-relevant. Therefore I begin this chapter by reading Said's *Orientalism* as a story about the failure of the Panopticon, about the disenchantment with, and breakdown of Westmoreland-like attempts to see the enemy and the other. I then turn to an empirical discussion of present technics being developed explicitly for the purpose of making the foe visible. Because visuality fails, in the sense that surveillance does not deliver the legibility that is expected of it, new means of acting upon the visual and making the invisible visible are pioneered. When direct surveillance is not up to the task, then Cuntz's Tower, as a technology of power, is drawn on. The digital mode of technics, with its limit-shapes and framing properties, comes into play. To this end a very particular ontology of the foe, 'the network', is developed. In a Global War on Terror the 'logistics of perception' extend beyond visual representations of the foe in the periphery to include training simulations, video games, and academic writings on the culture of 'the other' in the metropole. The fourth section therefore turns to these different areas and medias for the purpose of showing that even if the logistics of perception fail to reveal the other with reliability and fidelity in the field, the way a foe is represented in a videogame, training simulation, and academic text can still have far-reaching consequences.

VISION AND ORIENTALISM

When the poet Rainer Maria Rilke was a student his physics teacher built a phonograph. To the young poet the unfamiliar recorded sounds represented 'a new, still infinitely tender piece of reality'.[8] Today the live visual displays and layered interfaces of battle-spaces along with human terrain databases, video games and computer simulations represent a similarly new, yet far from tender, piece of the real. Used to manufacture, represent and augment visual information this crowded medium is an increasingly essential link in a global kill chain, as well as a method for the imagination and projection of meaning onto foreign bodies and territories. While these particular technological renditions, framings, and appropriations of the oriental other are new, they recapitulate an old central motif of Orientalism. As Edward Said teaches us, 'to divide, deploy, schematize, tabulate, index, and record everything in sight (and out of sight)' were 'features of Orientalist projection'.[9] In this desire to store, retain, and sort Orientalism 'embodies a systematic discipline of accumulation'.[10] Such accumulation entails a particular expertise. At present, the nature of that expertise is one of technical and methodical data management that subsumes knowledge about culture, history, and politics. Compared to earlier knowledge systems and scripts of othering, it becomes evident that the number—as code, data, and statistics—authorises orientalist images projected on screens. Enabled by digital power, contemporary Orientalism is more concerned with arithmetising and measuring the individual other than discovering any linguistic or civilizational essence.[11] This technical Orientalism is about making the invisible—culture, danger, and political stability—visible; it thereby constitutes a particular type of military visuality.[12]

Vision is frequently invoked in Said's *Orientalism* (1978). The thinkers Said discusses have visions, are visionaries, re-visionists and visualisers. 'Cromer envisions a seat of power in the West'; Dante has a vision of Mohammed; 'Averroes and Avicenna are fixed in a visionary cosmology'; Napoleon, de Lesseps, Balfour, and Cromer are 'men of vision'; 'the essential outlines of [Flaubert's] vision are clear'; Comte 'envisions' 'scientific regenerations of mankind'; Marx has a 'Romantic Orientalist vision'; Yeats too has 'visions of Byzantium'; then there is 'Smith's vision of the world'; 'Massignon's vision'; 'Glubb's later vision'; T.E Lawrence is a 'servant' of 'a certain conservative vision of the orient'.[13] Islam and the Orient are envisaged at the core of both *Orientalism* and Orientalism. 'Orientalism was ultimately a political vision of reality', a 'manner of regularized (or Orientalized) writing, vision, and study'. The Orient is visualised and is 'something one illustrates'; images of the Orient depend on a class of visualists and their practices. 'Neither "Europe" nor "Asia" was anything without the visionaries' techniques for turning vast geographical domains into treatable, and manageable, entities.' Methods of making the invisible visible, reign. 'Knowledge was essentially the *making visible of* material, and the aim of a tableau was the construction of a sort of Benthamite Panopticon.' Here the Panopticon is not so much understood as a mechanism for the self-disciplining of subjects, but rather as a regulative academic ideal, instrument for reform, and type of visuality in which an agent at the centre can see but not be seen. 'The Orientalist surveys the Orient from above', he must 'see every detail'. In the end though, this Panopticon itself is revealed as an untenable vision, a mirage, and a false presumption 'that the whole Orient can be seen panoptically'.[14]

When considering the relationship of the Panopticon to Orientalism it is worth retrieving a passage from Jeremy Bentham's twenty-first letter in his Panopticon writings entitled 'Schools'. Whatever its actual historic applications, Bentham himself had no intention of sharing his panoptic insights with the Orient. His reason for withholding 'the inspection principle' from the people of Constantinople is intriguing:

> Neither do I mean to give any instructions to the Turks for applying the inspection principle to their *Seraglios*: no, not though I were to go through *Constantinople* again twenty times, notwithstanding the great saving it would make in the article of *eunuchs*, of whom one trusty one in the inspection-lodge would be as good as half a hundred. The price of that kind of cattle could not fail of falling at least ten per cent., and the insurance upon marital honour at least as much, upon the bare hint given of such an establishment in any of the Constantinople papers. But the mobbing I got at *Shoomlo*, only for taking a peep at the town from a thing they call a *minaret* (like our monument) in pursuance of invitation, has cancelled any claims they might have had upon me for the dinner they gave me at the *Divan*, had it been better than it was.[15]

Although Bentham is convinced that the 'inspection principle' would bring economic benefits to 'the Turks'—'the price of that kind of cattle' (eunuchs) would fall 'at least ten per cent'—the 'mobbing' he received cancels any claims on hospitality or the reciprocal giving of gifts. This besieging occurs precisely when Bentham is seeking to undertake a quick visual inspection of the town, just a 'peep', from a religiously significant tower. Despite an initial invitation to do so, such alien panoptic appropriation of the minaret, albeit momentary, appears to have been met with great resistance. Many symbolic readings of this image of Bentham disoriented by the Orient, exactly at the instant of attempted surveillance, are feasible: the Orient itself rejects Orientalists' endeavours for a sovereign vision; religious sites resist foreign disciplinary annexation; technologies of surveillance have to be permitted to function by the population, etc. In this chapter I pursue a slightly different line of questioning: What happens when Bentham actually makes it up into the Minaret and Westmoreland's vision is fulfilled? What occurs when the technical means of informational accumulation about populations and visual representation of spaces achieve such a capacity that the Orient *can*, really, be seen continuously, perhaps even panoptically? Is this the 'highest stage of Orientalism', as some thinkers argue?[16] What does Bentham see?

SEEING THE FOE

On 23 February 2008, a group of enlisted U.S. soldiers made a little bit of history in the Diyala province of Iraq when they became the first to use an 'Armed Warrior Alpha Unmanned Aerial System' to 'neutralize targets'.[17] The significance of this event was that unlike predator drones, which are operated by trained pilots, the 'Armed Warrior Alpha Unmanned Aerial System' was controlled by ground troops—yet, it can also operate *fully autonomously*. This development was only the latest in a cluster of military tools for action at a distance. A full list would have to include Nikola Tesla's invention and demonstration of the remote control of a boat (1898), the first successful use of drones in battle (1982, Israel in the Bekka Valley), and the first time humans surrendered to a drone (1991, Iraqi soldiers surrendering to a U.S. Pioneer Drone).[18]

A seldom-discussed effect of these advances in the field of unmanned aerial systems is the vast amount of visual and other data produced by them. The present increase of drone flights is leaving the military with a huge, potentially debilitating, amount of visual data. This problem of figuring out what is 'junk' is a special characteristic of digital power.[19] Time is expanded and compressed as years of video footage are recorded in Afghanistan and Iraq in ever shrinking intervals. The developmental trajectory of these data streams is extremely steep, pointing to far more data being recorded in far less amounts of time. Reaper Drones will soon be able to record ten angles simultaneously, are projected to record thirty-five shortly thereafter, and should be up to sixty-five after that.[20] This optical multiplication coincides with an overall increase in the use of drones that has the potential to result in a startling total view of battle spaces; in 2008 the U.S. military already had twice as many drones as manned airplanes.[21] Northrup Grumman's marketing literature captures the spirit when it refers to its AN AAQ electro-optical distributed aperture system as 'seeing everything, everywhere, all the time'.[22]

Once in service and online, drones—or unmanned aerial vehicles (UAVs)—permit one to produce, record and replay an ocular reality that would previously have been lost to the past and friction of war, remaining consigned to memory and official accounts. One simple tactical practice is called 'backtracking': a fleet of drones maintains constant battlefield surveillance. When an improvised explosive device (IED) goes off, they simply rewind to see who placed it. The next obvious, more strategic, step enabled by sufficient digital power is to observe what kind of hitherto unrecognised patterns accompany the event to then begin to look for what phenomena might be tell-tale signs of similar future events.

The obvious danger of such an increase is the Stasi syndrome: drones may be looking 'everywhere, all the time' but actually see nothing, because there simply are not enough operators to watch and understand the images, to usefully archive them, and to produce coherent narratives with them. New technical systems are constantly being invented to grapple with the staggering amount of information and connectivity suddenly obtainable. In 2010 the basic operating platform for the military was Raytheon's Distributed Capability Ground System (DCGS). In Raytheon's words, emphasising dominance through speed, the 'DCGS provides continuous on-demand intelligence brokering to achieve full-spectrum dominance so that U.S. and coalition warfighters can change the course of events in hours, minutes or even seconds.'[23] In action DCGS looks like an assemblage of screens featuring live feeds and communication streams.

Technological artefacts and techniques developed by the sports casting industry are also being drawn on by the military. The means used to make a sports game legible to the disoriented viewer wondering 'are we winning?'—such as scores, overlays, tags keeping track of players, and commentators drawing on screens—are being studied and applied to live battle space images.[24] The system designed to do this is called the Full-Motion Video Asset Management Engine, or FAME. It uses metadata tags, like pictures placed into Google Earth:

One can then view data in ways as rich as depicted with football games on TV, which not only show what is happening from multiple angles, but the identity of teams, the current score, the line of the field where a play started, where the ball needs to go for first down, which quarter and down it is, time remaining, how many yards there are to go, as well as pop-up windows and scrolling data giving details on players and scores from others' games and audio commentary detailing plays.[25]

Deployed in a battle-space, these tools for tagging and labelling objects produce new kinds of hyper-visual experiences for operators behind screens; observed reality is en-framed in a novel way. John Delay, the Director of strategy for the company developing these technologies (Harris Corporation), uses a telling analogy to describe FAME. He is quoted as saying that 'you want to not only find a book in a library using the index card system. You want to be able to find a word on page 36 in chapter 12.' This is achieved through 'tagging information properly' to instantly 'review and analyze it'.[26] In other words, while today's military and entertainment needs exceed the capacity of the information technology of the card registry, these techniques stand squarely in a functional lineage with the card index and its mobile categorisation. What is now called for is not just greater specificity but a dynamic categorisation of images and observed reality. To continue the analogy, one could say that a 'card index' now needs to be constructed that contains all of a book's contents and not just information on its title, author, date and place of publication, and subject matter. Again, library management, this time in the form of Google Scholar, which represents precisely such a hyper-card index, appears to be leading the way. Considering the unexpected intellectual and bio-political revolution that the humble card index wrought, it is impossible to estimate the long-term knowledge management effects this tagging technology may have.

Arithmetising the Other and Data-Managing the Foe

The groundswell of data from drones and other visual streams is also accompanied by a stark increase of human terrain data. When the foe and the other, despite continuously being projected onto screens from drone feeds, still seem illegible, other 'techniques of visualisation' are deployed. The problems of legibility of the population, particularly *identifying* and *sorting*, are heightened in situations of warfare, and especially so in circumstances of 'small war'. The challenge is summarised well by a French officer in Algeria in 1845 who exclaimed 'that the essential thing is to gather into groups this people which is everywhere and nowhere; the essential thing is to make them something we can seize hold of'.[27] This 'gathering into groups' can occur physically through placement into camps and controlled zones of movement or exclusion. But it can also occur virtually, as a data-management practice by categorising individuals into groups in Cuntz's Tower.

Tagging and ethnic categorisation are the expression of an age-old desire to classify and taxonomise that which is not clearly understood, in this case the social and cultural world of the other. On the one hand, this tendency drives orientalist practices; as Said writes, the 'element preparing the way for modern Orientalist structures was the whole impulse to classify nature and man into types'.[28] On the other hand the empirical needs of empire develop classificatory techniques that spread and can find wider applications. For Scott '[a]ll empires, as cultural-political enterprises, are necessarily exercises in classification.'[29] Hannah Arendt, in a similar vein, regarded the imperial agent as a counterpart to bureaucracy, and the great tragedy of Nazism as brought about by the conjunction of racism with bureaucracy.[30] In the Global War on Terror one can see a combination of the empirical with the imperial in a complex technological assemblage that is used to keep track, identify and categorise the 'Muslim out of place'.[31]

The Handheld Interagency Identity Detection Equipment (Hiide) system is a mobile device used to capture the biometric information of individuals in Iraq and Afghanistan as well as criminals in the United States. A Hiide system can be used with Cross Match's Mission Oriented Biometric Software (MOBS), which sends data to a centralised database for registration, identification, and verification of suspected enemy personnel. Fingerprint data, biographic information (name, surname, tribe), birth date, birth place, weight, height, handscans, facial recognition data, voice recognition data, GPS data, and other information can all be stored on a database accessible from anywhere in the world by the right device. In this manner the machine can answer the question of whether the person is a recidivist or a 'Muslim out of place', or a previously unknown individual whose information is to be saved and added to the data baseline. Together with drones and Human Terrain Teams (HTTs), the Hiide and MOBS systems act as vacuum cleaners of data in modern battle spaces.

The ideal of total data capture is especially pronounced in Iraq and Afghanistan where the biometric details of individuals are gathered in many different instances and at many different stages: to get ID cards, to be permitted on a U.S. base, or simply to conduct a census. A Sergeant in Iraq undertaking such registration activity estimated that there are millions of irises stored on the database: 'I'd say a good percentage of Iraqis are already in the database'.[32] This total biometric registration—'*Restlose Erfassung*'—of the non-Western other coincides with an emphasis on clearly defined ethnic identities. 'We were Iraqis first,' said Saad Jawad, a professor of political science at Baghdad University. 'But the Americans changed all that. They made a point of categorizing people as Sunni or Shiites or Kurds.'[33]

Through the use of census and Geographic Information System (GIS) mapping tools commanders are supposed to be provided insight into the human terrain. This exercise too, is deeply constituted by the imperatives of seeing and taxonomising. As one member of an HTT wrote to me, 'Tribal identities are intact, with the exception of those who think they are "intelligentsia", and they deny their tribal identity (but they still know it, they just don't want to admit it).'[34] This brings to mind a letter written home by a British officer affiliated with a Sikh regiment during WWII: 'The Sikhs have many religious customs; we see that they keep them whether they like it or not'.[35] In these cases local ethnicity and culture are not just natural objects encountered in the field, but artefacts producing legibility and order for foreign powers that are drawn on to help interpret confusing circumstances—'they are tribal, they just don't want to admit it'. I return to this issue of a tribal ontology represented with digital power in the next chapter.

Through these technics of identification the recognition of whorls, loops, and ridges in fingerprints has been internalised by the machine, thereby bringing about a great reduction of the previously painstaking work of classification. The labours of Dewey's librarian, Bertillon's measuring policeman and of a fingerprint classification expert—more on that also in the next chapter—have all been mechanised, thereby radicalising an already on-going industrialisation of bio-political practices of identification and classification. Due to the ease with which data can be taken and stored it is, for the first time, possible to attempt the biometric census of an entire population. Providers of this technology treat it as an existential need: 'We believe that the use of biometrics, specifically iris recognition, in the War on Terror could help prevent another 9/11 from happening.'[36]

While there are accounts from the field of the Hiide and MOBS systems not always working and often 'crashing', the tendency of this technological apparatus is already apparent: as much data as possible is collected, tagged, combined, sifted, aggregated, weighted, and presented to produce states of hyper-legibility. The danger with any such enterprise is that the information is simply too much to be used or organised, that the tag covers too much of what is being sought. Is it possible that Hiides and drones are like the invention of movable type, churning out information that is swamping the systems built to organise it?

Bio-metric handheld devices coupled with globally accessible databases are the latest chapter in a history of tools deployed by the state to identify individuals; they are typically field-tested and perfected on the external and internal other, where sovereign power experiences the most urgent existential need to make human subjects legible. The technologies to identify individuals have gradually been moving away from visible physical markers—such as tattoos, conspicuous clothing, and badges—to more non-conspicuous identifiers, such as fingerprints, social security numbers, and IDs. Jane Caplan and John Torpey argue that new levels of centralised surveillance accompany this trend:

> The putatively universalist Enlightenment state gave up the selective outward identification of individuals and groups (e.g. marks on the body, sumptuary laws regulating dress) only by simultaneously asserting a newly comprehensive right of surveillance and identification that applied to all citizens.[37]

The tag, only visible on the screen of the authorised operator, is the logical conclusion of the disappearance of material markers of identity. It is accompanied by the biometric iris and fingerprint scan, captured with a HIIDE system, stored on a MOBS database, organised with a FAME system, connected with data collected with drones, and presented on a DCGS. One of the most interesting and indicative aspects of a fingerprint or iris scan is that, like a barcode, they are not intelligible without a technique and technological apparatus used to read, classify, retain, and remember them; they are highly meaningful read with the right apparatus, but complete gibberish when just seen with a plain eye. *Tekhne* and machines have become essential for these types of practices. All forms of *metis* that are required, such as proto-anthropological cultural information, appear to already be embedded within the technological system. In this way, the modern military requirements of academic knowledge are quite distinct from earlier periods: anthropological knowledge helps to establish the basic limit-shapes of tribes and ethnic groups as an interpretive grid, but much of this work occurs within a database. This means that it is sufficient to set up the system in a culturally attuned way, and then to let it run. It is through recourse to the categories and forms of particular databases that the culture of the other can then be read and deciphered. The growing non-materiality of markers of legibility also puts a different twist on the lament that the foe does not wear a uniform. Without uniforms it is easier to run wild with the identification and classification of a group, precisely because an empirical anchor of the identity has now been excised. In that way, one can sense an affinity, perhaps even an unexplored connection, between the salience of political categories and the technologies used to identify individuals.

The U.S. military's widely reported and discussed 'culture' turn in Counter-Insurgency (COIN)[38] is therefore not just characterised by proto-anthropological methods, but is also high-tech—at this conjunction of COIN and the Revolution in Military Affairs (RMA), databases and programs to represent cultural data spring forth. Whereas orientalist expertise used to be legitimated through linguistic and historical scholarship, it is now more oriented towards methods and technical mastery. Said provides a good description of this trajectory:

> No longer does an Orientalist try first to master the esoteric languages of the Orient; he begins instead as a trained social scientist and 'applies' his science to the Orient, or anywhere else. This is the specifically American contribution to the history of Orientalism, and it can be dated roughly from the period immediately following World War II, when the United States found itself in the position recently vacated by Britain and France.[39]

This transition is especially visible in the backgrounds of the academic advisors of HTTs; despite a mission statement emphasising the utility of anthropology, only a small minority of academic advisors have PhDs in anthropology.[40] Here one glimpses the possibility that there may be another stage of Orientalist after the social scientist: the Orientalist data-manager.

A characteristic of the widespread signifier of human terrain is that culture can be measured and subsequently visually represented in colourful graphs, maps, and diagrams with PowerPoint presentations. Applications have subsequently been custom-designed to facilitate the standardisation, quantification and representation of cultural knowledge, which is always necessary to making it utile and legible. A suite of programs designed for the Human Terrain System (HTS), and based on DCGS, is called MAP-HT. The fact that the software system for understanding culture is based on one designed to represent battlefields provides a good indication of the way culture is viewed in these systems. The HTS website describes MAP-HT in the following fashion:

> It facilitates research, analysis, storage, archiving, sharing and other applications of socio-cultural information relevant to the unit commander's operational decision-making processes. ... Map-HT Toolkit products include the following:
>
> – Maps: for example, spatial distribution of tribes and related social entities.
> – Link Charts: for example, power structures and social networks in informal economies.
> – Time lines: for example, time sequence of key religious holidays.
> – Visualization: for example, topographic views of Iraqi infrastructure.
> – Reports: for example, role of ethnicity in Iraqi power sharing.[41]

MAP-HT is a synthetic multi-medial perspective coupling select people to a shared ocular reality, one that visualises ethnicity along with infrastructure and topography. Images produced with this suite of programs are useless to the academic analyst if he treats them as some obvious representation or product of a surveilled reality. Instead these kinds of images need to be understood as profoundly enabled by statistics, as well as fitting into a particular history of a military visuality built on maps.

While there are accounts that the suite of programs is not being properly implemented in the field, the basic direction of this technology is apparent. HTTs collect and analyse data in the field, it is then sent to a knowledge centre based in the continental USA to be further processed, which means standardised, and uploaded to databases and servers. To make the data legible it is projected onto maps; in effect it is built on top of widespread Geographic Information Systems (GIS), and tagged. The abstraction of the map is further layered with a simplified representation of culture in the form of inkblots:

> The capability will provide a database augmented with specific sociocultural objects and an entity extraction capability for tagging narrative and freetext documents for ingestion into the local database.[42]

It has long been recognised that maps and the practice of cartography in general, are distinctly political. Mark Monmonier has pointed out that not only do maps often lie; they actually *have to misrepresent* to create a meaningful image.[43] As Thongchai Winichakul reminds us, 'A map may not just function as a medium; it could well be the creator of the sup-posed reality.'[44] A particularly significant example of the historically constitutive effects of such technics can be found in the nineteenth cen-tury history of Afghanistan. 'The idea that in Pashtun society there was widespread feuding'—which is completely central to contemporary notions of Pashtun and Pashtunwali—'was, in fact, the result of specific land arrangements implemented by the British which led to a particular peak in internal unrest.'[45] This unintended historical effect puts contem-porary efforts to standardise and visualise land ownership in Afghanistan into a special light.[46]

Moreover, one should recall Said's claim that 'neither "Europe" nor "Asia" was anything without the visionaries' techniques for turning vast geographical domains into treatable, and manageable, entities'.[47] What new cultural realities are then being produced—or old being repro-duced—through the widespread manufacture of 'ethnic maps'? That maps of ethnic identity and culture are profoundly political, necessarily fictitious and can easily be abused should become apparent to the mili-tary in due course. The consciousness-raising moment to watch out for is when the issue arises of handing over vast amounts of biometric and other data to 'host' governments.

In basic outlook, these Human Terrain datasets harken back to an age of anthropological research where the guiding principle was completion and standardised recording.[48] A recent critical report by an American Anthropological Association commission on the Human Terrain System raised 'questions about the integrity of data collected by HTTs, and where this data might end up'.[49] What else could be done with all of this data apart from providing the commander with cultural and political awareness? One answer to this question is discussed further below: the data could be used to simulate cultural environments for training pur-poses with higher fidelity and used to build more realistic models of the other and the foe.

Instead of understanding these new visual phenomena through the lens of surveillance, I argue that this phenomenon should be read in a tradition of statistical thought, one that in this case is being drawn on to supplement a malfunctioning Panopticon.[50] Gathered terabytes of visual and cultural data are combined with other bytes of information to form an aggregate baseline for the discovery of statistical patterns. Screens and computer programs offer opportunities for new immersive experiences, to see 'culture' and 'danger' on a map, to empirically encounter information, to have thick experiences from projected data. Yet, all of this occurs for distinctly martial and predatory reasons. In the words of Carlo Ginzburg, 'lurking behind this model for explanation or prophecy one glimpses something as old as the human race: the hunter crouched in the mud, examining a quarry's tracks'.[51] In this reading technology is simply animated by primal instincts and practices of the hunt. What we observe with the creation of these machines, however, exceeds its animating principles and intended consequences. Writing at the beginning of the Great War, Emil Lederer managed to capture the dynamic of this relationship well:

> Every military apparatus has as its aim the defeat of an enemy in war; there is, and can be, no military complex that does not have this aim. But as soon as this aim is fixed and held constant, the technology employed in the service of this end acquires an immanent necessity of its own.[52]

The military apparatus constructed for seeing the foe has the potential to become radically dis-embedded in a global military conflict. It entails a particular method of seeing, one that reveals and en-frames the world as data and indicators.

A World of Hidden Indicators

Searching for secret tell-tale signs of a terrorist has a strong pedigree in the visual arts. The 'Morelli method', developed in the second half of the nineteenth century, sought to identify paintings by the masters through looking at typically ignored details. Indicative clues were supposed to be the particular style in which a hand or an ear was painted. According to an anonymous article written by Sigmund Freud, deducing the secret character of a person, piece of art, or situation from obscure clues has much in common with the psychoanalytic method. 'It seems to me that this method of enquiry is closely related to the technique of psychoanalysis' which also 'is accustomed to divine secret and concealed things from despised or unnoticed features, from the rubbish-heap, as it were, of our observations'.[53] This basic pattern of seeking to identify a social group from a statistical study of their mundane, hidden, but shared characteristics and the invention of some new metric has resurfaced and failed with the development of every major technology to identify the individual, such as fingerprints, anthropometry, phrenology, and blood types.[54]

What is novel about the current iteration is that by seeking to observe, measure, and categorise movement patterns and, as we will encounter further below, cultural and social reality itself, it displaces essence into a dynamic context.

While some of the subtleties of this visuality, visual register, and visual repertoire are akin to writing—in that they can be recorded, replayed, edited, spliced; in that tags are 'written' onto objects and events—they also differ in two very important regards. (a) Deployed in situations where immediacy is the primary design restraint and the medium is characterised by the combination of a large variety of data streams it can be difficult to trace the origin of information. Information on screens thereby manifests as a kind of revelatory knowledge; it does not exist as a text with a bibliography, which is stable and can be cross-referenced. (b) The dissemination of these systems means that we have more, and will continue to have more, visual traces of real violence. It is easier to abstract and therefore stomach death and gross violence when it is described in a text (just consider books VIII and X of the *Iliad*) or a column of numbers. Images on the other hand, are more visceral and moving images even more emotive. As many have argued, this is one of the central grounds why drone pilots have been shown to have such high levels of Post-Traumatic-Stress-Disorder (PTSD).[55]

Since drones do not immediately fly away after firing their missiles, these pilots see more of the damage they do than earlier generations, as well as many soldiers in the field. The foe is no longer simply a blip on the radar screen but a clearly discernible, often unwitting, individual—posing no immediate existential threat to the drone operator—that disappears in flashes of firepower. Pilots are further faced with the knowledge that there is high definition visual evidence of the violence they commit, which can be replayed, copied, and leaked. This new visual battlefield record represents novel challenges for the military's information warfare and public relations. This was demonstrated with great impact when Wikileaks published classified footage of a gunship's video feed of two Reuters journalists being killed by U.S. soldiers.[56] The danger for the military is that it may lose control of the technical-visual narrative of the war, of the moving images produced through its own machines that have up until now stood for precision and competence. If one considers the importance of personal testimony, legitimised by the experience of existential danger, in the memorialisation of war, a further unexpected possible consequence of this technology comes into view. It is the chance that authenticity may only belong to the foe on the ground, the one who actually experiences being fired at and whose experience is not as apparently mediated by technology. How much empathy drone pilots can evoke in a global culture that understands heroism as action in the face of existential danger still remains to be seen. In the same way, it remains to be seen how the digital and technical enhancement and standardisation of anthropological knowledge for the military will affect anthropology as a type of knowledge, considering that it is fundamentally legitimated through long-standing and painstaking participant observer relations.

These panoptic technologies culminate in a martial optic in which the experience of quasi-instantaneous legibility of a complex situation is produced through swiftly circulating standardised information that labels objects and an archive in which information about events and individuals can be stored. Writing about the Cold War, Philip Mirowski argued that:

> It was hard not to notice that the colonels had grown fonder of their little Panopticons of bits than anything evoked by the formal theorems about game theory that their mathematicians were busy producing.[57]

If DCGS and MAP-HT are the modern equivalent of little Panopticons with the aim of seeing and finding the foe, and they are really as sophisticated as their marketing literature describes them, then why have the conflicts in Afghanistan and Iraq been such protracted illegible affairs? One answer could be that the panoptic mode provides an operator less than he would have wished for, but more than he bargained for. Finally, up in the Minaret, Bentham sees the whole oriental town laid out before him; but now the shortcomings of the ocular form become painfully apparent. Everybody looks the same. There is a difference between legibility and visibility. Seeing does not mean knowing or understanding. You can zoom in on one individual and not discover their essence; zoom out and not understand the town.

Who is that?

Are they dangerous?

How can one see the enemy in this environment? Can the enemy even be seen? How can we train for this?

WAR-GAMES, WARGAMES, WAR GAMES

This section looks at the recruitertainment war-game of America's Army, then considers the history of large-scale military simulations, and ends on a reading of entertainment war games. The danger of dividing games into these three different categories is that one may overlook the startling amount of design and aesthetic overlap between military training simulations, modern weaponry, and games created solely for entertainment.[58] Controls to operate a robot in the field are inspired by a video game controller. 'We modelled the controller after the PlayStation because that's what these 18-, 19-year old Marines have been playing with pretty much all of their lives.'[59] Visionary technologies showcased in movies spur development of similar tools for the military. Inspired by the interactive display Tom Cruise used in Steven Spielberg's adaptation of Philip K. Dick's *Minority Report*, the U.S. military hired Raytheon to create a real version for the U.S. military. Raytheon promptly hired the same person who had proposed the technology to Spielberg in the first place.[60] Today Oblong Industries's G-Speak Gestural Technology System looks just like the technological artefact used in the movie. Gaming environments built for commercial gain are also repurposed for training and simulation requirements:

> AMERICAS ARMY project is based on UNREAL TOURNAMENT from Blizzard Entertainment, and DARPA's DARWARS AMBUSH product is derived from OPERATION FLASHPOINT by Bohemia Interactive Games.[61]

We can expect new technologies, such as Microsoft's hand-free gaming systems, to quickly find military applications as well. This close connection between 'real' and 'fake', or virtual, visual machinery is an essential characteristic of simulation technologies.

Recruiting and Training with Games

Before the 9/11 attacks the U.S. Army already took on gaming as a recruitment strategy. In 1999, after some of the worst recruitment numbers in thirty years, the U.S. Congress invested heavily in new recruitment tools and techniques. It was during this time that the foundation for America's Army was laid by Colonel Casey Wardynski. America's Army is a widely popular freely available game that takes an Army recruit from training to different missions. In the midst of the global economic crisis, recruitment numbers were met for the first time in more than thirty-five years.[62] This success can, in part, be attributed to the popularity of America's Army.

To play a game such as America's Army is to undergo more training experiences than in any other popular shooter. The player's character has to spend a large amount of time running obstacle courses and qualifying on different weapons before they are 'ready' for combat. To play the game also means being constrained at every turn by strict rules of engagement (RoE). Soldiers get sent to 'Leavenworth' for punishment when they violate the RoE, where they miss stages of the gameplay. As such America's Army is a fantasy of individual agency embedded in a team that delivers expert and legal violence. What America's Army does is familiarise the player with a U.S. military habitus, by getting a sense of the practices at fire ranges, the rules and types of weapons used. It permits a player to encounter a community of martially minded teammates and to experience stages of success and qualification without having to leave their computer.

The gaming reality produced in America's Army should not just be considered for its power to mimic human physical confrontations, but rather for what it leaves out. America's Army does not provide an ideological narrative for violence in the confusing and disturbing world of actual conflict, but a repertoire of weaponry and a ritually ordered rehearsal for war. These games and simulations feel like the expression of a desire to control and rehearse, produce and perfect the delivery of force. While the kind of weapons you train on are hyper-realistic in America's Army, the fact that there is no 'collateral damage' is not. What is also highly unrealistic is the opponent. Whenever you see an enemy, he is to be shot—except if he is unconscious, which would be a violation of the RoE. The enemies exist in the game, but only as empty objects of violence. This cannot be said for new efforts to model cultural reality, in which the other arises as a highly complex set of behavioural functions.

Barry Silverman argues that human terrain data should be used to build serious games: training and simulation environments for cultural interaction.[63] The gaming environment he has helped construct for the U.S. military is called NonKin Village. In it the player has to enter the houses of Afghan civilians and interact with them; the player needs to be polite and learn the local cultural terrain. These simulations create thick immersive experiences from particular data. Drawing on theories of bargaining and political grievance drivers, behavioural models are constructed in which the other is capable of highly complex interaction. Silverman goes so far as to claim that the modelling and simulation community would be remiss if it did not rise to the task of producing serious games from human terrain data. Today the computer programmer, or serious games constructor, is the heir to Said's scientists and men of vision; the gaming platform appears as a descendant of the laboratory:

> To be able to sustain a vision that incorporates and holds together life and quasiliving creatures (IndoEuropean, European culture) as well as quasimonstrous, parallel inorganic phenomena (Semitic, Oriental culture) is precisely the achievement of the European scientist in his laboratory.[64]

Just like Said's 'laboratory' had much wider significance than the immediate output of its research, these types of training simulations fulfil many more important social functions than just the communication of information or technical know-how. Games and training simulations should also be read as modern forms of what James Frazer called homeopathic magic: 'the attempt which has been made by many peoples in many ages to injure or destroy an enemy by injuring or destroying an image of him'.[65] As such, these training simulations do not only fulfil an exercising function, but are also important ritualistic humiliations and recurring symbolic destructions of a foe that rehearse war as it should be.

A key question for Silverman is 'if we use the data of human terrain systems to help model the "parts" and their microdecision processes, can we observe macro-behaviors emerging that are useful for analysts to know about?'[66] In other words, can the minutiae of human terrain data describe larger societal processes and tendencies? This recapitulates a key question that has been haunting war games ever since their inception. Can these simulations somehow be used as a research methodology to provide different scenarios of what could happen in the real world? Are these gaming platforms actually laboratories? According to former Admiral of the U.S. Navy Thomas B. Hayward, the answer is a resounding no:

> It is my conviction that wargaming as a training tool constitutes the overriding value of the wargaming technique, whether tactical or strategic. I would almost go so far as to say the only value. For I contend that using the wargame beyond the training dimension is fraught with flotsam that endangers the utility of the outcome unless managed with great care by the experts.[67]

What are the effects of simulation even when only used as a training tool? One concern is that the training simulation itself, and all of the orientalist or technophile assumptions that underlie it, come to frame and over-determine real conflict, up to the point where simulation structures the narrative of what really happens. It is important to note that this fear of the power of copies over the real is not only associated with computer simulations. Daniel Ellsberg recounts the following incident occurring at the time of the Cuban Missile Crisis:

> [w]e were in ... the Policy Planning Room. There were various cables coming in from minute to minute. One of them looked almost identical to one of the cables of the year before. Namely that students were rioting and demonstrating in Berlin. It looked very much like the message from the [Berlin] game. I tapped Walt Rostow on the shoulder and I said, 'Read this.' He read it. I said, 'This shows how realistic the Berlin game was.' He said, 'Or how unrealistic this is.'[68]

The basic schema of a homeopathic ritual can be discovered amongst people of many different times and places. Usually the central logic of these rituals is conceptualised as 'like producing like'. But does the representation of the other, either as a hollow container of violence or a complex set of behavioural functions, in games mean that soldiers will view non-Western peoples they encounter in the same fashion? The anthropologist Jonathan Z. Smith argues, in the case of sympathetic hunting magic, that the power of the ritual can also be understood to lie in the fact that it is actually 'unlike the hunt. It is, once more, a perfect hunt with all the variables controlled.'[69] Read from this position, these games and their various representations of the other are primarily symptoms of the desire to clearly *see* the enemy; of the desire for a world in which collateral damage is minimised while force is delivered with technical precision and perfect legality. What is most important is how these games are different from, not similar to, reality.

War as Entertainment

The gaming entertainment industry needs to be taken seriously as an economic and cultural force. Sales of the popular shooter *Modern Warfare II* (MWII) have exceeded $1bn, with some $500m worth of games being sold in the first five days. More money was spent on advertising for *MWII* than for *Avatar*.[70] Considering the time and energy it takes to play these games, video game consumers are more continuously exposed to the assumptions and stereotypes of games than they are of individual movies. Due to this, special attention should be paid to how the other may be represented in them. A banal, blatant, and hackneyed kind of orientalism exists in video games.[71] At first playing such games it would appear that oriental stereotypes still hold sway over the public imagination:

One aspect of the electronic, postmodern world is that there has been a rein-forcement of the stereotypes by which the Orient is viewed. Television, the films, and all the media's resources have forced information into more and more standardized molds. So far as the Orient is concerned, standardization and cultural stereotyping have intensified the hold of the nineteenth-century academic and imaginative demonology of "the mysterious Orient."[72]

The genre of first person shooters, in particular, features multiple armed opponents who exist as copies and caricatures of North Koreans, Russians, Iraqis, Terrorists and Favela criminal gangs. Fictional narra-tives requiring the killing of many opponents are enriched through the hyper-realistic portrayal of certain aspects, such as the waves of a body of water or the military vehicles a game character can operate. This also applies to the game's politics: real reference points are embedded in imaginary worlds. For instance, the highly acclaimed *Crysis* (2007) is set in 2020 on an island in the Philippines. The first half of the gameplay is occupied with infiltrating an island and killing North Koreans. The North Korean characters all look alike and have a staple of simple lines: 'I see him!', 'Die, Yankee Scum', 'I kill you' and so on. But in the second half of the game, the enemy shifts. Now one plays a Special Forces sol-dier in a bionic suit that has to defend humanity itself from aliens.

Another example of a trace of politics within a fictional setting can be discovered in *Command and Conquer*. The gameplay takes place at the stra-tegic military-industrial level: players need to build weaponry and train soldiers to destroy enemy buildings and they require money to do so. The setting of the game is an entirely fictional world in which actors fight over some novel resource. The intro sequence, however, features the famous Bush-era terrorism threat chart—what President Obama referred to as the colour-coded politics of fear. There is no common thread con-necting the way the enemy is represented in these games. What binds all of them is an emphasis on technical know-how.

This affinity can also be discovered in the opening sequence of *Modern Warfare II* (*MWII*). While luminescent networks span the globe, inter-spersed by schematics of weapons and military vehicles, a single raspy voice delivers this monologue:

Shepherd's lament: The more things change, the more they stay the same. Boundaries shift, new players step in, but power always finds a place to rest its head.

We fought and bled alongside the Russians. We shoulda

known they'd hate us for it.

History is written by the victor. And here I am thinking we'd won.

But you bring down one enemy and they find someone even worse to replace him.

Locations change, the rationale, the objective.

Yesterday's enemies are today's recruits.

Train them to fight along you, and pray they don't eventually decide to hate you for it too.

Same shit, different day.

World politics exists here as a confusing and disorienting backdrop: the other is never what they seem, the foe is not stable. This is not the world of an unchanging, hostile Orient that can be known. A primitive kind of tragic realism can be sensed behind the account of sudden reversals of alliances, one in which the deep 'oriental' identity of the other is negligible. *MWII* continues:

We are the most powerful military force in the history of man.

Every fight is our fight.

…

Learning to use the tools of modern warfare is the difference between the prospering of our people, and utter destruction.

We can't give you freedom. But we can give you the know-how to acquire it.

What remains in *MWII* is not an identity or ideology based conflict, but a worldview in which everybody can be a foe: insurgents, Russian Mafia, and traitors from your own ranks. The only reliable constant is the cryptic organising concept of 'freedom' and an abiding faith in military technology. Does *MWII*'s emphasis on know-how over purpose, technique over ideology, recapitulate or coincide with the transition from what to how questions that has been taking place since the Middle Ages?[73] In this emphasis on know-how and utility we glimpse the possibility that there may be no extensive ideological investment in one or the other totalising representation of the other.

The real characters of the game are therefore the great variety of weapons one uses—from knives, to all forms of assault weapons and even military drones. The enemy you kill with this family of lethal objects is incidental. While the way you shoot a bullet is hyper-realistic in these games, the identity of the person it is shot at is not. Read in this way the foe, as a complex entity that challenges the self, is absent from this game and from all commercially available shooters.

Like many other games the first part of *MWII* is a training component to let the player familiarise themselves with controls before the real game begins. The training component of *MWII* has a twist though. In it the player is part of a training demonstration to foreign Arab-looking troops—named Fouad, Amin, Nasir, Fahd, Habib, and Bassam—who are being told that they are 'spraying from the hip too much'. This looks like Iraqi Security Sector Reform. The proper use of the 'tools of modern warfare' are treated here as a gift for the other.

Westmoreland's hopes and claims for automation appear hyperbolic forty years later. Especially so when contrasted to the pared-down assessment of General Norton A. Schwartz, the Air Force's chief of staff in 2010. In his account automation is only an inspiration for more efficiency: 'If automation can provide a cue for our people that would make better use of their time, that would help us significantly.'[74] In circumstances where technological fantasies and fixes for complex military tasks abound, it is useful to remind ourselves that in contrast to the popular notion that wars are fought and won with the newest technologies, most militaries are very reliant on surprisingly 'old' technologies. Consider, for instance, the B-52 Bomber. It 'first flew in 1952, and was last manufactured in 1962. Not only is it still in use, it is expected to continue in service to 2040 …'[75] Furthermore, there is a history of unrealistic expectations being placed on military technology.

With the advent of air power and air warfare on the horizon many believed that this weapon would serve to rein in destruction and possibly instantiate a kind of global peace that obliterated frontiers. 'The ultimate effect' wrote Octave Chanute in 1894 'will be to diminish greatly the frequency of wars and to substitute more rational methods of settling international misunderstandings.' He goes on to explain that 'this may come to pass not only because of the *additional horrors* which will result in battle, but because no part of the field will be safe, no matter how distant from the actual scene of conflict'.[76] Similar sentiments can be discovered in the writings of the Italian air power theorist Guilio Douhet, who advocated the use of airpower for a swift and early bombing campaign of population centres to end hostilities.[77] In the twentieth century the airplane was generally imagined as a destroyer of traditional time, space, and borders.[78] While the airplane has had a huge variety of effects, it has not ended warfare. In the same way, while modern applications of digital power are having a large range of effects, they do not entail the end of terrorism or warfare. The same dashed expectation is at work in both of these examples: if the capacity to fight in a battle or find a terrorist is dramatically increased, then the foe will experience such (potential) domination that he will choose not to fight. This expectation of a pacified global order both legitimates and pushes for the development of new technics.

. In this chapter I have sought to situate modern digital technics developed to see the foe in a history of attempts to visualise the Orient. I then argued that surveillance does not deliver on the legibility or domination that is expected of it. In its stead, different social ontologies are developed which circulate around the idea of a hidden collusion, and a world of hidden indicators. I then shifted to the realm of simulation, for purposes of training, research, and entertainment. Within the visual representation of the foe on the screen we encounter a rehearsal and recapitulation of clean and effective violence. These simulations need to be read as wish-fulfilment and regulative ideal and not just as brainwashing or propaganda. In these representations we encounter two different types of enemy. The first is an enemy that is filled to the brim with social scientific models and human terrain data, the second is an enemy that simply shoots and gets shot when he enters the picture. Both of these, inevitably, represent a 'closed world'[79] in which the other is either erased or modelled. The next chapter considers this relationship of self to other in the context of North to South outside of situations of warfare. How do the technics of politics fit into a world of radical unevenness, characterised by hyper-legibility in some locales and total disorientation in others?

10

DIGITAL POWER DOES DEVELOPMENT

In this chapter I follow the concept of the technics of politics further into the thicket of North–South relations. I begin with the notion of the periphery as a laboratory of social and political technologies for the core—exemplified by Michel Foucault's concept of the 'boomerang effect'. This is followed by a discussion of the way technology—from liberation technology to cyber-utopianism—is treated and imagined in relation to the global South. I then proceed to a study of the history of the development of fingerprinting that explicitly connects technologies used to identify individuals with colonialism while pointing to the constitutive, and globally interconnected, effects of such kinds of standardising technical innovations. In the main part of this chapter I offer an examination of the applications of digital power in a case study of Demobilisation, Demilitarisation and Reintegration (DDR) and Security Sector Reform (SSR) programmes in Liberia (2003–10). These programmes lend themselves well to the thematic focus of this book because they have particular information technology requirements; they are, for the main part, executed by foreign interveners; occur in geographic territories which, in a very short time-span, mix different modes of the technics of politics; and have as one of their primary, but overlooked, outputs a stable regime of individual documentation. The way human life is en-framed and measured by databases in these programmes is then contrasted to the social and political ontology enacted in the 2008 Obama Campaign's database. My guiding motif here is to 'treat metropole and colony in a single analytic field'.[1] The conclusion introduces the idea of the technics of politics as a global technology of identifying and sorting.

IMAGES OF TECHNOLOGY

In his famous short story 'In the Penal Colony' (*'In der Strafkolonie'*) (1918),[2] Kafka describes an intricate mechanical apparatus that inscribes the verdict on the back of the accused party, killing them in the process. Like in many of Kafka's stories, the guilty/accused party have no idea what the charge is levelled against them or what punishment lies before them. The process of inscription is a twelve-hour torture programme during which the victim begins to feel and understand their verdict only as it is being written into their back. Here, as is often the case, Kafka needs to be commended for his ability to distil important elements of modernity. By placing this machine in the penal colony, Kafka locates it squarely in a colonial reality of radical inequality. Imagining the process of writing the verdict with a machine as the punishment plays with the theme of the inequality of legibility. In this telling, the apparatus—technology—is built in the colony to deal with the problem of disciplining foreign bodies but also, crucially, of inscribing meaning on to them. It responds directly to the challenge of the illegibility of the other.

'Boomerang Effects', cut (crtl+c), and paste (ctrl+v)

In the classic 1980s movie *Robocop* (1987), Omnicron (a private contractor/corporation) has built a robot, Enforcement Droid 209 (ED-209), which is going to be first used to clean up the mean streets of Detroit, undertaking 'urban pacification', and then sold on to the army for a 'tour of duty'. Foucault writes about the same relationship, but from the other direction. That is, technologies coming back to the West from the colony and leading to a kind of self-colonisation. As he says in a lecture in 1976, the 'boomerang effect' describes '[a] whole series of colonial models ... brought back to the West, and the result was that the West could practice something resembling colonization ... on itself'.[3] A similar account has been provided by McCoy:

> In this process of imperial mimesis, a state such as the United States that creates a colony with circumscribed civil liberties and pervasive policing soon shows many of the same coercive features in its own society. As the metro-

pole's internal security apparatus starts to represent the imperial, so its domestic politics begin to exhibit many attributes of the colonial.[4]

This book emphasizes global interconnection by showing that there are many cases where more radical and sophisticated practices and technologies are first field-tested in the colonies—census, fingerprint, Hiide, drones, human terrain teams are all applied to the non-Western other—before then being shipped home. This ongoing dialectic of the technics of politics—between colony and metropole, core and periphery, hill and valley—has been captured well by some academics but has yet to be substantially theorised. Recognition of it is sorely missing from mainstream international relations or political science discourse, which through its basic nation-state orientation may also have difficulty theorising this.[5]

The case of Liberia, is especially useful for thinking through boomerang effects because it openly models its institutions after the United States. This even extends to the formal juridical domain: there is a law in the Liberian military code of justice that stipulates that if the code does not apply to a particular situation, then the U.S. code of justice should be consulted.[6] What these examples show is how a legal script can move from certain positions of power in the West and then be applied to societies in the global South. As the fingerprint case below demonstrates, practices that are successful in the periphery also travel back to the metropole. In contrast with this way of thinking about technics, as circulating between the South and the North, technology transfer is often thought of as one way: from the North to the South.

THE FINGERPRINT

The word digital comes from digits—as in toes or fingers. The problem of a stable identity, legibility, and reliable documentation of the other, is a recurring and central one, albeit underappreciated in the history of political thought. Through a breakthrough in identification and sorting technology British imperial agents developed a new solution to it in nineteenth-century India. In his seminal 1892 text, simply entitled 'Finger-prints', Francis Galton declares that the 'native clerks of Bengal give the name of *tipsahi* to the mark impressed by illiterate persons, who refusing to make either an X or their caste-mark, dip their finger into the ink-pot and touch the document'.[7] According to Galton it was through observing this practice in 1858 that Sir William Herschel had the idea to make 'regular and official employment' of fingerprints. Deployed first with the sole intention of frightening the illiterate person who would make and deny such a signature, Herschel became convinced that the method might have further utility. He finally introduced the use of fingerprints in several departments at Hooghly District in 1877, after seventeen years' experience of the value of the evidence they afforded.

A few years later in the metropole—London in 1893—the Troup Committee, tasked with discovering the best system of identifying recidivists, concluded that fingerprints and the technique of dactyloscopy (fingerprinting) could not be relied upon because the complexity that made fingerprints unique also made them very difficult to systematically catalogue. It recommended that a part of Bertillon's system, which we have already encountered in Chapters 3 and 6, be applied due to its superior classification.[8] With Bertillon's anthropometric technique, once a faceted number was produced with measurements one could more easily look it up to see if the body belonging to that number had already been arrested. This was not the case with fingerprints. For a technics of politics to be useful it needs to match its identifying capacity with its sorting and retention mechanisms.

Back in the periphery in 1897 Sir Edward R. Henry, the Inspector General of Police of Bengal, developed a new accurate fingerprint classification system. The breakthrough of Henry's system was the ease of reference it permitted. Fingerprint ridge patterns were divided into classifications of arches, loops, whorls, and composites—with a composite being a print that combined some of the other patterns. After discovering that the statistical incidence of loops was far higher than arches he combined whorls with composites and loops with arches. This created a binary system of classification where each digit could be placed into a category of either loop or whorl. For all five pairs of digits taken together there were now 1,024 combinations; Henry consequently used a cabinet with thirty-two sets of thirty-two pigeonholes. The individual filing number would look like the following, with the top part referring to the right hand and the bottom to the left.[9]

I aAra
I rRar

Fingerprinting was thereby made more efficient than Bertillon's system. This form of fingerprint classification was a bio-political practice exhibiting a mindset that had begun to internalise the easy access and configurable power of the card registry along with the specificity of the smart number. These are still archival technics, but their flexibility and speed already provide an indication of the digital technologies that will soon follow. This archival technology en-framed both the sovereign operator and the subject. Here 'the human being was significant principally as the occasion for a file', and as Edward Said continues, '[w]e must imagine the Orientalist at work in the role of a clerk putting together a very wide assortment of files in a large cabinet marked "the Semites."'[10] As a Dewey Decimal system of the organisation of the human epidermis, fingerprint classification brought together library, periphery, science, and criminality in an unexpected and powerful combination. The thrown boomerang returns: 'in the technologies of policing, as in many other areas, empire served as an important laboratory for the metropole'.[11] In particular, technologies used to identify and label the external, racial, other, are applied to the internal other.[12] With Henry's assistance Scotland Yard adopted fingerprinting in 1901; the New York Police Department followed in 1904. In 1905 the U.S. National Bureau of Identification card index that Dewey's Library Bureau had built began to add fingerprints to its cards of criminals. The FBI adopted them in 1924.

The fact that British imperial agents invented modern techniques of fingerprinting in India, which then spread through the world, was not obscured at the time. A prosecutor drawing on fingerprints as evidence in 1902 declares that the practice:

> was of the greatest importance in the administration of the criminal law, and was now being introduced into this country on a very large scale for the purpose of identifying habitual criminals, as well as being applied to the detection of individual crimes. *The system has had an extensive trial in our dependency in India.*[13]

The development of fingerprints can be abbreviated with the slogan: observe, operationalise, objectivise. This coincided with the formation of the signifier, moving from the conjunctural—*finger prints*—to the conjoined—*finger-prints*—to the concretised—*fingerprints*.

Here, in one special case, a close relationship is presented of the foreign need for legibility and identification of individuals in the global South, which subsequently returns to the North, first to identify recidivists and solve crimes and then, with contemporary biometric passports, to be applied to the whole population. This case complicates any notion that privacy is a stable right and the preserve of 'democratic man'.[14]

Instead, privacy appears as the result of a complex, global, circulation of technologies used to identify and track the individual. One that functions, in part, because the identification and arithmetisation of the other is securitised and commentators have inconsistent, paternalistic, standards: *what is privacy inhibiting here, is good over there.*

Fingerprints Redux

In 1906 the Transvaal government in South Africa, encouraged by the success of fingerprinting at Scotland Yard and by the NYPD, issued the draft Asiatic Law Amendment Ordinance, also known as the 'Black Law'. The ordinance would require all Indians in South Africa older than eight years to report to a 'Registrar of Asiatics' office. There they would submit complete sets of fingerprints for which they would receive a certificate, which would have to be shown on demand. Extreme penalties, including deportation, were proposed for those who failed to comply with the ordinance. A young Indian lawyer, Mohandas Gandhi, took issue with this. Gandhi told the press at the time that while the Indian community recognised 'the prejudice against color in the Transvaal' and 'accepted the principle of restriction of British Indian immigration' they only did so on 'terms as are not humiliating, and do not interfere with the liberty of those already in the country'.[15]

Because fingerprints were also to be required of Indian women and fingerprints were generally only taken from criminals at the time, Gandhi perceived a hatred of Indians in the legislation; a hatred that he believed conflicted with their rights as subjects of the British Empire. Leading protests and encouraging Indians to be arrested instead of complying, Gandhi developed Satyagraha, non-violent resistance, as the most effective way of countering the proposal. Indians gave oaths that they would never submit to the 'Black Laws'. In response to this confluence of bureaucratic bio-political techniques and racism[16] a powerful form of resistance was born which drew on elements of suffragette practices and would later provide an important foundation for independence struggles as well as the U.S. civil rights movement.

TECHNOLOGY AS GIFT AND DOMINATION

When considering the role of technology and information technology in North–South relations the first thing that becomes apparent is how difference in technological advancement is commonly used as an explanation for Western conquest and colonialism. A classic discussion of colonial history usually focuses on the hardware requirements of occupation and subjection. In these kinds of accounts, quinine, steamboats, guns and telegraphic cables figure prominently as the reasons why Europeans could colonise such large swathes of the world.[17] This understanding of the importance of technology for colonial domination also extends to post-colonial thinkers. Frantz Fanon, for instance, declares that '[i]n the colonies, the foreigner coming from another country imposed his rule by means of guns and machines.'[18] Michael Adas has taken this brute material explanation further and shown that accounts of differences in technological complexity also served important ideological functions.[19] As he demonstrates, a technological mastery of nature was a central point of comparison for the West to other peoples and thereby a means of legitimising domination.

Such historical matters of asymmetric conquest are reminiscent of the troubling question of how Cortés, with his relatively small cohort, could subdue and destroy the mighty Aztec Empire. As I sought to emphasise in Chapter 5, more was required for the conquest than simply gunpowder, horses, and armour. In particular, Cortés had recourse to an archival technics of politics—written forms of communication, identification, and reckoning—which the Aztecs did not. From this vantage point, a broad understanding of information technology also helps to account for the phenomenal colonial successes of Europe in Africa. Archival technics offered ways of simplifying and abstracting complex political realities and thereby provided the 'overwhelmed' colonial administrator with the experience of knowing the native.[20] A host of different factors could lead to colonial officialdom feeling overwhelmed; the most important though, was that the political, cultural, and even built environments were not familiar and legible. Timothy Mitchell's description of the Egyptian city is a good example of this:

> There were no names to the streets and no street signs, no open spaces with imposing facades, and no maps. The city refused to offer itself in this way as a representation of something, because it had not been built as one. It had not been arranged, that is, to effect the presence of some separate plan or meaning.[21]

Different archival technics—maps, ID cards, censuses, cadastre, and especially statistics—were all deployed to combat this illegibility and create a space for calculation and simplification.[22] At the same time, ethnographic categorisations and 'disambiguation protocols' were necessary to enable indirect rule to fully function.[23] In short, information technology played a crucial role in facilitating colonialism. Furthermore, information technologies connected the colonial sphere with the home world, inaugurating and articulating stereotypical images that still persist today: 'It was only by way of the written word and of the printed image that most Europeans knew anything at all about the places their countrymen were busy ruling.'[24] The technics of politics—information technology used to identify, document, and represent individuals—are an integral part of colonial and post-colonial relations.

Contemporary debates concerning the role of technology in North–South relations usually centre on the provision of technological access for less developed countries in the global South and technical assistance from developed countries in the global North. Technology plays the same material and ideological roles here as it does in regard to explanations of colonial domination. On the one hand, the lack of technological development in the global South is read as an indicator of the necessity for Western aid and assistance; on the other hand, it is precisely the technological progress of the West that enables it to intervene. From the inception of modern notions of 'development', technology has been read in these two ways. For instance, technology functions as a central organising concept in U.S. President Harry Truman's 1949 'Four Point' speech, widely accepted as the introduction of development as a U.S. foreign policy pillar. In the speech Truman states that 'our imponderable resources in *technical* knowledge are constantly growing and are inexhaustible' but also that 'we should make available to peace-loving peoples the benefits of our store of *technical* knowledge in order to help them realize their aspirations for a better life'.[25] Here one can find a powerful real-life precursor to the video-game character from *Modern Warfare II*, Shepherd, encountered in the preceding chapter. In his opening soliloquy Shepherd treats the gift of 'the tools of modern warfare' as a principle for U.S. Foreign Policy stating that: 'We can't give you freedom. But we can give you the know-how to acquire it.' For Truman and Shepherd alike, technology is used to liberate people from poverty and insecurity.

Information Technology as Liberator

Current discussions concerning information technology are similar to those on technology. The central emphasis is generally on how to overcome the 'digital divide', how to alleviate the situation of the 'information' poor in less developed countries.[26] The obvious presumption is that the more information people in the global South have, the better they will be informed, the better off they will be economically, the more democratic their system will be, and so on. It appears that information wants to be free and wants to set people free. Evgeny Morozov has labelled this thought 'cyber-utopian', although it has a wider basis and pedigree than simply the internet revolution.[27] This idea—while it may seem fantastically naive in the light of a twentieth century of psychoanalysis, marketing, and total war—endured throughout the Cold War and is widespread today. It is usually accompanied by the notion that closed authoritarian regimes would be swiftly undone and eventually democratised by the flow of free information.[28] Such a basic assumption inevitably leads to research into 'liberation technologies'.

The specific term of a 'liberatory technology' comes from a very different tradition and set of concerns, though. It can be traced to the anarchist Murray Bookchin, who, in his 1965 essay 'Towards a Liberatory Technology', saw in technological innovations 'the promise of decentralized, communitarian lifestyles' and the ability to shift 'economic power from national to local scale, and from centralized bureaucratic forms, to local, popular assemblies' to 'end the domination of man by man'.[29] This history is particularly interesting in light of the fact that the term 'liberation technology' no longer implies any anarchist or anti-capitalist position and is used today to refer to a whole set of centralising information technologies Bookchin did not initially consider. In his 1965 essay he only refers to computers in three paragraphs and mainly as an example of a miniaturisation that should be emulated in other industries. Today 'liberation technology' is sanitised of Bookchin's anarchism and now means 'any form of information and communication technology (ICT) that can expand political, social, and *economic* freedom'.[30] This approach goes hand in hand with the formulation of policies advocating internet freedom and Radio Free Europe/Radio Liberty, as well as a reading of the fall of the Soviet Union in which Western media plays a pivotal, perhaps even decisive, role.[31]

A clear continuation of this kind of thinking can be discovered in a succession of *Foreign Affairs* articles by George Schultz (1985), Robert Keohane and Joseph Nye (1998), Eric Schmidt and Jared Cohen (2010), and Clay Shirky (2011) that all present similar arguments.[32] The core notion connecting the different texts is that in a world with an information explosion, featuring 'information cascades', only a democratic and open society can be truly stable, technology is on the side of democracy; developing countries are recast as 'partially connected'[33] nations characterised by 'legacy media'. This idea, which categorises and en-frames countries by the level of information technology connectivity and openness they possess, receives its most extensive recent expression in Ian Bremmer's *J-Curve* (2006).[34] Bremmer's thesis is that all of the world's states can be mapped on to a J-shaped diagram—lying on its side like the Nike logo—in which the x-axis denotes openness and the y-axis stability. On the left side of the graph one would find relatively stable, closed, authoritarian regimes, in the lower-middle very unstable, opening, transitional, regimes, and on the top-right highly stable, open, and democratic countries. In an interconnected world, searching for stability, such a framework inadvertently leads to a securitisation of different political regimes and a national security need to transition them to openness and stability. This idea can be understood as an incarnation of 'modernisation theory' and is as fundamental, but not as statistically and critically examined, as the 'democratic peace theory', the notion that democracies do not go to war with each other.[35]

As with the belief that technological supremacy facilitated and legitimised Western domination, this pro-information, and therefore also always pro new information technology, bias has important ideological ramifications. One possible reading of the desires being expressed is offered by Morozov when he writes that this attitude:

> revealed the intense Western longing for a world where information technology is the liberator rather than the oppressor, a world where technology could be harvested to spread democracy around the globe rather than entrench existing autocracies.[36]

A wider interpretation of this idea is that it is the product of a democratic mindset that seeks more, external, justifications of democracy. Here, democracies not only do not wage war on each other, but they are also more stable than dictatorships. At the same time, it would seem that 'cyber-utopian' discourse attempts to tackle larger, and far more difficult to achieve, goals of emancipation and political change by proxy. The danger here is that 'information poverty' is battled against while old-fashioned economic poverty is treated as the inevitable result of sagacious markets. It is also worth pointing out a structural similarity to neo-liberalism: the very idea that unregulated free information would lead to the best possible consequence is isomorphic to the notion that unregulated markets deliver the most optimal outcome.

The complicated issue of how information relates to social organisation and freedom is often collapsed into two opposing camps, those who believe that innovations in information technology will have democratising and liberalising effects and those who do not.[37] While only time and more research can tell what the long-term political results of the connectivity and information explosion enabled by the internet will be, some tendencies are already apparent. Firstly, it is crucial not to lose sight of the material and capital basis of this sudden information and connectivity increase. Google, Facebook, et al. are multi-billion dollar industries whose product happens to be regarded as anti-authoritarian—this has at least as much to do with expensive public relations as it does with inherent technological tendencies. The statement that, 'Companies that provide access to the internet or software applications are critical for exchanging information' has an ominous ring to it when it comes from the CEO of the largest such company.[38]

Put differently, widespread expectations that new information technology liberates people need to be reassessed in light of the position of economic and political power those selling the technologies are in. The fact that information 'lost its body', that 'it came to be conceptualized as an entity separate from the material forms in which it is embedded',[39] appears to also have obscured the political and profit-seeking interests which drive the information technology industry. As a case in point, there would have been a healthy outcry of suspicion if the U.S. State Department had selected CEOs of oil and energy companies for a tour of Iraq and sought to enlist their help in the reconstruction process, yet when this occurred in April of 2009 with the executives of Twitter, AT&T, Google and Blue State Digital it was regarded as visionary thinking.

Secondly, a curious and radically inconsistent attitude is present in a lot of writings about information technology. For instance the fight for a free internet is fought mainly abroad and Google is treated as a technology that might make Americans and Europeans 'stupid', while 'it's presumed to be a tool of enlightenment' for the rest of the world.[40] This inconsistency also extends to innovations in the technics of politics: technologies of identification that are good 'over there' but privacy invading at home. This attitude receives a remarkably clear formulation in a short opinion piece for the *Foreign Policy* online magazine. In it the author argues that, '[i]n the developed world, high-tech personal IDs are the stuff of Orwellian dystopia. But for everyone else, they could be a path to a happier, healthier, less precarious life.'[41] This inconsistent, and extremely anti-egalitarian, attitude is reminiscent of the suspicion the English felt about having a census in their own country in the eighteenth century, while undertaking censuses and surveys in other quarters of the world. Proposing more high-tech tools for making the individual legible in the global South, while attempting to safeguard privacy in the global North, ignores the profoundly interconnecting powers and migratory tendencies of the technics of politics. Or, to put it differently, it forgets Foucault's returning boomerang—how colonial tools rebound back to the West for it to 'colonise' itself. A short history of fingerprints helps to illustrate the dynamic and constitutive relationship of technologies to identify the individual with colonialism, core and periphery.

POST-CONFLICT RECONSTRUCTION IN LIBERIA[42]

Liberia is difficult to navigate. Most roads in the countryside are not passable during the rainy season, which can last up to half a year. Large swathes of territory can only be reached from the capital with a helicopter. While this presents obvious operational difficulties to anybody trying to get around in the Liberian interior, it is also a symptom of the inability of the state to effectively project power, register its population, or levy taxes. This weakness, which is always also a limitation of legibility, has, in turn, historically led state military organisations and armed groups to pay themselves by plundering the countryside, thus undermining the public's perception of the legitimacy of the state's use of force. The basic logistical concern of a road network and travel conditions is therefore also an indication of the prevailing political and military structural circumstances that led to conflict and intervention in the first place: weak state institutions with infrastructure and capital concentrated in Monrovia, with fraught relations to the interior. This was part of the broader geographic and political background of the far-reaching DDR–SSR programmes. The most immediate cause of the programmes was the cessation of a brutal civil war.[43]

When human violence becomes too widespread to make sense of, data is turned to as a means to signify it. Some of the best numbers available for the Liberian Civil War are the following. The toll of the fourteen-year civil war (1989–2003) is an estimated 270,000 dead, with at least 320,000 long-term internally displaced people and 75,000 refugees—and this all in a country with less than four million people. Almost everybody in Liberia was affected by the war. A recent poll shows that 96 per cent of respondents had some direct experience of the conflict and, of these, an astonishing 90 per cent were at one point or another displaced from their homes.[44]

Liberia's international identity is documented and signalled through categorisations and rankings in a number of indexes, produced with digital power. In a data-centric order, the clearest indication that Liberia has undergone recent periods of chaos and illegibility is the absence of some parts of World Bank statistical data; these gaps are the digital mode's equivalent of Marlow's enticing blank spaces on a map.[45] The Civil War has pushed Liberia to the bottom of various health and development indexes. In 2009 it was ranked 169th out of 182 countries on the United Nations (UN) Development Programme (UNDP) Human Development Index.[46] The 2010 Gallup Global Wellbeing Survey puts it at 141st out of 155.[47] The 2010 Global Hunger Index ranks Liberia as 69th out of 84, which makes it the 15th most food insecure country in the world.[48] Legatum Institute's Prosperity Index—'the world's only assessment of wealth and well-being'—does not even list the country because of lacking data.[49]

What is the purpose of these indexes? Considered from a historical view that places an emphasis on the genealogy of information technology, there is obviously a design similarity to late nineteenth- and early twentieth-century tables of the hierarchy of races often based on skin colour, but sometimes on head shape.[50] This similarity even roughly extends to the content of the ranking. Scandinavians usually lead the rest of Europe and the USA at the top, Asia and Russia follow, and Africa constitutes the bottom. All the indexes I listed above, of course, are far removed from any purposive racial ordering or racist methodology. Rather, they seek to serve two related functions. The first is to produce information about where the good and bad cases are and how they are distributed, thus helping to direct funds and efforts to emulate 'best practices'. The second is to act as a kind of management tool. Transacting in the metrics of international development, these indices offer feedback on the success of development initiatives and domestic reform efforts. The crucial question then becomes: Does seeking to improve your standing on the Human Development Index lead to an improvement of human development? Or, to put it differently: Are improving one's rankings and improving what the ranking is supposed to measure identical? Can these kinds of complex systems be represented accurately and managed precisely with statistics?[51] In Liberia's case, to improve its standing it would have to improve education, health, the security sector, the legal sector, and the civil service; to improve these sectors financial resources and expertise would be required, and, crucially, a legible and stable regime of individual identification would have to be put in place.

In this section, I provide an account of the DDR–SSR programmes as primarily seeking to produce legibility and a stable individual identity. The problem of central reliable identification characterises the conflict and the post-conflict environment to a remarkable degree, and leads to a number of curious problems. From DDR, SSR, Truth and Reconciliation Commission (TRC), to efforts to reconnect children with their parents, databases and data-mining methods—*digital power*—play an important role.[52] This gives centre stage to the information technology tools of post-conflict reconstruction and, through the emphasis on identification and sorting, brings such programmes into relation with a history of state-formation in general. As many have pointed out, academic and policymaker conversations on state building are often curiously removed from a historical understanding of the development of the Western state:

> Controversies about state failure and state building are conducted without any reference to the violent process by which the modern states whose leaders are now concerned about these problems actually emerged.[53]

In contrast to such a removed discourse of state building and technical lessons learned, I seek to engage with what Talal Asad has called 'actually existing liberalism' and Nils Gilman has referred to as 'real existing development'.[54] An honest account of actually existing, real, post-conflict reconstruction in Liberia needs to begin by accepting the powerful distinction between what Robert Jackson has called 'positive' and 'negative sovereignty'. In reference to Isiah Berlin's notion of liberty,[55] negative sovereignty is 'a formal-legal entitlement' that means 'freedom from outside interference'.[56] But only a government that 'possesses the wherewithal to provide political goods for its citizens' enjoys 'positive sovereignty'.[57]

In the case of Liberia, the country represents a case of negative sovereignty. Founded in 1847, it is older than Germany. But, as widely signalled by its international rankings it did not have 'the wherewithal to provide political goods for its citizens', it did not have any 'positive sovereignty'. Here, we encounter a more recent equivalent of Carl Schmitt's argument that peoples 'who *don't demonstrate this technical competency* become protectorates'.[58] As a sort of bio-political update to Michael Adas's thesis on the way technology was understood in regard to colonialism, today a mastery of the means to provide goods to your population has replaced the means of the domination of nature as a civilisational measuring stick.[59] Yet presently the means of providing goods for one's citizens are intimately wound up with technologies to identify and sort them.

Who should be demobilised, who should be vetted, who should be permitted entry into the military are all questions that are answered by a bureaucratic apparatus with a stable means of identification and sorting. Due to a near absence of positive sovereignty in Liberia, these means were, and historically have been, constructed either by foreigners, mainly the USA, or with their assistance. A 2005 set of minutes of the Liberian Ministry of Defence describes the circumstances well: 'Hon. Wylie [Deputy Minister of Defence and former rebel commander] lauded ... our foreign partners who now seem to be dominating all DAMC [Demobilisation Advisory Monitoring Committee] meetings.'[60] This 'laudable domination' inadvertently results in a colonial configuration that requires careful assessment. In particular, what kind of human ontology is being enacted in the identifications and data-centric arithmetisations of the other?

DDR: Identity with no Record

In 2003, following the signing in Accra of the Comprehensive Peace Agreement (CPA) that ended the Liberian Civil War, and seven years after a failed demobilisation attempt in 1996, UN personnel were confronted by a complex logistical and political challenge. They were tasked with demobilising all rebel fighters almost simultaneously while ensuring that warring factions were not in the same vicinity. Yet it was not obvious who was a rebel. Due to the irregular nature of the fighting groups no records existed indicating who was actually a combatant. Furthermore, in the course of the fourteen-year civil war the bureaucratic mechanisms used to register and certify individuals at birth, or provide other forms of identification—such as driver's licences and national social security

IDs—had failed. This made it especially difficult to verify an individual's identity. Records and IDs seldom existed and when they did they were often assumed to be fraudulent.

The problem of identification was compounded by the widespread practice of fighters assuming *noms de guerre*. Memorable warlords included General Butt Naked, who is now a preacher, General Peanut-Butter, who is now a senator, General Cobra, General Mosquito, and General Mosquito Spray. But fighters would often also change their names to less conspicuous ones that could be confused with a 'regular' identity. It is worth recalling that stable surnames, as a register of identification, are state simplifications invented to make a population legible.[61] In a country where these technics break down, the practice of taking on a *nom de guerre* is not seen as a criminal offence. The uncertainty and plasticity of individual identity did not hinder an estimation of the quantity of rebels. During the 2003 CPA talks with Liberians United for Reconciliation and Democracy (LURD) and Movement for Democracy in Liberia (MODEL) faction leaders, the number of combatants, including those of the governmental Armed Forces of Liberia (AFL), had been put at approximately 38,000.[62] With around 13,000 AFL soldiers, one would have expected there to be around 25,000 rebels.

Yet establishing the correct size of the AFL was difficult because the part of the military responsible for the files, the G-1 Section of the Ministry of Defence, had suffered severe war damage. The Section had lost all its filing systems, including 201 files of Military Personnel Record Jackets (MPRJ).[63] A large re-documentation exercise was therefore launched. Personnel rosters, huge Excel spreadsheets, were constructed with assistance from the AFL leadership.

Without being able to rely on rosters, the UN implemented a system in which arms would be submitted to qualify for the DDR process. Threshold amounts of bullets and qualifying weaponry were established: one combatant could be qualified through the submission of 150 rounds of ammunition or a rifle, two per light machine gun, four for an anti-aircraft gun, six for a Howitzer, and so on. As a standard, U.S. $300, about six months of average salary in Liberia, was being spent per demobilised fighter. Demobilised fighters were also offered different educational opportunities. This approach had the advantage of incentivising the physical disarmament of combatants, yet was especially vulnerable to misuse in an impoverished country awash with small arms. Ex-combatant identity was suddenly something very valuable.

Following a shaky start in December of 2003, which involved government soldiers and militias rioting at a military base called Camp Schiefflin, the rest of the DDR process was peaceful and successful; major disarmament and demobilisation operations concluded in October 2004.[64] Due to the financial incentives and promised educational opportunities the DDR process was highly popular. Instead of having to coax individuals to demobilise, as in many other post conflict theatres, former rebels and AFL soldiers appeared to submit their weaponry gladly. This can partially be accounted for with the general attitude in the country, which was one of civil war fatigue. The departure of the president, Charles Taylor, and the arrival of the UN peacekeeping mission indicated a clear cessation of hostilities, which signalled to combatants that it was time to reorient towards a peacetime existence. A stronger explanation for the enthusiastic demobilisation was the combination of financial incentives and the nature of the political settlement, which placed rebel factions in the government that led various leaders—'bossmen'—to encourage their troops—'boys'—to demobilise. It was not uncommon for 'bossmen' to receive a percentage of the demobilisation benefits of their 'boys', further incentivising the leadership to demobilise their forces.

In the case of the AFL, which was demobilised by DynCorp International, the initial re-documentation exercise had enabled a system whereby, following questions by vetted officers, individuals could be confirmed as being on 'the list' and then subsequently paid and demobilised. DynCorp International's custom-built demobilisation site processed 13,770 AFL soldiers; grievance committees were established with AFL officers and international observers that worked to establish identity in questionable cases. Identity was verified by quizzing individuals about their own documented biographical information as well as details of life in the AFL, such as the names of cooks at certain training camps. Demobilisation benefits were determined on a points system that took rank and duration of service into consideration. The minimal amount awarded to AFL soldiers was U.S. $540. Former soldiers who successfully demobilised received ID cards documenting their identity; they also had their photograph and fingerprints stored in a database.

Once the UN's disarmament and demobilisation process was completed the large number of processed combatants startled many observers. At 101,495 demobilised fighters, the figure was significantly larger than most had estimated. As a reminder, in 2003 the total number of combatants had been put at approximately 38,000, with rebels expected to be 25,000. Either the estimate had been off by 400% or non-combatants demobilised. A look at the actual amount of submitted weaponry paints a clearer picture. It shows that fewer than 30,000 weapons were submitted, and the majority of DDR recipients qualified through the submission of ammunition.[65] Reviewing this data and considering the widespread references to DDR fraud encountered during vetting investigations for the new AFL, it is apparent that many had assumed, appropriated, and misrepresented an ex-combatant identity during the process. From later interviews it also became clear that the practice of rebels selling guns to ordinary civilians, so that these civilians could demobilise and receive the benefits of the ex-combatant identity, was widespread.[66] The DDR process had created a market for rebel identity—a political economy of identification.

In this case, the problem of a lack of legibility, stable means of identification and sorting obscured more than just the identity of individuals. It covered the dynamic nature of identity in the complicated conflict theatre that was Liberia. As we will see further below, the individual documentation produced through the DDR process, however flawed, provided a baseline that was referred to during the recruiting and vetting of the new AFL and thereby contributed to a disciplining and standardisation of individual identity.

SSR: Identified and Sorted

Following the Comprehensive Peace Agreement in 2003, the U.S. government agreed to assist the Liberian government in the Security Sector Reform (SSR) of the AFL.[67] The U.S. government in turn outsourced this treaty obligation to the private security company DynCorp International, which proceeded to design a plan to demobilise the entire standing military and then recruit, vet, and train a new 2,000 person strong military and 100-person strong Ministry of Defence.[68] To facilitate the recruitment and vetting of the new AFL a means for the verification and stabilisation of identity as well as sorting of applicants had to be constructed.

A database was built with Microsoft Access. Applicants to the new AFL, as well as Ministry of Defence, would fill out an application form and have their picture taken, which was then entered into a database by Liberian employees. Applicants would proceed to take an aptitude test, a physical fitness test, a medical examination, and a background check that vetted individuals for possible human rights abuses conducted during the civil war. With there being little to no reliable records available, all background checks had to be done through neighbourhood interviews by investigation teams, consisting of an international vetter (often former police or military) and a local counterpart.[69] The purpose of all of these tests was to generate data to rank applicants, first to determine who would be vetted, then to determine who would be in the military, and then, finally, to determine what kind of a role they would serve in the military.

To streamline the investigation, thresholds and disambiguation protocols were put in place. First off, a rule was established that any fraudulent or conflicting documentation was grounds for dismissal from the application process: 'fraudulent documentation will render an applicant "not recommended"' and 'if the documents conflict with other corroborated information, the application will be "not recommended"'.[70]

But, as I already pointed out above, assuming a different identity during the civil war was a widespread practice and not necessarily associated by the Liberian public with criminality. Close to a quarter of all vetting disqualifications took place because of these kinds of inconsistencies in a person's demobilisation files.[71] In this way the SSR vetting effort acted as a filtering and disciplining mechanism that only accepted those with a single, stable, identity.

To verify that identity different thresholds and disambiguation protocols were put in place, a constellation of testimonies was required to ratify the identity of an individual: 'a close family member who has known the subject for 15+ years', 'an unrelated source who can confirm professional experience', or a 'neighbor/colleague/acquaintance who has known the subject for 5+ years'.[72] It is important to note the necessarily arbitrary level of detail present in such disambiguation protocols. Even if a whole host of other characteristics and requirements had been used, it would have resulted in the same result: a sorted and identified population. With enough of these thresholds crossed, the identity of an individual was fixed and accepted. At this stage more vetting operations looking into the individual's character would usually take place. To determine who these expensive vetting operations would be conducted for a merit score was constructed, consisting of their physical fitness score and their aptitude test score along with a scoring of the biographical background.

Table 1: Order of Merit Score Formula[73]

1) Criteria	2) Number of Points	3) Points Awarded
4) Written Test		
5) Aptitude Test score divided by 2 + 5	6) ( ) / 2 + 5 =	
7) Physical Fitness Test Test score multiplied by 3 + 2	8) ( ) * 3+2 =	
9) Military Background	10) 5	
11) Education		
12) University Graduate	13) 15	
14) Vocational School Experience	15) 5	
16) Total Points Awarded	17)	18)

This merit score is a low-tech equivalent to the credit, risk, and support scores discussed in Chapter 7. Through it, the applicants were placed into a new hierarchy that determined who was worth vetting, and who wasn't.

Up to this point, digital power seems to be used for the same purposes in Liberia as in the other cases previously discussed: it identifies, ranks, and sorts the population so that resources can be concentrated on a subset of it. It does this through radical individuation and arithmetisation followed by ranking according to the sovereign's needs. Prominent differences only become apparent when one considers the typically mundane issue of applicant ID numbers. During the SSR process the ID numbers provided to individual applicants consisted of a two letter alphanumeric designator and consecutive numbers following that designator.[74]

AC 0000034

The alphanumeric designator, in the example above 'AC', represented the 'County of Origin'. What is important to note is that while the unit of analysis was the individual, the 'County of Origin' aggregated all applicants (ca. 12,000) into groups that correlated to ethnic identities. Here we encounter a contemporary example of Edward Said's description of 'the Orientalist at work in the role of a clerk putting together a very wide assortment of files in a large cabinet'.[75] Hence, the initial move of radical individuation was followed by re-organisation into a distinctly ontopological framework that connected tribe with county. Now, and this cannot be stressed enough, this framework was *entirely an invention of the U.S. contractors*. Indicating neither county of domicile, county of birth, nor ethnic group, the category was at times interpreted to mean what county a person's father came from and at other times what county applicants identified with most. Presented with the digital means to deal with each applicant in an individual fashion, to sort and organise them by any entry on the application form, DynCorp decided to openly distribute ID numbers that correlated to ethnicity but were a fictitious category. When partaking in one of the first large-scale reconstruction programmes in their country, Liberians were confronted with a view of their society that emphasised the importance of ethnic division and categorisation. It was the organisation of applicants into categories that existed only in the contractors' minds—a far cry from the notion that information technology would liberate and democratise people.

While there has been some superficial attention to, and criticism of, the role of contractors and lack of local ownership, this use of data itself has not been subject to critique or analysis. This is an essential part of the political power of these kinds of 'technical' details. The representation of the population is regarded as natural and neutral—as the apodictic recital of cold facts—and not as a foreign fantasy about African ethnicity. Furthermore, there is no developed rights discourse on such questions of identification that can easily be deployed to criticise them. Another strong reason for why this aspect of the programme has not been considered previously is that much of it takes place behind closed doors, just like the calculation of Obama support scores discussed in Chapter 7.

Private security companies generally enshrine their practices as confidential and their procedures as proprietary, with far ranging consequences for the public accountability of these kinds of projects and social memory of them.[76] Unlike other more apparent manifestations of discrimination and hierarchy (such as the segregation of bathrooms for Liberians and 'International staff') the 'order of merit' and 'County of Origin' coded ID card has a hidden logic, one that the population only experiences the results of. This logic responded to the problem of identification and sorting by constructing new powerful categories and hierarchies of Liberian society, which provided a response to the calls of 'who is worth being vetted' and 'who is worth being an officer in the new military'. The vexing paradox of this ID card was that its ethnographic structure contradicted the very principles of merit and citizenship that the new military was supposed to be built on. In light of that, and the fact that it had potentially disastrous consequences in a country which had experienced proto-genocidal tendencies in its recent history, it must have been the result of a fundamental assumption or served some wider purpose.

Tribal Ontology vs Obama's Database

While sometimes the practices of international actors can be accounted for by sheer incompetence, the case of the SSR ID card tells us something deeper about the manner in which this group of contractors imagined Liberia. DynCorp'—at odds with most scholarship on ethnicity in Liberia[77]—believed that the population consisted of pre-formed, stable categories that had become confused through migration during the war. DynCorp's impetus was to recognise these formations and then construct an intervention (recruitment of the new military that regarded them as the natural forms of identity within the country. Here the ethnic alphanumeric identifier acted as a limit-shape, providing conceptual order and legitimacy to the foreign interveners.

The use of high-tech digital means to represent the other as traditional and tribal can also be seen in the discussion of the Human Terrain Team software in the preceding chapter. These separate cases share a fascinating paradox: a stable, traditional, anti-modern, pre-technological, non-Western, identity is only fixed and instated through advanced digital power. These means also recapitulate important practical and ideological functions fulfilled by anthropology during the colonial era, where ethnographic constructions and the bureaucratic administration of tribes entailed each other.[78] The point here is to recognise the ideological and practical utility of 'ethnographic fictions'[79] for interveners, our overwhelmed colonial administrators. Not only do these classifications lend themselves to dividing the population, and creating a stable knowledge and strategy of interaction for dealing with it, but they also provide a significant ideological framework. In a second conceptual leap, these constructed 'natural' ethnic orders are often understood to be eroded or eroding due to war, external actors, etc. The only way forward then is a return to the past. Consider this passage as a particularly stark expression of such a belief:

> The central cultural fact about Afghanistan is that it is constituted of tribes. Not individuals, not Western-style citizens—but tribes and tribesmen. ... the answer to the problems that face the Afghan people, as well as other future threats to U.S. security in the region, will be found in understanding and then helping the tribal system of Afghanistan to flourish.[80]

This ethnic construction contributes to an ideology where interveners can imagine themselves on the side of modernity, but act as the agents of tribalism and feudalism. One must be careful, though, not to overstate the powers of the representations of foreign interveners. What matters here is not so much the content of the representation, but rather the 'appropriation of tribal images into structures of distribution and inter-pretation'.[81] The images and 'ethnographic fictions' of foreign interven-ers are always subject to appropriation by the population they are supposed to be about. It is also important to note that this return to an originary ontology—accompanied by a reading of the conflict as not being embedded in global capitalist relations and an amnesiac under-standing of the reconstruction process that does not speak of or consider previous interventions—is a necessary condition for the reform process, for the smooth functioning of the development and intervention dis-course.[82] The obvious question here is whether the model of human subjectivity instantiated in the Obama campaign's database may fulfil a similar ideological function.

It is through reading them in conjunction and considering the distance of these two representations of populations (Obama's America and DynCorp's Liberia) that we can begin to recognise some of the range of digital power. In both instances strong corporate industries supporting state power have created products which manufacture representations of a society that re-organises—Heidegger would say 'reveals'—it according to principles of particular utility: support scores and merit scores. Society is coded through these databases and the presuppositions of their design-ers, whether these are built on utility or a different ideology. In both cases, much of this occurs removed from the public gaze and deals with characteristics that are not immediately visible; one might call it the private realm of the public or the construction of identity out of incon-spicuous factors. What happens to individuals in both databases cannot simply be described as a form of discipline. Rather, a model of human ontology is used to organise society into groups, which then by being acted upon constitute this self-same model of human ontology. To put it differently, just like a map is necessarily false and marginalises alternating perceptions of political space, so too these identity constructions, as mod-els, are necessarily false but still succeed in displacing other models.

In our examples, Obama's America consists of individual liberal-democratic subjects; DynCorp's Liberia of individuals predetermined by their 'County of Origin'. In one case, radically dis-embedded individuals are produced; in another, all individuals are re-categorised into ill-fitting ethnic classes. Or to put it differently, one articulates individuals, the other supra-individual categories, as the fundamental ontology of a society—but both are located at the heart of modernity and both filter out other salient and constitutive categories, such as class.

This contrast offers an unambiguous demonstration of the underdetermined nature of both technology and population. The distance of our two examples also works as a more refined response to 'what is the question concerning technology'? Instead of asking what the essence of technology is, or how technology alters the social and political fabric, this question would be: 'Why does the same technology do different things in different places'? An obvious response to this type of question would be that these data-centric representations of human subjectivity represent things as they actually are. The same technology is showing different things because 'Liberians are tribal' and 'Americans are lonely consumers'.

The question of whether these representations are real is tricky. For instance, consider the following simple thought experiment. Imagine a Liberian immigrant to the United States, one who has previously demobilised and joined the AFL, and then decommissioned. Or think about a Liberian who lived and worked in the United States and is now returning to Liberia to join the AFL. Can one really maintain that this person is tribal in one country and a consumer category in another? If so, where does this transformation take place? The fact that people easily migrate from these different regimes of identification necessarily undermines their positivist basis and demonstrates that they are part of a global system, in which a technics of politics identifies and sorts them. To take it further, the issue of whether such identity constructions are false or represent reality needs to be rejected. These kinds of state simplifications are always necessarily false because they are simplifications, but they are also models with cultural, material, and political backing, which can instate these simplifications and thereby produce ontological realities. Just because 'the map' is necessarily false in one way or another, does not mean that it has the power to shape a reality on the ground, to become a referent object imbued with great political significance.

Presented with the results of such a similar technics of politics being transferred from one domestic locale to another the question arises if, instead of charting the various exchanges of different countries, it might be more fruitful to attempt to reject the reification of various societies and instead begin to think of the technics of politics as a global script that can be cited, quoted, plagiarised and rewritten in many different instances. For example, the fact that the AFL creed ('I am a Liberian Soldier. I am a Warrior and a member of a team. ... I will always place the mission first') is copied directly from the U.S. Army soldier's creed, with Liberia replacing America ('I am an American soldier'...) could lead to a hand-wringing search for authenticity, one that misses out on the fact that such a combination of words is a social technology, the usefulness of which is not delimited to a particular geographic territory. Or, in a similar vein, the fact that U.S. military manuals plagiarise both from academics and EU treaty documents[83] shows how the international is always already present in our instantiations of the national.

The conclusion of this book returns to this idea of a global technics of politics and considers the benefits and pathologies of a monopolistic regime of identification.

11

RESISTANCE ON OUR PLANETARY SHIP
OF STATE

The problem of identification and sorting is central to domestic politics and international relations. This book began with a discussion of the 'ship of state' in literature and philosophy to demonstrate the wide range of its uses, and thereby gesture towards the under-determined nature of technology in relation to politics, as well as to provide a spectrum of themes: technology, domination, colonialism, and world politics. Then we considered the history of the ear. I introduced my primary analytic category, the technics of politics, and undertook a study of the ritual mode. Next I turned to the archival mode and proposed a political metaphor for understanding it, called Cuntz's Tower. I then moved on to the digital mode and considered how digital power was being applied to create models of the U.S. population in the 2008 Obama campaign, as well as to control international migration in the face of terrorism. This was followed by a study of digital power in warfare, one that placed special emphasis on issues of visuality. Here, I argued that because vision does not deliver the legibility that is expected of it, digital power, as tagging, sorting and identifying tools, needs to be drawn on. The last chapter assessed how the technics of politics fits into North–South relations. Through all of these cases a picture of digital power was painted which is characterised by an unevenness of legibility. While experiences of hyper-legibility exist for the operator plugged into the network, near illegibility pertains for the average subject seeking to manoeuvre in a world increasingly stripped of conspicuous markers of identity.

After an eclectic mix of theory and history, I end this book by proposing that our contemporary technics of politics should be thought of as an increasingly standardised, global, script, one that can be deployed, edited, and spliced for a variety of different purposes. What would it mean, borrowing a phrase from Buckminster Fuller, to think of the technics of politics as individual operating instructions for 'spaceship earth'?[1] Although the last chapter argued that a similar technology of identification and sorting could result in radically different models of the human subject, it is worth recalling that these separate ontologies are embedded in a remarkably stable and standardised global system of identification one which is trending towards a universal convergence. After all, whether the individuals voting for Obama are imagined as ethnic or consumer categories, they are still interpolated as U.S. subjects.

A global technics of politics so normalised and standardised that it is obscured, copied and rebuilt up to the point where it becomes uncertain as to what is original (national) and what is copied (international) can also be thought of as a ship. In Greek philosophy the Ship of Theseus symbolises the following paradox: If all of the components of a ship have been replaced over time, is it still the same ship as it was in the beginning?[2] Thomas Hobbes had a follow-up question: What if the planks taken from the old vessel are used to build a new one? Which then is the original ship?[3] To this, let us add another query, especially pertinent in an age of digital reproduction: What if it is copied and the original is destroyed? What if the ship of state is a simulacrum?[4]

This image of a ship, whose essence and origin are displaced, needs to be added to our broad repertoire of possible meanings of the ship of state in world politics. At the end of this book it should be apparent that the fundamental constitutive means of identification and sorting states deploy come from a huge range of global sources. It would appear that there is more than one 'boomerang effect'; perhaps 'boomerang effects' is more appropriate. Technologies and techniques bounce back from library to prison, theory to practice, fiction to reality, and periphery to metropole constantly legitimated and constrained by specific requirements. Practices developed over there are applied here; knowledge needed to produce legibility in the periphery is funded in the metropole; and specific technologies of identification enable particular scripts of resistance.

Identities that are imagined as natural and neutral are standardised and sorted through a worldwide-disseminated set of technics; in this sense, the national is a clear product of the international. Furthermore, the homogeneity of the tools to render a political subjectivity legible contributes to the homogeneity of political subjectivity. The conjunction of cadastre, census, passports, maps, and databases has resulted in a notable standardisation of political power and subjectivity. This mono-culture of political subjectivity, the nation-state's citizen, has certain benefits as well as pathological tendencies; it does well with some tasks and fails spectacularly with others (climate change is a case in point). A pertinent question for further research is whether such a *Gleichschaltung* ('equalisation', 'bringing into line') of political subjectivity is desirable or sustainable. Would it be better for the human condition if a plethora of notions of time, space, and subjectivity existed in world politics?

Such inquiry generates a number of further research questions. Are other modes and forms of the technics of politics possible? What would a different mode look like? Would some lend themselves to more democratic use? Is the digital mode so pervasive that future political activists need to be hackers? What is the connection of illegibility caused by a lack of data and a return to ethnic and tribal ontologies? How many identities in the global system can be understood as solutions to the sovereign problem of identification and sorting? To push it further, can the nation-state system itself be regarded as such a solution? A solution that by 'segment[ing] off the exploited and impoverished regions within discrete national compart-ments with "their own problems"' obscures profoundly inter-connected political relations 'behind the false fronts of a sovereignty and independ-ence that have never existed'.[5] Since we know that every globalisation also produces a 'deviant globalization',[6] we need to ask: What kind of deviant globalisation is being produced by our current technics of politics? To be more precise, how do current technological solutions to the problem of identifying and sorting create novel opportunities for the 'deviant' com-modification of false identities? A more philosophical question is how a 'self' constructed through digital power fits into a history of 'the idea of the self'?[7] Finally, if a standardised global subjectivity en-framed by a homogenous technics of politics turns out to be profoundly undesirable, what kinds of strategies of resistance or engagement are available? Can these technics of politics be destabilised?

Resistance and Appropriation

To consider the history of the ear, the map, the fingerprint, and the technics of politics in general, means to recognise that we have already

177

become subject to the tools developed to identify and measure the other and find the foe. The present is haunted by the unintended consequences of earlier means for the documentation and arithmetisation of individual identity. Considering the history of the fingerprint to resistance also brings a peculiarity of our present mode into focus: the type of resistance through refusal Gandhi articulates in response to the 'Black Laws' would not function as well today. As classification and identification techniques improve they appear less targeted and are no longer directly experienced as discrimination. An ear that is digitally captured from afar is not experienced as a privacy violation, just like an anonymous database storing all of our conversations does not trigger the same visceral response as a neighbour eavesdropping on us.

A biometric border does not discriminate: it demands data from all the people that seek to pass through it; airport security gets around violating the rights of a sub-group by invading everybody's privacy. Instead of targeting the equivalent of the Indian population in South Africa, modern means of data-managing the foe and arithmetising the other exhibit their own supra-political logic. That is to say, they don't engage with groups with political consciousness, but with huge numbers of individuals who are then aggregated into categories of risk, thus producing new groups without group consciousness.

Established forms of resistance and refusal work well in response to blatant discrimination or open networks: such as radio, even television, and websites. It works well when we see that all the women are being discriminated against, or all the Arabs, or all the short people, or all the disabled people. These, however, are not the crude categories with which digital power works. The modern technics of politics can sidestep these salient and protected categories of identity. Closed networks and coded, segmenting discrimination—like batteries of biometric databases—leave little opportunity for any appropriation or resistance. Here, even refusal to be made subject to the technology is a complicated affair. Drones can collect information without being seen from the ground. Data-management practices can produce digital imprints of individuals without their knowledge. Tallying all of an individual's Facebook activities and connections produces a digital fingerprint[8] without the individual feeling singled out and violated, and therefore ever having an impetus to organise to resist.

With traditional forms of resistance and refusal not appearing feasible in regard to today's technics of politics, the main avenue left for activists is one of appropriation: a whole-hearted embrace of, firstly, one's identified and sorted political subjectivity for the purpose of redefining it, and, secondly, of the tools of identification and sorting. In a world where context, use, and users matter, a global regime of a technics of politics is not ultimately determined by those who operate it or by the content of its representations, but by how the representations are appropriated, circulated and interpreted by those subject to them. Such a development must begin with the solidarist recognition that we are all already identified and sorted. It must next be followed by demanding that sites of private and public power provide us with an annual account of the information they have of us, as individuals. Think of it as a kind of reverse tax day on which sites of power have to show the cards they are holding on all of us.

A good place to start is by looking at modern European legal history. In 1983 the West German Federal Constitutional Court, in response to widespread political resistance to a census, introduced the right of *Informationelle Selbstbestimmung* ('informational self-determination').[9] Informational self-determination is, in its essence, an anti-totalitarian perception of privacy. It exists to ensure that individuals will not be subject to external control—it stands squarely in a tradition of individual security only being granted through individual rights and freedoms. In the words of the German law professor and former data protection commissioner Spiros Simitis, modern information technologies 'threaten the very fabric of democracy' through their 'labeling of individuals, manipulative tendencies, magnification of errors, and strengthening of social control'.[10] Informational self-determination attempts to respond to this challenge by granting a right in the individual to control how their data is used. This is a start, but it does not bring us far enough to be useful in our current moment. The main problem is that the entire framework is built on the shifting sands of individual versus statistical information. For the West German Federal Constitutional Court, an individual has informational self-determination over identifiable information about them, and not about statistical 'anonymous' information. But, through digital power that which appears statistical and anonymous today is not statistical and anonymous tomorrow. Today, big data is teaching us that our purchase patterns, medical history, and travel are surprisingly unique, much like fingerprints. For instance, a study demonstrated that given only four referent points of cell-phone activity, time and location—information freely posted by many individuals on Twitter or Facebook when they 'check in'—it was possible to identify a person's 'anonymous' record out of a freely available dataset of 1.5 million with 95 per cent accuracy.[11] As the means of identifying and sorting this unique data improve, anonymity as we currently understand it, will be greatly curtailed. The battle for anonymity is practically over. But the war about how the information about individuals is used, first by political power and second by private parties, continues. A more capacious concept than anonymity is needed for our time.

The right to the property of one's personal data is not merely a right to be left alone or anonymity, but rather a right to maintain and build up a stable and coherent self-representation. It is what I call a right to *nymity*.[12] But why *nymity* and not anonymity? Protecting anonymity is no longer a realistic endeavour; the coming technological innovations will remove the last shred of any anonymous public sphere. Instead of attempting to prevent this development, it is more prudent to ensure that the individual maintains a property and control right over their personal data. *Nymity* is the property of one's personal data, the right to control one's self-representation. The *nymity* principle seeks to place informational privacy on a more stable footing. The *nymity* principle does not apply to the collection of information—that cat is well out of the bag at this point—but instead places a subsequent right of access and influence over this data in the individual. The first step in this direction is to offer legibility to individuals about the information collected and aggregated about them. One practical way of achieving this is to grant individuals regular access to the information institutions have assembled on them.

It is easy to imagine an institutional, legal, and technological system in which citizens once they turn eighteen, and responsible guardians, are provided an annual report—a kind of reverse tax filing—where information is sent back down to the individual by political and corporate entities detailing the information they hold on the individual. Within this structure, proper *nymity* would require people to be given a legal right to contest, correct, and erase the data held on them.

There is already a growing movement underway granting a kind of *nymity* right to persons. In the UK, a person has a right to request CCTV footage of themselves and receive a copy of the footage within forty days.[13] In California, a law was recently passed permitting minors to delete social media posts.[14] And in the summer of 2014, the Court of Justice of the

European Union ruled that a person can receive a legal injunction forcing Google to remove search results that appear when the person's name is searched: 'An internet search engine operator is responsible for the processing that it carries out of personal data which appear on web pages published by third parties'.[15] These are all expressions of the *nymity* principle: the right to control personal data. Here, privacy as an anti-totalitarian principle and property as an anti-feudal principle meet.

It is only by creating and subsequently globalising such new arrangements—which short circuits and undermines the growing chasm of unequal legibility—that we can hope for a semblance of popular control of the technics of politics.

APPENDIX

Cuntz's Letter

Mein Fuehrer!

I turn to you confidentially in the hope that your chancellery will know to honour my proposal and that this letter may be fortunate enough to be read by you. These are ideas that have been engaging me for close to 30 years. I have the feeling that they can no longer be treated as fantasies, but that their time has now come.

You will notice that, especially in regard to the proposal for a 'German Registry', this only deals with the creation of an external frame with practical side effects, but that my desire extends further: 'To the "Volks"-community through the "*Altersgenossenschaft*" [generational community].' The article 'Bund der Deutschen' indicates the way for the Germanic people of the entire world to unify into one league. Of course everything is only sketched in a short fashion here. Perhaps I may once be permitted to present my ideas to you personally.

With German Greeting/*Heil Ihnen* [Heil to you]
Erwin Cuntz

German Registry.

To date, there is no office where one could find out the address of every German and other worthwhile information about him in a single step, although such an office would be highly desirable and its construction would not be especially difficult, as is shown in the following.

One only needs to advance to the insight that the human is a movable, itself moving, being [*Wesen*], that one therefore should not select as the basis for an organisation something which can continuously change and continuously changes for millions, namely domicile and address, but something which is solid and always remains the same, namely date of birth and place of birth, and, in a more developed framework, race and family origin.

Instead of the territorial principle, one must apply the personage principle [*Personalitätsprinzip*], for which I have fought for years. This is especially true because it is the only way in which human affairs can be brought into harmony with the progress of technology. It is the bringing into line [*Gleichschaltung*] with technology that is the challenge.

The goal that I envisage can therefore not be achieved by amassing directories of addresses from all of Germany. Directories age too quickly. Besides it would require an incredible effort to search through all of these directories for a particular person. Not even considering the fact that many areas don't have directories yet and that many people prefer not to register themselves.

My proposal, which I have called 'the German Registry', calls for the establishment of a single German registration office, in which every change of residence, every journey lasting more than six weeks, every change of occupation, every death and every birth would have to immediately be reported. Failure to report these occurrences would result in severe punishment. The incoming data shall be sorted by year of birth in such a way that those born in the same 25-year interval are grouped together, with further subdivisions by birth months and birthdays.

It would be helpful if in Berlin or in another centrally located German city a round tower with 25 storeys were erected, every story of which had twelve circular ordered rooms, one for each month, with 30 or 31 cabinets, one for each day of the month, to hold all the actual registration files. On the first storey would be kept the files of people whose names began with 'A' and who were born in the years 1901, 1926, 1876, 1851, and perhaps 1826. On the third story there would be the age group corresponding to the years 1828, 1853, 1878, 1903, 1928, and so forth, and on the 25th floor the age group corresponding to the years 1850, 1875, 1900, 1925, and so forth.

I have attempted to represent this better in a small sketch.

In this context it should be indicated what kind of numbers this would entail. The strange fact should be considered that the numbers of those born in individual years and months would not be substantially different, if special conditions, such as war do not exist. If we assume around 60 million Germans, there would be 2.4 million on every floor, 200,000 in each of the 12 rooms, and in every of the 30 filing cabinets around 7,000 names to be registered.

When registering these names the organisation should first be according to gender, then according to the alphabet and the place of birth. The registry cards should be arranged in such a manner that, for instance all of those born on 11 June 1828, then those born on the same day in 1853, 1878, 1903, and then finally at the top level there are all those born in 1928.

If the individual residence is continuously updated on the card, then, when the place of birth of the person in question is known, only one step is needed to discover their current address.

APPENDIX

A further device will enable the discovery of the current address even if the place of birth is unknown. In each of the rooms for those born in the same month, totalling 300, because it is 25 times 12 rooms, in each of which there are 30 to 31 filing cabinets, the names (ca. 2,000,000) are to be kept alphabetically in a ledger. Whereby next to the names the address does not need to be entered, since this would require constant correction, but only the date of birth. Such a ledger would for now and ever establish the names of all of those born in one and the same month and year or 25, 50, and 75 years earlier or later. It would probably come to pass on its own course that the 12 ledgers of every floor would be combined into one volume with around 2.4 million names, yes that one would come to a unitary index of all Germans, if one were to combine all 25 ledgers into one volume. Of course this would not have to be printed.

Should a request for a name arrive without an indication of the birth, it would be added to the daily search lists sent from the central post reception point [*Centralposteinlaufstelle*] via letter chute in 300 copies to the individual rooms. One would then only have to check in the registry volume whether a person with such a name is registered in the room, and if they are to look up their current address on the card.

The establishment of such a registry could take place in a relatively short amount of time. The building, the tower for the German registry, would be constructed in a few years. The basic addresses could be obtained from sorting the existing material that has been collected through the census at the statistical office. Apart from this it could be made the duty of the Germans that on their birthday everybody mails in their address and other information on an official form, which is to be certified and mailed free of charge. Everything could happen in a year, the 200,000 to 250,000 daily received registrations could then be processed by good civil servants. Yet, as soon as the registry is fully established, 1,500 civil servants should be able to handle the day-to-day operations.[1]

NOTES

1. THE SOVEREIGN'S DATA

1. John Hart Ely, *Democracy and Distrust: A Theory of Judicial Review* (Cambridge, MA: Harvard University Press, 1980), 135.
2. 1 yottabyte is 1000000000000000000000000 bytes or 1 trillion terabytes or 1 quadrillion gigabytes. An academic research library is in the range of 2 terabytes.
3. Siobhan Gorman, 'NSA Officers Spy on Love Interests', *The Wall Street Journal*, 23 Aug. 2013.
4. 'In time … the Cartographers Guilds struck a Map of the Empire whose size was that of the Empire, and which coincided point for point with it. The following Generations, who were not so fond of the Study of Cartography as their Forebears had been, saw that that vast Map was Useless, and not without some Pitilessness was it, that they delivered it up to the Inclemencies of Sun and Winters. In the Deserts of the West, still today, there are Tattered Ruins of that Map, inhabited by Animals and Beggars; in all the Land there is no other Relic of the Disciplines of Geography.' Jorge Luis Borges, 'On Exactitude in Science', in *Collected Fictions* (London: The Penguin Press, 1999), 325.
5. F.A. Hayek, 'The Use of Knowledge in Society', *The American Economic Review* 35, no. 4 (1945): 519. The emphasis is mine.
6. Bruce A. Ackerman, *We the People* (Cambridge, MA: Belknap Press of Harvard University Press, 1991).
7. Langdon Winner, *The Whale and the Reactor: A Search for Limits in an Age of High Technology* (Chicago: The University of Chicago Press, 1986), 29.
8. As an analogy we can think of a subway. Once a main infrastructure that does not take physically impaired persons into account has been completed it is difficult to simply add mobility and access, as is the case with London's tube or New York's subway.

9. Alexis de Tocqueville, *Democracy in America* (Cambridge: Sever and Francis, 1862), 7.

10. James C. Scott, *Seeing Like a State: How Certain Schemes to Improve the Human Condition Have Failed* (New Haven: Yale University Press, 1998).

11. See Wendell Wallach and Colin Allen, *Moral Machines: Teaching Robots Right from Wrong* (Oxford: Oxford University Press, 2009).

12. Adam L. Alter et al., 'Overcoming Intuition: Metacognitive Difficulty Activates Analytic Reasoning', *Journal of Experimental Psychology: General* 136, no. 4 (2007); Connor Diemand-Yauman, Daniel M. Oppenheimer, and Erikka B. Vaughan, 'Fortune Favors the Bold *(and the Italicized)*: Effects of Disfluency on Educational Outcomes', *Cognition* 118, no. 1 (2011).

13. Ferdinand de Saussure, *Course in General Linguistics*, revised ed. (London: Fontana, 1974).

14. Andrew Feenberg, *Alternative Modernity: The Technical Turn in Philosophy and Social Theory* (Berkeley: University of California Press, 1995), 83.

15. Michel Foucault, *The History of Sexuality* (New York: Vintage Books, 1988), 139. By 'bio-power … I mean the mechanisms through which the basic biological features of the human species became the object of a political strategy, of a general strategy of power, or, in other words, how, starting from the eighteenth century, modern Western societies took on board the fundamental biological fact that human beings are a species.' *Security, Territory, Population: Lectures at the Collège de France, 1977–1978*, trans. Arnold Ira Davidson (Houndmills: Palgrave Macmillan, 2007), 1.

16. Scott, *Seeing Like a State*.

17. While vision refers to the physical act of seeing, visuality refers to the social fact of seeing. The difference is 'between the mechanism of human sight and its historical techniques'. Hal Foster, 'Preface', in *Vision and Visuality*, ed. Hal Foster (Seattle: Bay Press, 1988), ix.

18. Max Weber, 'Wissenschaft Als Beruf', in *Schriften 1894–1922*, ed. Dirk Kaesler (Stuttgart: Kroener, 2002 [1919]), 504. The translation is mine.

19. Jean-Jacques Rousseau, 'On Social Contract or Principles of Political Right', in *Rousseau's Political Writings: New Translations, Interpretive Notes, Backgrounds, Commentaries* (New York: W.W. Norton, 1988 [1762]), 137.

20. Niklas Luhmann, *Die Gesellschaft Der Gesellschaft I* (Frankfurt am Main: Suhrkamp, 1997), 520.

21. For a similar idea see Lewis Mumford, *The Myth of the Machine* (New York: Harcourt, 1967), 64.

22. For a classic discussion of these problems see Quentin Skinner, *Visions of Politics, Regarding Method*, 3 vols, vol. 1 (Cambridge: Cambridge University Press, 2002), 57–89.

23. Quentin Skinner, *Liberty before Liberalism* (Cambridge: Cambridge University Press, 1998), 112.

24. I find that the process of translation, even of previously translated texts, opens an avenue to different latent interpretations and constitutes an important research methodology for political theory.

25. Feenberg, *Alternative Modernity*, 4–6.

26. Carl Schmitt, *Der Leviathan in Der Staatslehre Des Thomas Hobbes* (Stuttgart: Klett-Cotta, 1995 [1938]), 53.

27. Martin Heidegger, *Die Technik Und Die Kehre* (Pfullingen: Günther Neske, 1962), 7.

28. Carl von Clausewitz, *Vom Kriege* (München: Cormoran Verlag, 2000), 86–90.

29. Alf Hornborg, *The Power of the Machine: Global Inequalities of Economy, Technology, and Environment* (Oxford: Rowman & Littlefield Publishers, 2001); Carl Schmitt, *Politische Theologie II: Die Legende Von Der Erledigung Jeder Politischen Theologie* (Berlin: Duncker & Humblot, 1996); *Politische Theologie: Vier Kapitel Zur Lehre Von Der Souveränität* (Berlin: Duncker & Humblot, 2004 [1922]).

2. THE SHIP

1. Langdon Winner, *The Whale and the Reactor: A Search for Limits in an Age of High Technology* (Chicago: The University of Chicago Press, 1986), 31; Plato, *Republic* (Oxford: Oxford University Press, 1998), 208–9.

2. Plato, *Republic*, 209.

3. '... the exact *definition* and *criteria* of securitization is constituted by the inter-subjective establishment of an existential threat with a saliency sufficient to have substantial political effects'. Barry Buzan, Ole Waever, and Jaap de Wilde, *Security: A New Framework for Analysis* (London: Lynne Riener, 1998), 25. For a take on securitisation as being 'concerned with making life accessible to different social technologies' see Michael Dillon and Julian Reid, 'Global Liberal Governance: Biopolitics, Security and War', *Millennium: Journal of International Studies* 30, no. 1 (2001): 51.

4. Horace, 'Ode I.14', in *Horace, the Odes*, eds Robert Bly and J.D. McClatchy (Princeton: Princeton University Press, 2002), 51.

5. Henry Wadsworth Longfellow, *Poems and Other Writings* (New York: Library of America, 2000), 126.

6. Phyllis A. Hall, 'The Appreciation of Technology in Campanella's "The City of the Sun"', *Technology and Culture* 34, no. 3 (1993).

7. Carl Schmitt, *Der Leviathan in Der Staatslehre Des Thomas Hobbes* (Stuttgart: Klett-Cotta, 1995 [1938]), 70; Tommaso Campanella, *City of the Sun: A Poetical Dialogue* (Berkeley: University of California Press, 1992).

8. Friedrich Engels, 'On Authority', in *Philosophy of Technology: An Anthology*, eds Val Dusek and Robert C Sharff (Oxford: Blackwell Publishing, 2003 [1873]), 79; Winner, *The Whale and the Reactor*, 29–30.

9. Lenin quoted in James C. Scott, *Seeing Like a State: How Certain Schemes to Improve*

189

the Human Condition Have Failed (New Haven: Yale University Press, 1998), 162–3. But see Lenin's response to Luxemburg's reply to 'One Step Forward, Two Steps Back': 'Comrade Luxemburg declares that I glorify in the educational influence of the factory. That is not so. It was my opponent, not I, who said that I pictured the Party as a factory. I properly ridiculed him and proved with his own words that he confused two different aspects of factory discipline, which, unfortunately, is the case with Comrade Luxemburg too.' V.I Lenin, '(Reply by N. Lenin to Rosa Luxemburg) One Step Forward, Two Steps Back', Marxists Internet Archive, http://www.marxists.org/archive/lenin/works/1904/sep/15a.htm.

10. Michael Oakeshott, *Rationalism in Politics* (New York: Basic Books, 1962), 127.

11. Paul Gilroy, *The Black Atlantic: Modernity and Double Consciousness* (London: Verso, 1993), 4.

12. Peter Linebaugh and Marcus Buford Rediker, *The Many-Headed Hydra: Sailors, Slaves, Commoners, and the Hidden History of the Revolutionary Atlantic* (Boston: Beacon Press, 2000), 163.

13. Otto Neurath, *Anti-Spengler* (München: G.D.W. Callwey, 1921).

3. THE EAR

1. James C. Scott, *Decoding Subaltern Politics: Ideology, Disguise, and Resistance in Agrarian Politics* (New York, NY: Routledge, 2013), 131.

2. James Q. Whitman, *Harsh Justice: Criminal Punishment and the Widening Divide between America and Europe* (New York: Oxford University Press, 2003), 27.

3. Art. 205. This punishment also extended to slaves who denied the identity of their owners. 'If a slave say to his master: "You are not my master," if they convict him his master shall cut off his ear.' Article 282. Code of Hammurabi. Michael Oliver, *The Politics of Disablement: A Sociological Approach* (New York: St. Martin's Press, 1990).

4. James Henry Breasted, *Ancient Records of Egypt*, vol. IV (Chicago: University of Chicago Press, 1906), § 451ff.

5. Ibid.

6. George Smith, *The Hebrew People* (New York: Carlton & Phillips, 1856), 672.

7. 'Having cut off his ears, bade him live, a memorial of his own clemency, and a disgrace to us.' Tacitus, 'The Annals', http://classics.mit.edu/Tacitus/annals.8.xii.html. An analogous case occurred in the early eighteenth century when a contender to the Emperorship of Ethiopia—Nebahne Yohannes—had his ears and nose cut off as punishment.

8. Mary Douglas, *Purity and Danger: An Analysis of Concepts of Pollution and Taboo* (London: Routledge & K. Paul, 1966), 54.

9. John (18:10); Matthew (26:51); Mark (14:47).

10. A famous Roman statue from 200 BC, the Dog of Alcibiades, shows cropped

ears. The British Museum, Collection Online. http://www.britishmuseum. org/research/collection_online/collection_object_details. aspx?objectId=467443&partId=1

11. Lucien M. Turner, 'Ethnology of the Ungava District, Hudson Bay Territory', in *Eleventh Annual Report of the Bureau of Ethnology to the Secretary of the Smithsonian Institution*, ed. J.W. Powell (Washington: Government Printing Office, 1894), 201.

12. Alexander Stewart, *Twixt Ben Nevis and Glencoe: The Natural History, Legends, and Folk–Lore of the West Highlands* (Edinburgh: William Paterson, 1885), 235–8.

13. Chase J. Smeaton, 'Cropping Animals' Ears', *Folklore* 17, no. 1 (1906): 72–3.

14. Roger D. Groot, 'Petit Larceny, Jury Lenity and Parliament', in *The Dearest Birth Right of the People of England: The Jury in the History of the Common Law*, eds John W. Cairns and Grant McLeod (Oxford: Hart Publishing, 2002), 58.

15. Groot, 'Petit Larceny', 52.

16. 27 Henry VIII, c. 25.

17. John Macgregor, *The History of the British Empire from the Accession of James the First* (London: Chapman and Hall, 1852), cccxxi.

18. 'Offentlich inn branger gestelt, beyde oren abgeschnitten, vnnd des landts biß auff kundtlich erlaubung der oberkeyt verweist werden soll.' Art. 198. Peinliche Halsgerichtsordnung Kaiser Karls V (Constitutio Criminalis Carolina) (1532).

19. Friedrich Engels, *Der Deutsche Bauernkrieg* (Leipzig: Verlag der Expedition des 'Volksstaat', 1870), 24.

20. Engels, *Der Deutsche Bauernkrieg*, 59.

21. Blackstone, William. *Commentaries on the Laws of England*, http://avalon.law. yale.edu/18th_century/blackstone_bk4ch15.asp.

22. Ibid.

23. Richard Heath, *The English Peasant. Studies: Historical, Local, and Biographic* (London: T. Fisher Unwin, 1893), 27.

24. While there are punishments such as burning, being drawn and quartered, branding, fine, public whipping, whipping, pardon, being executed, etc, there is none for ear cutting or similar mutilation. Pillory did exist as a punishment, but this pillory punishment did not appear to entail a nailing and cutting off of ears. Moreover, the punishment of pillory was extremely infrequent (0.16% of all punishments) and practically disappeared from use in the eighteenth century. The last time somebody was pilloried at the Old Bailey was in 1831. (http://www.oldbaileyonline.org)

25. 'An Act to prevent Clandestine Marriage' passed in the Isle of Man in 1757, and repealed in 1849, proscribed ear cropping for foreign priests without a marriage licence. *The Lex Scripta of the Isle of Man; Comprehending the Ancient Ordinances and Statute Laws. From the Earliest to the Present Date* (Douglas:

G. Jefferson, 1819), 372. Here too, it is unclear whether this punishment was ever actually executed on an individual.

26. Georg Stephan Wieland, *Juristisches Hand-Buch* (Jena: Johann Gottfried Hanisch, 1762), 793.

27. R.S. Rattray, 'Ashanti Law and Constitution', in *Readings in African Law*, eds Neville Rubin and Eugene Cotran (New York: Frank Cass & Company Limited, 1970), 80.

28. Whitmore, William Henry. *The Colonial Laws of Massachusetts* (Boston: Published by order of the City Council of Boston, under the supervision of William H. Whitmore, Rockwell and Churchill, city printers, 1889), 127.

29. Philip B. Kurland and Ralph Lerner, *The Founders' Constitution*, 5 vols, vol. 5 (Indianapolis: Liberty Fund, 2000), Amendment VIII, Document 14.

30. Lawrence M. Friedman, *Crime and Punishment in American History* (New York: Basic Books, 1993), 40.

31. Exodus (21:2–6).

32. American Anti-Slavery Society, *American Slavery as It Is: Testimony of a Thousand Witnesses* (New York: The American Anti-Slavery Society, 1839), 84.

33. *Owens v. Ford*, 1823 WL 736 (Nov. 1823).

34. American Anti-Slavery Society, *American Slavery as It Is*, 79.

35. On the history of barbed wire, see the excellent Reviel Netz, *Barbed Wire: An Ecology of Modernity* (Middletown, CT: Wesleyan University Press, 2004).

36. Josiah Lafayette Seward, *A History of the Town of Sullivan, New Hampshire, 1777–1917* (Keene, NH: Sentinel Printing Co., 1921), 569–70.

37. Dorvil Miller Wilcox, *Records of the Town of Lee from Its Incorporation to A.D. 1801* (Lee: Press of the Valley Gleaner, 1900), 128.

38. Seward, *A History of the Town of Sullivan*, 570.

39. Francis Olcott Allen, ed. *The History of Enfield Connecticut*, vol. III (Lancaster: The Wickersham Printing Co., 1900), 2495.

40. *Buck v. Davenport Sav. Bank*, 29 Neb. 407, 45 N.W. 776 (1890).

41. *Andregg v. Brunskiel*, 87 Iowa 351, 54 N.W. 135 (1893).

42. 'Talbot, seeing the headless carcass of the hog, and believing it to be all that was left of his blue barrow, called for the head, which, after some parleying, was produced, but without the ears, which had once adorned it, while they served to identify their possessor as the property of Talbot, whose mark they bore.' *Burch v. State*, 1881 WL 4583 (Miss. Nov. 21, 1881). 'Both ears were cut off to such an extent that it was impossible to tell whether or not the ears of the hog had been marked, and if so, the character of such marks.' *Fletcher v. State*, 97 Ark. 1, 132 S.W. 918, 919 (1910). '[I]t had previously been marked with a crop off each ear thus, (symbol), and that, when found in possession of the defendant, this mark had been changed thus, (symbol).' *Brite v. State*, 43 S.W. 342, 343 (Tex. Crim. App. 1897).

43. *Musgrove v. State*, 68 Ga. App. 561, 23 S.E.2d 201, 202 (1942).

44. *Com. v. Crawford*, 2011 PA Super 122, 24 A.3d 396 (Pa. Super. Ct. 2011).

45. 'It is unlawful for any person willfully to cut, sever, detach or mutilate more than one-half (1/2) of either ear of any sheep or to unlawfully have in his possession or under his control any sheep which have more than one-half (1/2) of either ear removed or mutilated unless the same are so described in a bill of sale or other certificate of title covering the sheep.' Wyo. Stat. Ann. § 11–30–113 (West).

46. '[D]isfigure a gelding, the horse beast of Benjamin Birdwell, of the value of $100, by then and there, etc., cutting off the hair of the tail of said horse beast, and by then and there cutting off the mane of said horse beast, etc.' *Boyd v. State*, 21 Tenn. 39, 40 (1840).

47. *Elisea v. State*, 777 N.E.2d 46, 47 (Ind. Ct. App. 2002). *United States v. Berry*, 09-CR-30101-MJR, 2010 WL 1882057 (S.D. Ill. May 11, 2010) *aff'd sub nom. United States v. Courtland*, 642 F.3d 545 (7th Cir. 2011).

48. Alphonse Bertillon, *Signaletic Instructions: Including the Theory and Practice of Anthropometrical Identification*, trans. R.W. McClaughry (Chicago: The Werner company, 1896), 46.

49. Bertillon, *Signaletic Instructions*, 45.

50. Ibid., 46.

51. Ibid., 116.

52. Ibid., viii.

53. '[T]he science of ear identification' developed by Alfred Iannarelli, a police official of thirty years. 'For 30 years, he had worked as a deputy sheriff in Alameda County, California, as the chief of campus police at California State University at Hayward, and in several other law enforcement positions. … He became interested in ears in 1948, and over the next 14 years classified perhaps 7,000 ears from photographs (but not from latent prints).' *State v. Kunze*, 97 Wash. App. 832, 839–41 (1999).

54. L. Neil Burcham and Jason L. Turner, 'Guide B-602: Identify Pigs by Ear Notching' (Las Cruces, NM: NM State University Cooperative Extension Service, College of Agricultural, Consumer and Environmental Sciences, 2011).

55. A.J. Hoogstrate, H. Van Den Heuvel, and E Huyben, 'Ear Identification Based on Surveillance Camera Images', *Sci Justice* 41, no. 3 (2001).

56. Li Yuan, Zhichun Mu, and Fan Yang, 'A Review of Recent Advances in Ear Recognition' (paper presented at the Biometric Recognition: 6th Chinese Conference, CCBT 2011, Beijing, 2011), 252.

57. Bertillon, *Signaletic Instructions*, 46.

58. *State v. Kunze*, 97 Wash. App. 832, 855, 988 P.2d 977, 991 (1999).

59. *People v. Lawson*, 302128, 2012 WL 2402033 (Mich. Ct. App. June 26, 2012) *appeal denied*, 493 Mich. 896, 822 N.W.2d 597 (2012).

60. Bertillon, *Signaletic Instructions*, 13.

61. Hui Zhang et al., 'Ethnic Classification Based on Iris Images' (paper presented at the Biometric Recognition: 6th Chinese Conference, CCBT 2011, Beijing, 2011), 82.

4. TECHNICS AND TOWERS

1. Lewis Mumford, *The Myth of the Machine* (New York: Hacourt, 1967), 9. See also Stanley Rosen, 'Technē and the Origins of Modernity', in *Technology in the Western Political Tradition*, eds Arthur M Melzer, Jerry Weinberger, and Richard M Zinman (Ithaca: Cornell University Press, 1993); Keekok Lee, '*Homo Faber*: The Unity of the History and Philosophy of Technology', in *New Waves in Philosophy of Technology*, eds Jan Kyrre Berg Olsen, Evan Selinger, and Søren Riis (New York: Palgrave Macmillan, 2009), 17–18.

2. Bernard Stiegler, *Technics and Time* (Stanford: Stanford University Press, 1998), 1.

3. For an argument that *phronesis* should be the basis of political science see Bent Flyvbjerg, *Making Social Science Matter: Why Social Inquiry Fails and How It Can Succeed Again* (Cambridge: Cambridge University Press, 2001), 55–65.

4. James C. Scott, *Seeing Like a State: How Certain Schemes to Improve the Human Condition Have Failed* (New Haven: Yale University Press, 1998), 311–23; Marcel Detienne and Jean Pierre Vernant, *Cunning Intelligence in Greek Culture and Society* (Hassocks: Harvester Press, 1978).

5. Aristotle, *The Complete Works of Aristotle*, ed. Jonathan Barnes, 2 vols. (Princeton: Princeton University Press, 1984), bk. 6, 4.

6. Leo Marx, 'Technology: The Emergence of a Hazardous Concept', *Technology and Culture* 51, no. 3 (2010). For a good treatment of how technology fits into American culture see his *The Machine in the Garden: Technology and the Pastoral Ideal in America* (Oxford: Oxford University Press, 1964).

7. Here technique is to be understood as uses and practices of technical artefacts. On practices in international relations in general see Emanuel Adler and Vincent Pouliot, 'International Practices', *International Theory* 3, no. 01 (2011).

8. Niklas Luhmann, *Die Gesellschaft Der Gesellschaft I* (Frankfurt am Main: Suhrkamp, 1997), 524.

9. Scott, *Seeing Like a State*, 77.

10. Bernard S. Cohn, *Colonialism and Its Forms of Knowledge: The British in India* (Princeton: Princeton University Press, 1996), 162.

11. Mark S. Monmonier, *How to Lie with Maps* (Chicago: University of Chicago Press, 1996), 1. The emphasis is mine.

12. Scott, *Seeing Like a State*, 183.

13. Carl Schmitt, 'Das Zeitalter Der Neutralisierungen Und Entpolitisierungen', in *Der Begriff Des Politischen* (Berlin: Duncker & Humblot, 2002 [1929]), 84.

14. David Bates, 'Political Theology and the Nazi State: Carl Schmitt's Concept of the Institution', *Modern Intellectual History* 3, no. 3 (2006).

15. Jan-Werner Müller, *A Dangerous Mind: Carl Schmitt in Post-War European Thought* (New Haven: Yale University Press, 2003).

16. Giorgio Agamben, *State of Exception* (Chicago: The University of Chicago Press, 2005).

17. For a recent appraisal of Carl Schmitt's relevance to international relations see Louiza Odysseos and Fabio Petito, *The International Political Thought of Carl Schmitt* (Abingdon: Routledge, 2008). For a critique see David Chandler, 'The Revival of Carl Schmitt in International Relations: The Last Refuge of Critical Theorists?', *Millennium* 37, no. 1 (2008).

18. Notable exceptions are Duncan Kelly, *The State of the Political: Conceptions of Politics and the State in the Thought of Max Weber, Carl Schmitt, and Franz Neumann* (Oxford: Oxford University Press, 2003), 212–17; John P. McCormick, *Carl Schmitt's Critique of Liberalism: Against Politics as Technology* (Cambridge: Cambridge University Press, 1997); Pier Paolo Portinaro, 'Kulturpessimismus Und Die Grenzen Der Entzauberung. Diagnosen Zur Technik, Kultur Und Politik Nach Der Jahrhundertwende', in *Kultur Und Kulturwissenschaften Um 1900*, eds Rüdiger vom Bruch, Friedrich Wilhelm Graf, and Gangolf Hübinger (Stuttgart: Franz Steiner Verlag, 1989).

19. Schmitt, 'Das Zeitalter Der Neutralisierungen Und Entpolitisierungen', 85.

20. Ibid., 88.

21. ....

22. Schmitt, 'Das Zeitalter Der Neutralisierungen Und Entpolitisierungen', 89.

23. Ibid., 90.

24. Luhmann, *Die Gesellschaft Der Gesellschaft I*, 518.

25. Jürgen Habermas, *Technik Und Wissenschaft Als 'Ideologie'* (Frankfurt am Main: Suhrkamp, 1989 [1968]), 83.

26. Habermas, *Technik Und Wissenschaft*, 81.

27. Schmitt, *Leviathan*, 53.

28. Ibid., 72–3. The emphasis is mine.

29. For the most prominent discussion see Michel Foucault, *Discipline and Punish: The Birth of the Prison* (New York: Pantheon Books, 1977).

30. Wendy Brown, *Walled States, Waning Sovereignty* (New York: Zone Books, 2010), 7–28.

31. Foucault, *Discipline and Punish*, 211.

32. Joseph Schumpeter, 'The Analysis of Economic Change', in *Essays on Entrepeneurs, Innovations, Business Cycles and the Evolution of Capitalism*, ed. Richard V Clemence (New Brunswick: Transactions Publishers, 2000), 142.

33. For a critique of such an idea see Paul J. DiMaggio and Walter W. Powell, 'The Iron Cage Revisited: Institutional Isomorphism and Collective Rationality in Organizational Fields', *American Sociological Review* 48, no. 2 (1983). Cf. Adam McKeown, *Melancholy Order: Asian Migration and the Globalization of Borders* (New York: Columbia University Press, 2008), 320–1.

34. James C. Scott, *The Art of Not Being Governed: An Anarchist History of Upland Southeast Asia* (New Haven: Yale University Press, 2009), 111–12. See also Oliver Wolters, *History, Culture, and Region in Southeast Asian Perspective* (Singapore: Institute for Southeast Asian Studies, 1982).

35. For a theory of mimicry in colonial relations see Michael Taussig, *Mimesis and Alterity: A Particular History of the Senses* (New York: Routledge, 1993).

36. Norbert Wiener, *Cybernetics: Or Control and Communication in the Animal and the Machine* (Cambridge, MA: The MIT Press, 1948), 11–12.

37. *Cybernetics: Or Control and Communication in the Animal and the Machine* (Cambridge, MA: The MIT Press, 1948), 8.

38. For a social theory inspired by cybernetic principles see Luhmann, *Die Gesellschaft Der Gesellschaft I.*

39. Hal Varian, Joseph Farrell, and Carl Shapiro, *The Economics of Information Technology: An Introduction* (Cambridge: Cambridge University Press, 2004), 3. For a description of 'the cycle' of innovation, monopoly, and decay of these industries see Tim Wu, *The Master Switch: The Rise and Fall of Information Empires* (New York: Knopf, 2010).

40. Varian, Farrell, and Shapiro, *The Economics of Information Technology*, unpaginated foreword.

41. On increasing returns see W. Brian Arthur, 'Competing Technologies, Increasing Returns, and Lock-in by Historical Events', *The Economic Journal* 99, no. 394 (1989).

42. To be specific, Moore's law claims that there is a doubling of the number of transistors that can be placed on an integrated circuit every two years. On Metcalfe's Law cf. David Singh Grewal, *Network Power: The Social Dynamics of Globalization* (New Haven: Yale University Press, 2008), 305, n. 17.

43. Jeremy Bentham, *The Panopticon Writings* (London: Verso, 1995), 35.

44. ....

45. For a good discussion of the Panopticon and vision in Foucault see Martin Jay, *Downcast Eyes: The Denigration of Vision in Twentieth-Century French Thought* (Berkeley: University of California Press, 1994), 381–434.

46. François Cusset, *French Theory: How Foucault, Derrida, Deleuze, & Co. Transformed the Intellectual Life of the United States* (Minneapolis: University of Minnesota Press, 2008).

47. Foucault, *Discipline and Punish*, 200–1.

48. Ibid., 207–9.

49. Some indicative statements are Roy Boyne, 'Post-Panopticism', *Economy and Society* 29, no. 2 (2000); Kevin D Haggerty, 'Tear Down the Walls: On Demolishing the Panopticon', in *Theorizing Surveillance: The Panopticon and Beyond*, ed. David Lyon (Cullompton, Devon: Willan Publishing, 2006); Daniel J. Solove, 'Privacy and Power: Computer Databases and Metaphors for Information Privacy', *Stanford Law Review* 53, no. 6 (2001); Zygmunt Bauman, 'On Postmodern Uses of Sex', in *Love and Eroticism*, ed. Mike Featherstone (London: Sage, 1999).

50. Gertrude Himmelfarb, 'The Haunted House of Jeremy Bentham', in *Ideas in History: Essays Presented to Louis Gottschalk by His Former Students*, eds Richard Herr and Harold Parker (Durham: Duke University Press, 1965), 219–20.

51. Jane Caplan, '"This or That Particular Person": Protocols of Identification in Nineteenth-Century Europe', in *Documenting Individual Identity: The Development of State Practices in the Modern World*, eds Jane Caplan and John Torpey (Princeton: Princeton University Press, 2001), 65. The practice of tattooing citizens was widely used to control their movement in a variety of places. For one example from early nineteenth-century southern Lao see Scott, *The Art of Not Being Governed*, 163.

52. Matthew S. Anderson, 'Samuel Bentham in Russia, 1779–1791', *American Slavic and East European Review* 15, no. 2 (1956); Timothy Mitchell, *Colonising Egypt* (Cambridge: Cambridge University Press, 1988), 185.

53. Martha Kaplan, 'Panopticon in Poona: An Essay on Foucault and Colonialism', *Cultural Anthropology* 10, no. 1 (1995): 89.

54. A similar note is struck by Louise Amoore and Alexandra Hall, 'Taking People Apart: Digitised Dissection and the Body at the Border', *Environment and Planning D: Society and Space* (2009): 18.

55. Michel Foucault, *Security, Territory, Population: Lectures at the Collège de France, 1977–1978*, trans. Arnold Ira Davidson (Houndmills: Palgrave Macmillan, 2007), 66. The emphasis is mine.

56. Cuntz's proposal is used to illustrate the horrors of Nazi demography in Götz Aly et al., *The Nazi Census: Identification and Control in the Third Reich* (Philadelphia: Temple University Press, 2004); Götz Aly and Karl Heinz Roth, *Die Restlose Erfassung: Volkszählen, Identifizieren, Aussondern Im Nationalsozialismus* (Berlin: Rotbuch Verlag, 1984). Apart from this discussion, and later German references to it in Götz Aly, there appear to be no published works dealing with his proposal.

57. For a fascinating discussion of a manual database design from eighteenth-century Paris called 'The Paperholder' see Grégoire Chamayou, '"Every Move Will Be Recorded": A Machinic Police Utopia in the Eighteenth Century', Max Planck Institute For the History of Science, http://www.mpiwg-berlin.mpg.de/en/news/features/feature14.

58. Foucault, *Discipline and Punish*; Charles Tilly, *Coercion, Capital, and European States, AD 990–1990* (Cambridge: Blackwell, 1990).

59. For more on this see Markus Krajewski, *Zettelwitschaft: Die Geburt Der Kartei Aus Dem Geiste Der Bibliothek* (Berlin: Kulturverlag Kadmos, 2002).

5. THE RITUAL

1. Victor Witter Turner, *The Forest of Symbols; Aspects of Ndembu Ritual* (Ithaca: Cornell University Press, 1967), 19.

2. See Catherine M. Bell, *Ritual Theory, Ritual Practice* (New York: Oxford University Press, 1992); *Teaching Ritual* (Oxford: Oxford University Press, 2007); *Ritual: Perspectives and Dimensions* (New York: Oxford University Press, 1997); Victor Witter Turner, *The Ritual Process* (London: Routledge & Kegan Paul Ltd, 1969); *The Forest of Symbols*; *The Drums of Affliction: A Study of Religious Processes among the Ndembu of Zambia* (Oxford: Clarendon, 1968); Edward Shils, *Center and Periphery: Essays in Macrosociology* (Chicago: University of Chicago Press, 1975); Walter Burkert et al., *Violent Origins* (Stanford: Stanford University Press, 1987).

3. In particular see David I. Kertzer, *Ritual, Politics, and Power* (New Haven: Yale University Press, 1988); Sean Wilentz, *Rites of Power: Symbolism, Ritual, and Politics since the Middle Ages* (Philadelphia: University of Pennsylvania Press, 1985); Bruce Lincoln, *Discourse and the Construction of Society: Comparative Studies of Myth, Ritual, and Classification* (Oxford: Oxford University Press, 1989). For related discussions of the role of myth in politics see Christopher Flood, *Political Myth: A Theoretical Introduction* (New York: Garland Pub. Inc., 1996).

4. Kertzer, *Ritual, Politics, and Power*, 58–61.

5. Edward Shils and Michael Young, 'The Meaning of the Coronation', in *Center and Periphery: Essays in Macrosociology*, ed. Edward Shils (Chicago: University of Chicago Press, 1975 [1956]).

6. Bruce Lincoln, *Discourse and the Construction of Society: Comparative Studies of Myth, Ritual, and Classification* (Oxford: Oxford University Press, 1989), 53–71.

7. Lincoln, *Discourse and the Construction of Society*, 43.

8. Emile Durkheim, *The Elementary Forms of Religious Life*, translated by Karen E. Fields (New York: Free Press, 1995), 34, 38.

9. Turner, *The Forest of Symbols*, 19. The emphasis is mine.

10. Jeffrey C. Alexander, 'Marxism and the Spirit of Socialism: Cultural Origins of Anti-Capitalism (1982)', *Theses Eleven* 100, no. 1 (2010): 85.

11. Bell, *Ritual Theory, Ritual Practice*, 106.

12. Jonathan Z. Smith, 'The Bare Facts of Ritual', *History of Religions* 20, no. 1/2 (1980): 117.

13. Lewis Mumford, *The Myth of the Machine* (New York: Hacourt, 1967), 69.

14. Walter J. Ong, *Orality and Literacy: The Technologizing of the Word* (London: Routledge, 1991), 46–9.

15. Mumford, *The Myth of the Machine*, 64.

16. Grewal, *Network Power*, 42–3.

17. Alf Hornborg, *The Power of the Machine: Global Inequalities of Economy, Technology, and Environment* (Oxford: Rowman & Littlefield Publishers, 2001), 46.

18. Hornborg, *The Power of the Machine*, 81.

19. For more on this see Maurice Godelier, *The Mental and the Material: Thought, Economy, and Society* (London: Verso, 1988); John V. Murra, *The Economic Organization of the Inka State* (Greenwich: JAI Press, 1980).

20. Durán quoted in Tzvetan Todorov, *The Conquest of America: The Question of the Other* (Norman: University of Oklahoma Press, 1999), 67.

21. Todorov, *The Conquest of America*, 71.

22. Mumford, *The Myth of the Machine*, 69.

23. Inga Clendinnen, *The Cost of Courage in Aztec Society* (Cambridge: Cambridge University Press, 2010), 15.

24. C.A. Bayly, *Empire and Information: Intelligence Gathering and Social Communication in India, 1780–1870* (Cambridge: Cambridge University Press, 1996), 6; James C. Scott, *The Art of Not Being Governed: An Anarchist History of Upland Southeast Asia* (New Haven: Yale University Press, 2009), 68.

25. James C. Scott, *Seeing Like a State: How Certain Schemes to Improve the Human Condition Have Failed* (New Haven: Yale University Press, 1998), 186. For more on the problem of mobile populations see Michael Adas, 'From Avoidance to Confrontation: Peasant Protest in Precolonial Southeast Asia', *Comparative Studies in Society and History* 23, no. 2 (1981).

26. Mumford, *The Myth of the Machine*, 111.

27. This experience was not just particular to the Aztecs. For a discussion on officers, distinctive dress and courage in Europe see John Keegan, *The Face of Battle* (New York: Penguin, 1978), 190.

28. Todorov, *The Conquest of America*, 89.

29. Duncan Bell, *The Idea of Greater Britain: Empire and the Future of World Order, 1860–1900* (Princeton: Princeton University Press, 2007), 63.

30. Marcia Ascher and Robert Ascher, *Mathematics of the Incas: Code of the Quipu* (Mineola, New York: Dover Publications, 1997), 7.

31. Cieza de León quoted in ibid.

32. De Acosta quoted in Todorov, *The Conquest of America*, 70.

33. Ascher and Ascher, *Mathematics of the Incas*; Gary Urton, *Signs of the Inka Khipu: Binary Coding in the Andean Knotted-String Records* (Austin: University of Texas Press, 2003); Gary Urton and Carrie J. Brezine, 'Khipu Accounting in Ancient Peru', *Science* 309, no. 5737 (2005), 1065–7; Richard L. Burger et al., *Variations in the Expression of Inka Power: A Symposium at Dumbarton Oaks, 18*

and 19 October 1997 (Washington, D.C.: Dumbarton Oaks Research Library and Collection, 2007). Reference to similar information systems in Southeast Asia can be found in Scott, *The Art of Not Being Governed*, 117.

34. Bruno Latour, *Science in Action: How to Follow Scientists and Engineers through Society* (Cambridge: Harvard University Press, 1987), 227.

35. Urton and Brezine, 'Khipu Accounting in Ancient Peru', 1066.

36. Urton, *Signs of the Inka Khipu*, 31.

37. Named after the Italian mathematician Leonardo Fibonacci (1170–1250), the sequence is generated by adding the preceding two values: 0, 1, 1, 2, 3, 5, 8, 13, etc.

38. Donna Haraway, 'A Cyborg Manifesto: Science, Technology, Socialist-Feminism in the Late Twentieth Century', in *Simians, Cyborgs and Women: The Reinvention of Nature*, ed. Donna Haraway (New York: Routledge, 1991), 149.

39. For a discussion of the encounter see Todorov, *The Conquest of America*, 51–124. An important supplement to Todorov's account is provided in Inga Clendinnen, *The Cost of Courage in Aztec Society: Essays on Mesoamerican Society and Culture* (Cambridge: Cambridge University Press, 2010), 49–90. See also Paul Hirst, *Space and Power: Politics, War and Architecture* (Cambridge: Polity Press, 2005), 86–90.

40. Todorov, *The Conquest of America*, 74.

41. Clendinnen, *The Cost of Courage in Aztec Society*, 49.

42. Todorov, *The Conquest of America*, 61, 73.

43. Ibid., 87.

44. Ibid., 112.

45. Ibid., 127.

46. Ibid., 69.

47. Cortés quoted in Clendinnen, *The Cost of Courage in Aztec Society*, 89.

48. Clendinnen, *The Cost of Courage in Aztec Society*, 63.

49. Ibid., 58.

50. Ibid., 75.

51. Ibid., 6–48.

52. Cortés quoted in Ibid., 84.

53. Cortés quoted in Ibid., 87.

54. Clendinnen, *The Cost of Courage in Aztec Society*, 84–85.

55. Diaz quoted in Ibid., 85.

56. Thomas C Schelling, *Arms and Influence* (New Haven: Yale University Press, 1966), 136, note 7.

57. Lincoln, *Discourse and the Construction of Society*, 165.

58. Sigmund Freud, *Jenseits Des Lustprinzips*, 2nd ed., Beihefte Der Internationalen Zeitschrift Für Psychoanalyse, Nr. 2 (Zürich: Internationaler Psychoanalytischer Verlag, 1921), 52–64.

59. James George Frazer, *The Golden Bough: A Study in Magic and Religion* (Harmondsworth: Penguin Books, 1996), 15.

60. Jonathan Z. Smith, 'The Bare Facts of Ritual', *History of Religions* 20, no. 1/2 (1980), 127.

61. Bell, *Ritual Theory, Ritual Practice*, 110.

6. THE ARCHIVE

1. John C. Torpey, *The Invention of the Passport: Surveillance, Citizenship, and the State* (Cambridge: Cambridge University Press, 2000), 25–26.

2. Anthony Giddens, *The Consequences of Modernity* (Stanford: Stanford University Press, 1990), 64.

3. Bell, Duncan. *The Idea of Greater Britain: Empire and the Future of World Order, 1860–1900* (Princeton: Princeton University Press, 2007), 64.

4. Cf. Stephen Kern, *The Culture of Time and Space, 1880–1918* (Cambridge: Harvard University Press, 2003).

5. Mark S. Monmonier, *How to Lie with Maps* (Chicago: University of Chicago Press, 1996), 189.

6. Markus Krajewski, *Restlosigkeit: Weltprojekte Um 1900* (Frankfurt am Main: Fischer Taschenbuch Verlag, 2006), 11. For more on Sandford Fleming see Clark Blaise, *Time Lord: Sir Sandford Fleming and the Creation of Standard Time* (New York: Pantheon Books, 2000).

7. C. A. Bayly, *The Birth of the Modern World, 1780–1914: Global Connections and Comparisons* (Malden: Blackwell Publishers, 2004), 17. For more on the history of time see David S. Landes, *Revolution in Time: Clocks and the Making of the Modern World* (Cambridge, MA: Belknap Press, 2000); Gerhard Dohrn-van Rossum, *History of the Hour: Clocks and Modern Temporal Orders* (Chicago: University of Chicago Press, 1996). For discussions explicitly connecting time to international relations see Kimberly Hutchings, 'Happy Anniversary! Time and Critique in International Relations Theory', *Review of International Studies* 33 (2007); *Time and World Politics: Thinking the Present* (Manchester: Manchester University Press, 2008); Andrew R. Hom, 'Hegemonic Metronome: The Ascendancy of Western Standard Time', *Review of International Studies* 36 (2010).

8. For an account of how the problem of scientific coordination was more of a driver than that of transportation see Ian R. Bartky, 'The Adoption of Standard Time', *Technology and Culture* 30, no. 1 (1989).

9. 'Standard Time and Measures', *Science* 9, no. 205 (1887): 7.

10. John Maynard Keynes, *A Treatise on Money*, vol. 2 (New York: Harcourt, 1930), 332.

11. Thomas C. Schelling, *The Strategy of Conflict* (Cambridge: Harvard University Press, 1960), 55. For more on conventions see David Singh Grewal, *Network*

Power: The Social Dynamics of Globalization (New Haven: Yale University Press, 2008), 58–62; Jon Elster, *The Cement of Society: A Study of Social Order* (Cambridge: Cambridge University Press, 1989), 11–13.

12. As a reminder, while vision refers to the physical act of seeing, visuality refers to the social fact of seeing. The difference is 'between the mechanism of human sight and its historical techniques'. Foster, 'Preface', in *Vision and Visuality*, ed. Hal Foster (Seattle: Bay Press, 1988), ix.

13. Ontopology is a neologism coined by Jacques Derrida that refers to an ontology that is tied to topography, such as states, cities, counties, etc. Jacques Derrida, *Specters of Marx: The State of the Debt, the Work of Mourning, and the New International* (New York: Routledge, 1994), 82.

14. Jordan Branch, 'Mapping the Sovereign State: Technology, Authority, and Systemic Change', *International Organization* 65, no. 01 (2011): 15. For particular histories of mapping states see Rachel Hewitt, *Map of a Nation: A Biography of the Ordnance Survey* (London: Granta Books, 2011); David Gugerli and Daniel Speich, *Topografien Der Nation: Politik, Kartografische Orndung Und Landschaft Im 19. Jahrhundert* (Zürich: Chronos Verlag, 2002).

15. Branch, 'Mapping the Sovereign State', 28–9.

16. R.J.P. Kain and Elizabeth Baigent, *The Cadastral Map in the Service of the State: A History of Property Mapping* (Chicago: University of Chicago Press, 1992), 344.

17. James C. Scott, *Seeing Like a State: How Certain Schemes to Improve the Human Condition Have Failed* (New Haven: Yale University Press, 1998), 33–4.

18. Thongchai Winichakul, *Siam Mapped: A History of the Geo-Body of a Nation* (Honolulu: University of Hawai'i Press, 1994), 130.

19. Winichakul, *Siam Mapped*, 114.

20. Joseph Conrad, *Heart of Darkness* (New York: Bendford Books, 1996), 22. See also Edward Said, *Orientalism* (London: Penguin Books, 2003), 216.

21. For more on censuses see Ian Hacking, *The Taming of Chance* (Cambridge: Cambridge University Press, 1990); Margo J. Anderson, *The American Census: A Social History* (New Haven: Yale University Press, 1988); Margo J. Anderson and Stephen E. Fienberg, *Who Counts?: The Politics of Census-Taking in Contemporary America*, 1st pbk. ed. (New York: Russell Sage Foundation, 2001); D. V. Glass, *Numbering the People: The Eighteenth-Century Population Controversy and the Development of Census and Vital Statistics in Britain* (Farnborough: D.C. Heath, 1973); David I. Kertzer and Dominique Arel, *Census and Identity: The Politics of Race, Ethnicity, and Language in National Census* (Cambridge: Cambridge University Press, 2002); Mark S. Monmonier, *Bushmanders & Bullwinkles: How Politicians Manipulate Electronic Maps and Census Data to Win Elections* (Chicago: University of Chicago Press, 2001). For a disturbing account of how demographic knowledge was used to undertake population control see Matthew

Connelly, *Fatal Misconception: The Struggle to Control World Population* (Cambridge: Harvard University Press, 2008).

22. Hernan Cortés quoted in Tzvetan Todorov, *The Conquest of America: The Question of the Other* (Norman: University of Oklahoma Press, 1999), 175.

23. Arnold Joseph Toynbee, *Lectures on the Industrial Revolution in England* (Kessinger Publishing, 2004 [1884]), 5.

24. Hacking, *The Taming of Chance*, 17.

25. William Petty, 'The Political Anatomy of Ireland', in *Economic Writings* (1691), 129. See also Theodore M. Porter, *The Rise of Statistical Thinking, 1820–1900* (Princeton: Princeton University Press, 1986), 19.

26. Hacking, *The Taming of Chance*, 19.

27. Rousseau, Jean-Jacques. 'On Social Contract or Principles of Political Right', translated by Alan Ritter and Julia Conaway Bondanella, in *Rousseau's Political Writings: New Translations, Interpretive Notes, Backgrounds, Commentaries* (New York: W.W. Norton, 1988 [1762]), 137.

28. Hacking, *The Taming of Chance*, 19.

29. Ibid., 24.

30. Ibid., 23.

31. W Boehlich, ed. *Der Berliner Antisemitismusstreit* (Frankfurt am Main: 1965).

32. Hacking, *The Taming of Chance*, 193.

33. Solomon Neumann, *Die Fabel Von Der Jüdischen Masseneinwanderung: Ein Kapitel Aus Der Preussischen Statistik*, 2nd ed. (Berlin 1880).

34. 'Décret qui indiqué les formalités a observer pour sortir du royaume' of 28 June 1791 quoted in Torpey, *The Invention of the Passport*, 27.

35. Torpey, *The Invention of the Passport*, 38. For an account of how the Milanese Duke Ludovico almost escaped disguised, see Valentin Groebner, 'Describing the Person, Reading the Signs in Late Medieval and Renaissance Europe: Identity Papers, Vested Figures, and the Limits of Identification, 1400–1600', in *Documenting Individual Identity: The Development of State Practices in the Modern World*, eds Jane Caplan and John C. Torpey (Princeton: Princeton University Press, 2001), 25.

36. B. Traven writing in 1926 quoted in John Torpey, 'The Great War and the Birth of the Modern Passport System', in *Documenting Individual Identity: The Development of State Practices in the Modern World*, eds Jane Caplan and John Torpey (Princeton: Princeton University Press, 2001), 270.

37. Torpey, *The Invention of the Passport*, 4.

38. Adam McKeown, *Melancholy Order: Asian Migration and the Globalization of Borders* (New York: Columbia University Press, 2008), 90–1.

39. Anthony Giddens, *The Nation-State and Violence* (Berkeley: University of California Press, 1987), 47.

40. Max Weber, *Schriften 1894–1922*, ed. Dirk Kaesler (Stuttgart: Kröner, 2002),

177–8. Foucault does not have much to say on card registries, but Weber does. In his late great *Economy and Society* (1922) he writes at some length about the importance of filing technology for a bureaucracy See *Wirtschaft Und Gesellschaft* (Tübingen: J.C.B Mohr, 1922), 128. 129, 651

41. Scott, *Seeing Like a State*, 311–23; Marcel Detienne and Jean Pierre Vernant, *Cunning Intelligence in Greek Culture and Society* (Hassocks: Harvester Press, 1978).

42. Neil Rhodes and Jonathan Sawday, 'Paperworlds: Imagining the Renaissance Computer', in *The Renaissance Computer: Knowledge Technology in the First Age of Print*, eds Neil Rhodes and Jonathan Sawday (New York: Routledge, 2000), 3.

43. Groebner, 'Describing the Person', 17. On the increase in written communication during this period see Claudius Sieber-Lehmann, *Spätmittelalterlicher Nationalismus* (Göttingen: Vandenhoek und Ruprecht, 1995).

44. Michael E. H and Zachary S. Schiffman, *Information Ages: Literacy, Numeracy, and the Computer Revolution* (Baltimore: The Johns Hopkins University Press, 1998), 88.

45. Christoph Gottlieb von Murr quoted in Krajewski, *Zettelwitschaft*, 29.

46. Ann M. Blair, *Too Much to Know: Managing Scholarly Information before the Modern Age* (New Haven: Yale University Press, 2010).

47. Krajewski, *Zettelwitschaft*, 20.

48. For more on punch-card systems see Lars Heide, *Punch-Card Systems and the Early Information Explosion, 1880–1945* (Baltimore: Johns Hopkins University Press, 2009).

49. Bruno Latour, *Science in Action: How to Follow Scientists and Engineers through Society* (Cambridge: Harvard University Press, 1987), 227.

50. Walter Benjamin, 'Einbahnstraße', in *Gesammelte Schriften* (Frankfurt am Main: Suhrkamp Verlag, 1929), 103.

51. Krajewski, *Zettelwitschaft*, 151.

52. Paul Ladewig, *Politik Der Bücherei* (Leipzig: Ernst Wiegandt Verlagsbuchhandlung, 1912), 254–5.

53. Herbert E. Davidson and W.E. Parker, *Classified Illustrated Catalog of the Library Bureau. A Handbook of Library and Office Fittings and Supplies* (Boston: Library Bureau, 1891), 27.

54. Krajewski, *Zettelwitschaft*, 117.

55. For more on his methods see Alphonse Bertillon, *Signaletic Instructions: Including the Theory and Practice of Anthropometrical Identification*, trans. R.W. McClaughry (Chicago: The Werner company, 1896). Major R. W. McClaughry, the General Superintendent of the Police of Chicago, edited the English edition.

56. Raymond B. Fosdick, 'The Passing of the Bertillon System of Identification', *Journal of the American Institute of Criminal Law and Criminology* 6, no. 3 (1915): 363. The emphasis is mine.

57. Alfred McCoy, *Policing America's Empire: The United States, the Philippines, and the Rise of the Surveillance State* (Madison: The University of Wisconsin Press, 2009), 21.

58. Michel Foucault, *Discipline and Punish: The Birth of the Prison* (New York: Pantheon Books, 1977); Tilly, *Coercion, Capital, and European States, AD 990–1990* (Cambridge: Blackwell, 1990).

59. Torpey, *The Invention of the Passport*; Salter, *Rights of Passage*; McKeown, *Melancholy Order*.

60. Max Weber, 'Wissenschaft Als Beruf', in *Schriften 1894–1922*, ed. Dirk Kaesler (Stuttgart: Kroener, 2002 [1919]), 504.

61. Weber, 'Wissenschaft Als Beruf,' *Schriften 1894–1922*, 488.

62. Max Weber, 'Vorbemerkung Zu Den "Gesammelten Aufsätzen Zur Religionssoziologie"', in *Schriften 1894–1922*, ed. Dirk Kaesler (Stuttgart: Kroener, 2002 [1919]), 568.

63. GStA, Rep. 77, Tit. 343, vol. no. 107, quoted in Götz Aly et al., *The Nazi Census: Identification and Control in the Third Reich* (Philadelphia: Temple University Press, 2004), 35.

64. Max Weber, 'Die protestantische Ethik und der "Geist" des Kapitalismus', in *Schriften 1894–1922*, 177–8, ed. Dirk Kaesler (Stuttgart: Kroener, 2002 [1922]).

65. Max Weber, 'Die Drei Reinen Typen Der Legitimen Herrschaft. Eine Soziologische Studie', in *Schriften 1894–1922*, ed. Dirk Kaesler (Stuttgart: Kroener, 2002 [1922]), 273.

66. Weber, 'Die Protestantische Ethik', *Schriften 1894–1922*, 719.

67. Weber, *Schriften 1894–1922*, 184.

68. Frederick Winslow Taylor, *The Principles of Scientific Management; and Shop Management* (London: Routledge/Thoemmes Press, 1993).

69. Weber, *Schriften 1894–1922*, 224. Ever since Talcott Parsons' 1930 translation of *The Protestant Ethic*, 'steel-hard housing' has been rendered as the far more dramatic 'iron cage', see *The Protestant Ethic and the Spirit of Capitalism*, trans. Talcott Parsons (New York: Scribner, 1930), 177. For a discussion of the translation difference see Peter Baehr, 'The "Iron Cage" and the "Shell as Hard as Steel": Parsons, Weber, and the Stahlhartes Gehäuse Metaphor in the Protestant Ethic and the Spirit of Capitalism', *History and Theory* 40, no. 2 (2002). For Parsons' 'smiley-faced updating of Weber' see Nils Gilman, *Mandarins of the Future: Modernization Theory in Cold War America* (Baltimore: Johns Hopkins University Press, 2003), 74, 92–4; Tracy B Strong, '"What Have We to Do with Morals?" Nietzsche and Weber on History and Ethics', *History of the Human Sciences* 5, no. 3 (1992): 9.

70. Weber, 'Vorbemerkung', *Schriften 1894–1922*, 566. Emphasis in original.

71. Max Weber, 'Die "Objektivität" Sozialwissenschaftlicher Und Sozialpolitischer

Erkenntnis,' in *Schriften 1894–1922*, ed. Dirk Kaesler (Stuttgart: Kroener, 2002 [1904]), 119.

72. Weber, 'Wissenschaft als Beruf', *Schriften 1894–1922*, 508.

73. Weber, 'Vorbemerkung', *Schriften 1894–1922*, 568.

74. More on the Panopticon, including a definition, can be found below.

75. For more on this see James Holston, *The Modernist City: An Anthropological Critique of Brasília* (Chicago: University of Chicago Press, 1989).

76. 'The despot is not a man. It is the plan. The correct, realistic, exact plan, the one that will provide your solution once the problem has been posited clearly, in its entirety, in its indispensable harmony. This plan has been drawn up well away from the frenzy in the mayor's office or the town hall, from the cries of the electorate or the laments of society's victims. It has been drawn up by serene and lucid minds.' Le Corbusier, *The Radiant City: Elements of a Doctrine of Urbanism to Be Used as the Basis of Our Machine-Age Civilization* (New York: Orion Press, 1967), 154.

77. Marcia Ascher and Robert Ascher, *Mathematics of the Incas: Code of the Quipu* (Mineola, New York: Dover Publications, 1997), 43.

78. Scott, *Seeing Like a State*, 126.

79. These are 'disqualified as inadequate to their task or insufficiently elaborated: naïve knowledges, located low down on the hierarchy, beneath the required level of cognition or scientificity'. Michel Foucault, *Power/Knowledge: Selected Interviews and Other Writings, 1972–1977*, edited and translated by Colin Gordon (Brighton, Sussex: Harvester Press, 1980), 82.

80. Walter Benjamin, *Illuminationen: Ausgewählte Schriften 1* (Frankfurt am Main: Suhrkamp Verlag, 1974), 137.

81. Benjamin, *Illuminationen: Ausgewählte Schriften 1*, 139.

82. Ibid.

83. Benjamin, *Illuminationen: Ausgewählte Schriften 1*, 143.

84. Ibid., 145.

85. Ibid., 167–8.

86. Ibid., 168.

87. See Laikwan Pang, '"China Who Makes and Fakes": A Semiotics of the Counterfeit', *Theory, Culture & Society* 25, no. 6 (2008).

88. Benjamin, *Illuminationen: Ausgewählte Schriften 1*, 169.

7. THE DATABASE

1. For an early theoretical investigation into hypertext see George P. Landow, ed. *Hyper/Text/Theory* (Baltimore: Johns Hopkins University Press, 1994).

2. For a recent update on one of the first anthropological studies of human relations to computers published in 1987 see Lucy A. Suchman, *Human-Machine*

Reconfigurations: Plans and Situated Actions (Cambridge: Cambridge University Press, 2007).

3. For more on 'information' see the magisterial 10,000 word entrance in the Oxford English Dictionary Online Version, 'Information, *n*.', Oxford English Dictionary, www.oed.com/viewdictionaryentry/Entry/95568. For good popular histories and theories of information see Alex Wright, *Glut: Mastering Information through the Ages* (Ithaca: Cornell University Press, 2007); James Gleick, *The Information: A History, a Theory, a Flood* (New York: Pantheon Books, 2011); Michael E. Hobart and Zachary S. Schiffman, *Information Ages: Literacy, Numeracy, and the Computer Revolution* (Baltimore: The Johns Hopkins University Press, 1998); Theodore M. Porter, 'Speaking Precision to Power: The Modern Political Role of Social Science', *Social Research* 73, no. 4 (2006): 1278–80.

4. Bit was defined as 'A unit for measuring information' in 1948 by Claude Shannon, a Bell Labs employee and significant intellectual influence on the discipline of cybernetics. Gleick, *The Information*, 4.

5. Edmund Husserl, 'Die Krisis Der Europäischen Wissenschaften', in *Gesammelte Werke*, ed. H.L. Van Breda (The Hague: Martinus Nijhoff, 1962 [1937]).

6. Max Weber, 'Wissenschaft Als Beruf', in *Schriften 1894–1922*, ed. Dirk Kaesler (Stuttgart: Kroener, 2002 [1919]), 504.

7. Arnold Mitchell, *The Nine American Lifestyles: Who We Are and Where We're Going* (New York: Macmillan, 1983).

8. For more on this see David Lyon, 'Surveillance after September 11, 2001', in *The Intensification of Surveillance: Crime, Terrorism, and Warfare in the Information Age*, eds Kristie Ball and Frank Webster (London: Pluto Press, 2003), 23.

9. David Gugerli, *Suchmaschinen. Die Welt Als Datenbank* (Frankfurt am Main: Suhrkamp, 2009), 63–5.

10. Biometrics Identity Management Agency (BIMA), 'Biometrics Glossary 5.0' (2010), 4, 17, 35, 58.

11. Arthur Schlesinger Jr. quoted in Nils Gilman, *Mandarins of the Future: Modernization Theory in Cold War America* (Baltimore: Johns Hopkins University Press, 2003), 39.

12. The IR literature on norms and practices is useful for thinking through the spread of these databases. Martha Finnemore, 'Review: Norms, Culture, and World Politics: Insights from Sociology's Institutionalism', *International Organization* 50, no. 2 (1996); Emanuel Adler and Vincent Pouliot, 'International Practices', *International Theory* 3, no. 01 (2011): 1–36.

13. Michael Barnett and Raymond Duvall, 'Power in International Politics', *International Organization* 59, no. 01 (2005): 42, 45.

14. Quoted in Jeffrey C. Alexander, *The Performance of Politics: Obama's Victory and the Democratic Struggle for Power* (Oxford: Oxford University Press, 2010), 45.

15. For an insider rendition of the marketing techniques applied during the 1968

Nixon campaign, see Joe McGinniss, *The Selling of the President, 1968* (New York: Trident Press, 1969).

16. Kim Zetter, '22 Million E-Mails Missing from Bush White House Found', WIRED, www.wired.com/2009/12/22-million-emails-found/; cnn.com, 'Clinton's Gift to Internet Age: Only 2 E-Mails,' http://edition.cnn.com/2004/TECH/internet/01/28/clinton.email.reut/.

17. For an earlier example of this see Sarah Elizabeth Igo, *The Averaged American: Surveys, Citizens, and the Making of a Mass Public* (Cambridge: Harvard University Press, 2007).

18. Alexander, *The Performance of Politics*, 41, 51–2. On the positive effects of increased voter turnout for the Obama campaign see Tracy Osborn, Scott D. McClurg, and Benjamin Knoll, 'Voter Mobilization and the Obama Victory', *American Politics Research* 38, no. 2 (2010).

19. On practices of micro-targeting and use of other technologies in election campaigns see Oscar H. Gandy, Lance W. Bennett, and Robert M. Entman, *Dividing Practices: Segmentation and Targeting in the Emerging Public Sphere* (Cambridge University Press, 2000); Lance W. Bennett and Robert M. Entman, *Mediated Politics: Communication in the Future of Democracy* (Cambridge: Cambridge University Press, 2001); Rasmus Kleis Nielsen, 'Mundane Internet Tools, Mobilizing Practices, and the Coproduction of Citizenship in Political Campaigns', *New Media & Society*, 13, no. 5 (2011), 755–771.

20. Ethan Roeder, Data Manager for Obama for America, telephone interview, 16 Jan. 2009.

21. An analogy might be the significance of double entry book keeping as accounting practice which not only influences capitalist processes but also theories about capitalism. Eve Chiapello, 'Die Geburt Des Kapitalismus Aus Der Idee Der Doppelten Buchfuehrung', *WestEnd: Neue Zeitschrift für Sozialforschung* 4, no. 2 (2007); Max Weber, Schriften 1894–1922, ed. Dirk Kaesler (Stuttgart: Kroener, 2002 [1922]), 273.

22. I am indebted to Chris Brown of the LSE for impressing this point upon me.

23. The Obama campaign successfully applied an organisational model developed by Marshall Ganz and Ruth Wageman at Harvard University and were supported in their efforts by Chris Hughes, a co-founder of Facebook. Sarah Lai Stirland, 'Obama's Secret Weapons: Internet, Databases and Psychology', WIRED Blog Network, http://blog.wired.com/27bstroke6/2008/10/obamas-secret-w.html.

24. Jeff Zeleny, 'Obama Battles Block by Block to Get Voters to Polls', *New York Times*, 12 Oct. 2008. Also quoted in Alexander, *The Performance of Politics*, 43.

25. Flavius Vegetius Renatus, *The Military Institutions of the Romans*, translated by John Clarke, edited by Thomas R. Phillips, Military Classics (Harrisburg, PA: The Military Service Publishing Company, 1944).

26. Roeder, interview, 16 Jan. 2009.

27. One of the things the campaign did was to—based on prior email receipts—send out personalised emails to their supporters at a time when they were most likely to read them. Shailagh Murray and Matthew Mosk, 'Under Obama, Web Would Be the Way', *Washington Post*, 10 Nov. 2008.

28. Blue State Digital worked with the State Department on a project restoring the Iraqi National Museum. For more on Blue State Digital see www.bluestatedigital.com and Tobias Moorstedt, *Jeffersons Erben: Wie Die Digitalen Medien Die Politik Verändern* (Frankfurt am Main: Suhrkamp, 2008), 27–33. For a similar company that also offers the opportunity to buy voter data and software to manage voters see www.electionmall.com.

29. Jonathan Simon, 'The Ideological Effects of Actuarial Practices', *Law & Society Review* 22, no. 4 (1988): 772.

30. Mike Madden, 'Barack Obama's Super Marketing Machine', Salon.com, www.salon.com/news/feature/2008/07/16/obama_data. Of course there has been a close relationship with marketing and U.S. presidential politics all through the twentieth century.

31. Robert Putnam, *Bowling Alone: The Collapse and Revival of American Community* (New York: Simon & Schuster, 2000).

32. Alexander, *The Performance of Politics*, 40.

33. 'Five Years after the Intelligence Reform and Terrorism Prevention Act: Stopping Terrorist Travel,' ed. TERRORIST SCREENING CENTER DIRECTOR, FEDERAL BUREAU OF INVESTIGATION (2009).

34. Ibid.

35. Ibid. The problem of misspelling is a perennial problem when dealing with foreign names and scripts but is especially pronounced when the data is only heard and not seen. The way the Stasi dealt with this problem was to store names according to the phonetic alphabet.

36. Dataveillance is 'the systematic use of personal data systems in the investigation or monitoring of the actions or communications of one or more persons', Roger Clarke, 'Introduction to Dataveillance and Information Privacy, and Definitions of Terms', www.anu.edu.au/people/Roger.Clarke/DV/Intro.html; 'Dataveillance: Delivering 1984', in *Framing Technology: Society, Choice and Change*, eds Lelia Green and Roger Guinery (London: Routledge, 1994).

37. Peter Walker, 'Database of Every Phone Call and Email "a Step too Far"', *The Guardian*, 15 July 2008.

38. Colin J. Bennett, 'What Happens When You Book an Airline Ticket? The Collecting and Processing of Passenger Data Post-9/11', in *Global Surveillance and Policing: Borders, Security, Identity*, eds Elia Zureik and Mark B. Salter (London: Willan Publishing, 2005), 115.

39. Edward Hasbrouck, 'What's in a Passenger Name Record (PNR)?', www.hasbrouck.org/articles/PNR.html.

40. Ibid.

41. John Markoff, 'Chief Takes over at Agency to Thwart Attacks on U.S.', *The New York Times*, 13 Feb. 2002.

42. Bradley Graham, 'Poindexter Resigns but Defends Programs: Anti-Terrorism, Data Scanning Efforts at Pentagon Called Victims of Ignorance', *Washington Post*, 13 Aug. 2003.

43. Shane Harris, 'Tia Lives On,' *National Journal*, 23 Feb. 2006. For a comprehensive history of the NSA see Matthew M. Aid, *The Secret Sentry: The Untold History of the National Security Agency* (New York: Bloomsbury Press, 2009).

44. James Bamford, 'Who's in Big Brother's Database?', *The New York Review of Books* 56, no. 17 (2009).

45. Louise Amoore and Marieke De Goede, 'Governance, Risk and Dataveillance in the War on Terror', *Crime, Law & Social Change* 43, no. 2–3 (2005): 162.

46. Amoore and De Goede, 'Governance, Risk and Dataveillance', 154.

47. In Chapter 5 the ritual mode was identified as being strongly characterised by an 'apotropaic' logic. An apotropaic ritual is one that is undertaken to ward off evil, making it difficult to refute.

48. For the relationship of a cybernetic machine to the perception of an enemy see Peter Galison, 'The Ontology of the Enemy: Norbert Wiener and the Cybernetic Vision', *Critical Inquiry* 21, no. 1 (1994).

49. While fingerprints are as popular as ever for documenting the identity of individuals, they have been discredited as a means to discover the inherent, biological class or criminality of an individual. For failed attempts and dashed hopes at connecting fingerprints with race and class see Francis Galton, *Finger Prints* (London: Macmillan and Co., 1892), 17–19, 192–7.

50. Alan Travis and Richard Norton-Taylor, 'Private Firm May Track All Email and Calls: "Hellhouse" of Personal Data Will Be Created, Warns Former DPP', *The Guardian*, 31 Dec. 2008.

51. Home Secretary Jacqui Smith quoted in ibid.

52. 'Leitsätze Zum Urteil Des Ersten Senats Vom 11. März 2008', in *1 BvR 2074/05* ed. Bundesverfassungsgericht (2008).

53. See Tadayoshi Kohno et al., 'Analysis of an Electronic Voting System', in *IEEE Symposium on Security and Privacy* (2004).

54. Travis and Norton-Taylor, 'Private Firm May Track All Email and Calls'.

55. See Robert J. Dostal, 'Time and Phenomenology in Husserl and Heidegger', in *The Cambridge Companion to Heidegger*, ed. Charles B Guignon (Cambridge: Cambridge University Press, 1993).

56. For another important essay connecting the character of calculation to money economy see Georg Simmel, 'Die Grossstradt Und Das Geistesleben', in

Jahrbuch Der Gehe-Stiftung Zu Dresden, Vol. 9, ed. K Bücher (Dresden: von Zahn & Jaensch, 1903). This text was translated by Edward Shils into English in the 1930s under the title of 'The Metropolis and Mental Life'.

57. Husserl, 'Die Krisis Der Europäischen Wissenschaften', 6.

58. Ibid., 18, 20.

59. Ibid., 25. The emphasis is mine.

60. In an etymology that implies the political foundation of abstract thought, the term *limes* referred to the border defence that marked the limits of the Roman Empire.

61. Husserl, 'Die Krisis Der Europäischen Wissenschaften', 26.

62. Ibid., 31.

63. Ibid.

64. Ibid., 32.

65. Ibid., 40.

66. Ibid., 44. In their discussion of the *Krisis* Herbert Marcuse and Bernard Stiegler both place special emphasis on this passage; Bernard Stiegler, *Technics and Time* (Stanford: Stanford University Press, 1998), 3.

67. Husserl, 'Die Krisis Der Europäischen Wissenschaften', 43.

68. Husserl, 'Die Krisis Der Europäischen Wissenschaften', 50.

69. Husserl, 'Die Krisis Der Europäischen Wissenschaften', 33.

70. Husserl, 'Die Krisis Der Europäischen Wissenschaften', 43.

71. Heidegger's being philosophically gifted but politically retarded has caused much to be written about his relationship to Nazism. For a good account see Philippe Lacoue-Labarthe, *Heidegger, Art, and Politics: The Fiction of the Political* (Oxford: B. Blackwell, 1990).

72. Cited in Petzet's preface to Martin Heidegger and Erhart Kästner, *Briefwechsel, 1953–1974*, ed. Heinrich W Petzet (Frankfurt a. M.: Insel Verlag, 1986), 10.

73. Martin Heidegger, 'Das Rektorat, 1933/34: Tatsachen Und Gedanken', in *Die Selbstbehauptung Der Deutschen Universität* (Frankfurt a. M.: Vittorio Klosterman, 1983), 39.

74. '[E]very thinking of being, all philosophy, can *never* be confirmed by "facts", i.e., by beings. Making itself intelligible is suicide for philosophy. Those who idolise "facts" never notice that their idols only shine in a borrowed light. They are also meant not to notice this; for thereupon they would have to be at a loss and therefore useless.' *Contributions to Philosophy: From Enowning* (Bloomington: Indiana University Press, 1999), 307.

75. Martin Heidegger, *Die Technik Und Die Kehre* (Pfullingen: Günther Neske 1962), 7.

76. Ibid.

77. Ibid., 15–16.

78. Ibid., 20. The emphasis is mine.

79. Martin Heidegger, 1967, 'What is a Thing?', 63 quoted in Stiegler, *Technics and Time*, 206.

80. Heidegger, *Die Technik Und Die Kehre*, 24.

81. It is important to bear in mind that in German, *Wesen* can be translated as both being and essence. Heidegger writes that *Wesen* stems from *die Weserei*, which means the city hall, where 'the life of the community gathers and village existence is constantly in play, i.e., comes to presence'. *Die Technik Und Die Kehre*, 27, 30.

82. Heidegger, *Die Technik Und Die Kehre*, 35.

83. Ibid.

84. Nah ist

        Und schwer zu fassen der Gott.

        Wo aber Gefahr ist, wächst

        Das Rettende auch.

Friedrich Hölderlin, 'Patmos', in *Friedrich Hölderlin: Die Gedichte*, ed. Jochen Schmidt (Frankfurt a.M.: Insel Verlag, 2001 [1800–5]), 350. Heidegger, *Die Technik Und Die Kehre*, 35.

85. Martin Heidegger, *Sein Und Zeit* (Tübingen: Max Niemeyer Verlag, 2001 [1926]), 176.

86. Max Weber, 'Vorbemerkung Zu Den "Gesammelten Aufsätzen Zur Religionssoziologie"', in *Schriften 1894–1922*, ed. Dirk Kaesler (Stuttgart: Kroener, 2002 [1919]), 568.

8. THE NETWORK: ONTOLOGY IN THE DIGITAL AGE

1. Peter Linebaugh and Marcus Buford Rediker, *The Many-Headed Hydra: Sailors, Slaves, Commoners, and the Hidden History of the Revolutionary Atlantic* (Boston: Beacon Press, 2000), 39.

2. A Google search for 'Al-Qaeda' and 'Hydra' produces 35,800 hits.

3. National Commission on Terrorist Attacks upon the United States, *The 9/11 Commission Report: Final Report of the National Commission on Terrorist Attacks Upon the United States*, 1st ed. (New York: Norton, 2004), 364.

4. For a good overview of U.S. constructions of otherness in the past see David Campbell, *Writing Security: United States Foreign Policy and the Politics of Identity* (Minneapolis: University of Minnesota Press, 1992).

5. For more on networks see Manuel Castells, *The Rise of the Network Society: The Information Age* (Chichester: Wiley-Blackwell, 2010); Dirk Messner, *The Network Society: Economic Development and International Competitiveness as Problems of Social Governance* (London: Frank Cass, 1997); Alex Wright, *Glut: Mastering Information through the Ages* (Ithaca: Cornell University Press, 2007), 5–21. For an assessment that networks may not be as dangerous as is widely assumed see Mette Eilstrup-

Sangiovanni and Calvert Jones, 'Assessing the Dangers of Illicit Networks: Why Al-Qaida May Be Less Threatening Than Many Think', *International Security* 33, no. 2 (2008).

6. United States Corps, *Small Wars Manual* (Honolulu, Hawaii: University Press of the Pacific, 2005 [1940]), 2–46, f (2). The emphasis is mine.

7. United States Dept. of the Army and United States Marine Corps, *The U.S. Army/Marine Corps Counterinsurgency Field Manual: U.S. Army Field Manual No. 3–24: Marine Corps Warfighting Publication No. 3–33.5* (Chicago: University of Chicago Press, 2007), 1–94.

8. Ibid.

9. 'This enemy is better networked than we are'. General John Abizaid, 20 June 2007, Tranformation Warfare Conference, 2007; 'In bitter, bloody fights in both Afghanistan and Iraq, it became clear to me and to many others that to defeat a networked enemy we had to become a network ourselves. … It takes a network to defeat a network.' Stanley McChrystal, 'It Takes a Network', *Foreign Policy*, online edition, 22 Feb. 2011, www.foreignpolicy.com/articles/2011/02/22/it_takes_a_network.

10. For the use of ecological concepts in military strategy and tactics see Daniel Bertrand Monk, 'Hives and Swarms: On the "Nature" of Neoliberalism and the Rise of the Ecological Insurgent', in *Evil Paradises: Dreamworlds of Neoliberalism*, eds Mike Davis and Daniel Bertrand Monk (New York: The New Press, 2007).

11. Duncan Bell, 'Writing the World: Disciplinary History and Beyond,' *International Affairs* 85, no. 1 (2009): 18; Peter Galison, 'The Ontology of the Enemy: Norbert Wiener and the Cybernetic Vision', *Critical Inquiry* 21, no. 1 (1994).

12. Confidential email exchange with U.S. Army Intelligence Officer, 24 May 2010.

13. I am indebted to John Mowitt for bringing this to my attention. For more on the Battle of Algiers see John Mowitt, 'The Battle of Algiers: Pentagon Edition', in eds Tina Chen and David Churchill, *History, Film and Cultural Citizenship: Sites of Production* (Oxford: Routledge, 2007).

14. Said, *Orientalism*, 240.

15. Galison, 'The Ontology of the Enemy', 264.

9. DIGITAL POWER GOES TO WAR

1. Stanley McChrystal, 'It Takes a Network', *Foreign Policy*, online edition, 22 Feb. 2011, www.foreignpolicy.com/articles/2011/02/22/it_takes_a_network

2. David Galula, *Counterinsurgency Warfare: Theory and Practice* (New York: Praeger, 1964), 85.

3. William Westmoreland, *Address to the Association of the U.S. Army* (1969).

4. McChrystal, 'It Takes a Network'.

5. Biometrics Identity Management Agency (BIMA), 'Biometrics Glossary 5.0' (2010), 35.

6. Paul Virilio, *War and Cinema: The Logistics of Perception* (London: Verso, 1989), 20. See also Rey Chow, *The Age of the World Target: Self-Referentiality in War, Theory, and Comparative Work* (London: Duke University Press, 2006).

7. Derek Gregory, *The Colonial Present: Afghanistan, Palestine, and Iraq* (Malden, MA: Blackwell, 2004).

8. Friedrich A. Kittler, *Aufschreibesysteme 1800/1900* (München: Fink, 1985), 239.

9. Said, *Orientalism*, 86.

10. Said, *Orientalism*, 123.

11. This, however, does not mean that the number sets or statistical images cannot be read as a text. Like texts, statistical data also contain coded symbols that are used to facilitate communication; they also have preconceived archetypes that are used to organise information.

12. Visuality is the socially constructed mode of sight. Foster, 'Preface', in *Vision and Visuality*, ed. Hal Foster (Seattle: Bay Press, 1988), ix. For more on vision see Denis Cosgrove, *Geography and Vision: Seeing, Imagining and Representing the World* (London: I.B Tauris, 2008); John Pickles, *A History of Spaces: Cartographic Reason, Mapping and the Geo-Coded World* (New York: Routledge, 2004).

13. Said, *Orientalism*, 44, 68, 70, 95, 113, 14, 54, 230, 37, 70, 76, 40.

14. Ibid., 43, 202, 40, 113, 27, 239, 40.

15. Jeremy Bentham, 'Panopticon', in *The Complete Works of Jeremy Bentham*, vol. 4, ed. John Bowring (Edinburgh: William Tait, 1843), 65–6.

16. Mike Davis, *Planet of Slums* (London: Verso, 2007), 205. See also Derek Gregory, '"The Rush to the Intimate" Counterinsurgency and the Cultural Turn', *Radical Philosophy*, no. 150 (2008); Stephen Graham, 'The Urban "Battlespace"', *Theory, Culture & Society* 26, no. 7–8 (2009).

17. Multi-National Force in Iraq, Official Website, 'Unmanned Aerial System First to Fire Missiles in Combat', www.mnf-iraq.com/index.php?option=com_content&task=view&id=25656&Itemid=128.

18. For more on the military applications of robots and artificial intelligence see Manuel De Landa, *War in the Age of Intelligent Machines* (New York: Zone Books, 1991); P.W. Singer, *Wired for War: The Robotics Revolution and Conflict in the 21st Century* (New York: The Penguin Press, 2009).

19. For a philosophical inquiry into junk see Thierry Bardini, *Junkware* (Minneapolis: University of Minnesota Press, 2011).

20. Christopher Drew, 'Military Is Awash in Data from Drones', *New York Times*, 10 Jan. 2010.

21. Singer, *Wired for War*, 37.

22. Northrup Grumman, 'An AAQ-37 Eo Das for the F-35', www.es.northropgrumman.com/solutions/f35targeting/assets/eodasvideo.html.

23. See http://www.raytheon.com/capabilities/products/dcgs/

24. Charles Q Choi, 'Military to Adopt NFL's Instant Replay Technology', *LiveScience.Com*, 1 June 2010.
25. Ibid.
26. Ibid.
27. James C. Scott, *The Art of Not Being Governed: An Anarchist History of Upland Southeast Asia* (New Haven: Yale University Press, 2009), 98.
28. Said, *Orientalism*, 119.
29. Scott, *The Art of Not Being Governed*, 123.
30. Hannah Arendt, *The Origins of Totalitarianism* (New York: Schocken Books, 2004), chapter 7. Said, *Orientalism*, 240.
31. Darryl Li, 'A Universal Enemy?: "Foreign Fighters" and Legal Regimes of Exclusion and Exemption under the "Global War on Terror"', *Columbia Human Rights Law Review* 41, no. 2 (2010): 358.
32. Quoted in Cali Bagby, '"I'd Say a Good Percentage of Iraqis Are Already in the Database"', *KVAL.com*, 7 Nov. 2009.
33. Rajiv Chandrasekaran, *Imperial Life in the Emerald City: Inside Iraq's Green Zone* (New York: Vintage Books, 2007), 222.
34. Confidential email exchange with HTS member, 14 Sep. 2008.
35. Cited in Tarak Barkawi, 'Peoples, Homelands, and Wars? Ethnicity, the Military, and Battle among British Imperial Forces in the War against Japan', *Comparative Studies in Society and History* 46, no. 1 (2004): 141.
36. Lieutenant Colonel Kathy DeBolt, U.S. Army Battle Laboratory, quoted in L1 Identity Solutions: Biometrics Division, 'Portable Multimodal Enrollment and Recognition Device: The Handheld Interagency Identity Detection Equipment,' (www.l1id.com/HIIDE2009).
37. Introduction in Jane Caplan and John C. Torpey, *Documenting Individual Identity: The Development of State Practices in the Modern World* (Princeton: Princeton University Press, 2001), 8.
38. United States Dept. of the Army and United States Marine Corps, *The U.S. Army/Marine Corps Counterinsurgency Field Manual: U.S. Army Field Manual No. 3–24: Marine Corps Warfighting Publication No. 3–33.5* (Chicago: University of Chicago Press, 2007); Patrick Porter, *Military Orientalism: Eastern War through Western Eyes* (New York: Columbia University Press, 2009).
39. Edward W. Said, *Orientalism*, 1st Vintage Books ed. (New York: Vintage Books, 1979), 290.
40. AAA Commission on the Engagement of Anthropology with the U.S. Security and Intelligence Communities (CEAUSSIC), 'Final Report on the Army's Human Terrain System Proof of Concept Program', 2009, 12.
41. US Army, 'HTS Components', http://humanterrainsystem.army.mil/components.html.
42. Erin Flynn Jay, 'Mapping the Human Terrain,' *Geospatial Intelligence Forum* 7, no. 4 (2009).

43. Mark S. Monmonier, *How to Lie with Maps* (Chicago: University of Chicago Press, 1996), 189.

44. Thongchai Winichakul, *Siam Mapped: A History of the Geo-Body of a Nation* (Honolulu: University of Hawai'i Press, 1994), 56.

45. Robert Johnson, 'The Pashtun Way of War: A Contested History, 1809–2010', in *Orientalism at War*, eds Tarak Barkawi and Keith Stanski (University of Oxford 2010), 6.

46. See for example Douglas E. Batson, *Registering the Human Terrains: A Valuation of Cadastre* (NDIC Press 2008).

47. Said, *Orientalism*, 113.

48. For an extreme example see Rebecca Lemov, 'Towards a Data Base of Dreams: Assembling an Archive of Elusive Materials, C. 1947–61', *Hist Workshop J* 67, no. 1 (2009).

49. AAA Commission (CEAUSSIC), 'Final Report', 15.

50. On statistical thought, see Ian Hacking, *The Taming of Chance* (Cambridge: Cambridge University Press, 1990); Theodore M. Porter, *The Rise of Statistical Thinking, 1820–1900* (Princeton: Princeton University Press, 1986).

51. Carlo Ginzburg, 'Morelli, Freud and Sherlock Holmes: Clues and Scientific Method,' *Hist Workshop J* 9, no. 1 (1980): 14.

52. Emil Lederer, 'On the Sociology of World War', *European Journal of Sociology* 47, no. 02 (2006): 247.

53. Sigmund Freud, 'Der Moses Des Michelangelo', *Imago. Zeitschrift für Anwendung der Psychoanalyse auf die Geisteswissenschaften* III (1914): 24. See also Ginzburg, 'Morelli, Freud and Sherlock Holmes,' 10.

54. For failed attempts and dashed hopes at connecting fingerprints with race and class see Francis Galton, *Finger Prints* (London: Macmillan and Co., 1892), 17–19; 192–7. For the colonial history of fingerprints see Chandak Sengoopta, *Imprint of the Raj: How Fingerprinting Was Born in Colonial India* (Oxford: Macmillan, 2003). I discuss fingerprints in more detail in the next chapter.

55. William Saletan, 'Ghosts in the Machine: Do Remote-Control War Pilots Get Combat Stress', *Slate*, 11 Aug. 2008; For more on drones see Singer, *Wired for War*, 36–7, 47, 58, 59, 64, 119, 45, 306. For more on drones see Matt J. Martin and Charles W. Sasser, *Predator: The Remote-Control Air War over Iraq and Afghanistan* (Minneapolis: Zenith Press, 2010). For a science fiction exploration of the psychological dynamics of drone piloting see William Gibson and Michael Swanwick, 'Dogfight', *Omni*, 7, no. 10 (1985).

56. WikiLeaks, 'Collateral Murder,' www.collateralmurder.com.

57. Philip Mirowski, *Machine Dreams: Economics Becomes a Cyborg Science* (Cambridge: Cambridge University Press, 2002), 480.

58. There are also fascinating connections between science fiction writings and military future planning and weapon development. See Duncan Bell, 'Writing

the World: Disciplinary History and Beyond,' *International Affairs* 85, no. 1 (2009): 14; Charles Gannon, *Rumors of War and Infernal Machines: Technomilitary Agenda-Setting in British and American Speculative Fiction* (Liverpool: Liverpool University Press, 2005). See also Matt Carr, 'Slouching Towards Dystopia: The New Military Futurism', *Race & Class* 51, no. 13 (2010).

59. Official in charge of a ground robot programme quoted in Singer, *Wired for War*, 68.

60. Singer, *Wired for War*, 69.

61. Roger Smith, 'The Long History of Gaming in Military Training', *Simulation Gaming* 41, no. 1 (2010): 6.

62. Ann Scott Tyson, 'A Historic Success in Military Recruiting', *Washington Post*, 14 Oct. 2009.

63. Barry Silverman, 'Human Terrain Data—What Should We Do with It?,' *Departmental Papers (ESE)* (2007). Barry Silverman et al., 'Nonkin Village: An Embeddable Training Game Generator for Learning Cultural Terrain and Sustainable Counter-Insurgent Operations', *Agents for Games and Simulations: Lecture Notes in Computer Science*, 5920 (2009): 135–54.

64. Said, *Orientalism*, 145.

65. James George Frazer, *The Golden Bough: A Study in Magic and Religion* (Harmondsworth: Penguin Books, 1996), 15.

66. Silverman, 'Human Terrain Data', 1.

67. Admiral Thomas B. Hayward, USN (Ret.), foreword in Peter P. Perla, *The Art of Wargaming: A Guide for Professionals and Hobbyists* (Annapolis: Naval Institute Press, 1990), xiii.

68. Quoted in Sharon Ghamari-Tabrizi, *The Worlds of Herman Kahn* (Cambridge, Massachusetts: Harvard University Press, 2005), 158–9.

69. Jonathan Z. Smith, 'The Bare Facts of Ritual', *History of Religions* 20, no. 1/2 (1980): 127.

70. See http://www.trustedreviews.com/video-games/news/2010/01/15/ Modern-Warfare-2-As-Successful-As-Avatar/p1

71. For more on Orientalism in video games see Johan Höglund, 'Electronic Empire: Orientalism Revisited in the Military Shooter', *Game Studies: The International Journal of Computer Game Research* 8, no. 1 (2008).

72. Said, *Orientalism*, 26.

73. Niklas Luhmann, *Die Gesellschaft Der Gesellschaft I* (Frankfurt am Main: Suhrkamp, 1997), 520.

74. Drew, 'Military Is Awash in Data from Drones'.

75. David Edgerton, *The Shock of the Old: Technology and Global History since 1900* (London: Profile Books, 2008), 95.

76. David MacIsaac, 'Voices from the Central Blue: The Air Power Theorists', in *Makers of Modern Strategy: From Machiavelli to the Nuclear Age*, ed. Peter Paret (Oxford: Oxford University Press, 1986), 626. The emphasis is mine.

77. Giulio Douhet, *The Command of the Air*, USAF Warrior Studies (Washington, D.C.: Office of Air Force History, 1983).

78. Jenifer L. Van Vleck, 'The "Logic of the Air": Aviation and the Globalism of the "American Century"', *New Global Studies* 1, no. 1 (2007).

79. Paul N Edwards, *The Closed World: Computers and the Politics of Discourse in Cold War America* (Cambridge: MIT Press, 1996).

10. DIGITAL POWER DOES DEVELOPMENT

1. Frederick Cooper and Ann Laura Stoler, *Tensions of Empire: Colonial Cultures in a Bourgeois World* (Berkeley: University of California Press, 1997), 4.

2. Franz Kafka, 'In Der Strafkolonie', in *Das Urteil Und Andere Erzählungen* (Frankfurt am Main: Fischer Taschenbuch Verlag, 1935).

3. Michel Foucault, *Society Must Be Defended: Lectures at the Collège de France, 1975–76*, trans. David Macey (New York: Picador, 2003), 103.

4. Alfred McCoy, *Policing America's Empire: The United States, the Philippines, and the Rise of the Surveillance State* (Madison: The University of Wisconsin Press, 2009), 295.

5. James C. Scott, *The Art of Not Being Governed: An Anarchist History of Upland Southeast Asia* (New Haven: Yale University Press, 2009); McCoy, *Policing America's Empire*; Martin Thomas, *Empires of Intelligence: Security Services and Colonial Disorder after 1914* (Berkeley: University of California Press, 2008).

6. A journalist describes a similar situation occurring after the invasion of Iraq, where large sections of the Maryland traffic code were copied from the internet and inserted into the new Iraq traffic law. Rajiv Chandrasekaran, *Imperial Life in the Emerald City: Inside Iraq's Green Zone* (New York: Vintage Books, 2007), 268.

7. Galton, *Finger Prints*, 24; see also Ginzburg, 'Morelli, Freud and Sherlock Holmes: Clues and Scientific Method.'

8. Sengoopta, *Imprint of the Raj*, 32; Anne M. Joseph, 'Anthropometry, the Police Expert, and the Deptford Murders: The Contested Introduction of Fingerprinting for the Identification of Criminals in Late Victorian and Edwardian Britain,' in *Documenting Individual Identity: The Development of State Practices in the Modern World*, eds Jane Caplan and John Torpey (Princeton: Princeton University Press, 2001), 166–72.

9. Sengoopta, *Imprint of the Raj*, 212–14.

10. Edward W. Said, *Orientalism* (New York: Pantheon Books, 1978), 234.

11. Nicholas B. Dirks, *Castes of Mind: Colonialism and the Making of Modern India* (Princeton, NJ: Princeton University Press, 2001), 187.

12. See Robert J.C. Young, *Colonial Desire: Hybridity in Theory, Culture and Race* (London: Routledge, 1995). In many ways a similar dynamic can be discov-

ered in contemporary discussions on the role race plays in intelligence. James R. Flynn, *What Is Intelligence?* (Cambridge: Cambridge University Press, 2007).

13. Sengoopta, *Imprint of the Raj*, 7. The emphasis is mine.

14. For good works on privacy see Daniel J. Solove, *Understanding Privacy* (Cambridge, MA: Harvard University Press, 2008); Daniel J. Solove, Marc Rotenberg, and Paul M. Schwartz, *Privacy, Information, and Technology* (New York: Aspen Publishers, 2006).

15. James D. Hunt, *An American Looks at Gandhi: Essays in Satyagraha, Civil Rights, and Peace* (New Delhi: Promilla & Co. Publishers, 2005), 178. For a recent controversial biography of Gandhi see Joseph Lelyveld, *Great Soul: Mahatma Gandhi and His Struggle with India* (New York: Alfred A Knopf, 2011).

16. It is worth recalling that Hannah Arendt located Nazism at the conjunction of bureaucracy and racism Hannah Arendt, *Elemente Und Ursprünge Totaler Herrschaft: Antisemitismus, Imperialismus, Totale Herrschaft* (München: Piper, 1986), 405–7.

17. Daniel Headrick, *The Tools of Empire: Technology and European Imperialism in the Nineteenth Century* (Oxford: Oxford University Press, 1981). Paul S Landau, 'Empires of the Visual: Photography and Colonial Administration in Africa', in *Images & Empires: Visuality in Colonial and Postcolonial Africa*, ed. Paul S Landau and Deborah D Kaspin (Berkeley: University of California Press, 2002), 142.

18. Frantz Fanon, *The Wretched of the Earth* (London: Penguin, 2001), 31.

19. Michael Adas, *Machines as the Measure of Men: Science, Technology, and Ideologies of Western Dominance* (Ithaca: Cornell University Press, 1989).

20. Ashis Nandy, *The Intimate Enemy: Loss and Recovery of Self under Colonialism* (Oxford: Oxford University Press, 1988), 32. See also Bernard S. Cohn, *Colonialism and Its Forms of Knowledge: The British in India* (Princeton: Princeton University Press, 1996).

21. Timothy Mitchell, *Colonising Egypt* (Cambridge: Cambridge University Press, 1988), 33.

22. For an account of the uses of calculation in surveying by the British in Egypt during the late nineteenth and early twentieth century see *Rule of Experts: Egypt, Techno-Politics, Modernity* (Berkeley: University of California Press, 2002), 80–119.

23. I define disambiguation protocols as rules of thumb used to classify entities, mainly humans, into categories. See the first chapter of this book for a longer definition.

24. Landau, 'Empires of the Visual,' 141.

25. Harry S Truman, 'Inaugural Address' (1949). The emphasis is mine.

26. A few examples are Coetzee Bester, 'The Management of Information in Development Projects: A Proposed Model for Enhancing Community Participation in Democracy and Policy Making in Africa', *European View* 7,

no. 1 (2008); Pippa Norris, *Digital Divide: Civic Engagement, Information Poverty, and the Internet Worldwide* (Cambridge: Cambridge University Press, 2001); Johannes J. Britz, 'Making the Global Information Society Good: A Social Justice Perspective on the Ethical Dimensions of the Global Information Society', *Journal of the American Society for Information Science and Technology* 59, no. 7 (2008). For a critical assessment of these debates see Mark Thompson, 'Discourse, "Development" & the "Digital Divide": ICT & the World Bank', *Review of African Political Economy* 31, no. 99 (2004); Julian Reid, 'Politicizing Connectivity: Beyond the Biopolitics of Information Technology in International Relations', *Cambridge Review of International Affairs* 22, no. 4 (2009).

27. Evgeny Morozov, *The Net Delusion: How Not to Liberate the World* (London: Allen Lane, 2011), 19–21.

28. See Ithiel de Sola Pool, 'Communication in Totalitarian Societies,' in *Handbook of Communication*, eds Ithiel de Sola Pool and Wilbur Schramm (Chicago: Rand McNally, 1974); Ithiel de Sola Pool, *Technologies of Freedom: On Free Speech in an Electronic Age* (Cambridge: Harvard University Press, 1983).

29. Murray Bookchin, 'Towards a Liberatory Technology,' in *Post-Scarcity Anarchism*, ed. Murray Bookchin (Edinburgh: AK Press, 2004), 49, 63, 84.

30. Larry Diamond, 'Liberation Technology', *Journal of Democracy* 21, no. 3 (2010): 70. The emphasis is mine.

31. See for instance Scott Shane, *Dismantling Utopia: How Information Ended the Soviet Union* (Chicago: I.R. Dee, 1995); Renée de Nevers, *Comrades No More: The Seeds of Political Change in Eastern Europe* (Cambridge: The MIT Press, 2003), 286–7.

32. George P. Schultz, 'New Realities and New Ways of Thinking', *Foreign Affairs* 63, no. 4 (1985); Joseph S. Nye and Robert O. Keohane, 'Power and Interdependence in the Information Age', *Foreign Affairs* 77, no. 5 (1998); Eric Schmidt and Jared Cohen, 'The Digital Disruption: Connectivity and the Diffusion of Power' *Foreign Affairs* 89, no. 6 (2010); Clay Shirky, 'The Political Power of Social Media,' *Foreign Affairs* 90, no. 3 (2011).

33. Schmidt and Cohen, 'The Digital Disruption'.

34. Ian Bremmer, *The J Curve: A New Way to Understand Why Nations Rise and Fall* (New York: Simon and Schuster, 2006).

35. For critical assessments of modernisation theory see Michael Latham, *Modernization as Ideology: American Social Science and 'Nation Building' in the Kennedy Era* (Chapel Hill: University of North Carolina Press, 2000); David Engerman, *Modernization from the Other Shore: American Intellectuals and the Romance of Russian Development* (Cambridge: Harvard University Press, 2003); Nils Gilman, *Mandarins of the Future: Modernization Theory in Cold War America* (Baltimore: Johns Hopkins University Press, 2003). For critical literature on the idea that

democracies don't fight each other see Christopher Layne, 'Kant or Cant: The Myth of the Democratic Peace, *International Security* 19, no. 2 (1994); Joanne Gowa, *Ballots and Bullets: The Elusive Democratic Peace* (Princeton: Princeton University Press, 2000).

36. Morozov, *The Net Delusion*, 5.

37. On the pro new social media side there are Clay Shirky, *Here Comes Everybody* (London: Allen Lane, 2008); *Cognitive Surplus: Creativity and Generosity in a Connected Age* (London: Penguin, 2010); Schmidt and Cohen, 'The Digital Disruption.' Against it there are Morozov, *The Net Delusion*; Malcolm Gladwell, 'Small Change: Why the Revolution Will Not Be Tweeted', *The New Yorker*, 4 Oct. 2010.

38. Schmidt and Cohen, 'The Digital Disruption'.

39. Katherine N. Hayles, *How We Became Posthuman: Virtual Bodies in Cybernetics, Literature, and Informatics* (Chicago: University of Chicago Press, 1999), 2.

40. Morozov, *The Net Delusion*, 233, 41.

41. Jamie Holmes, 'Identification, Please,' *Foreign Policy*, http://www.foreignpolicy.com/articles/2011/03/08/identification_please.

42. This section draws on archival work and interviews, as well as my experience working in the Security Sector Reform Programme in Liberia from 2005–7.

43. For literature on Liberia and the Civil War see Stephen Ellis, *The Mask of Anarchy: The Destruction of Liberia and the Religious Dimension of an African Civil War* (London: Hurst, 1999); Joseph Tellewoyan, *The Years the Locusts Have Eaten: Liberia, 1816–2004* (Philadelphia: Xlibris Corporation, 2006); Jeremy I. Levitt, *The Evolution of Deadly Conflict in Liberia: From 'Paternaltarianism' to State Collapse* (Durham: Carolina Academic Press, 2005).

44. International Monetary Fund, 'Liberia: Interim Poverty Reduction Strategy Paper' (Washington, DC: IMF, 2007), x; IDP Advisory Team Policy Development and Evaluation Service, 'Real-Time Evaluation of UNHCR's IDP Operation in Liberia' (Geneva: United Nations High Commissioner for Refugees (UNHCR), 2007), 7; UNHCR, 'Liberia: Regional Operations Profile—West Africa', www.unhcr.org/cgi-bin/texis/vtx/page?page=49e48 4936#; ICRC, 'Liberia: Opinion Survey and in-Depth Research' (Geneva: International Committe of Red Cross, 2009), 1.

45. Joseph Conrad, *Heart of Darkness* (New York: Bendford Books, 1996), 216.

46. United Nations Development Programme (UNDP), 'Human Development Report' (New York: United Nations Development Programme, 2009), 145.

47. Gallup, 'Global Wellbeing Surveys Find Nations Worlds Apart,' Gallup.com, www.gallup.com/poll/126977/global-wellbeing-surveys-find-nations-worlds-apart.aspx.

48. Klaus von Grebmer et al., 'Global Hunger Index, the Challenge of Hunger:

Focus on the Crisis of Child Undernutrition' (Bonn, Washington D.C., Dublin: Welthungerhilfe, International Food Policy Research Institute, Concern Worldwide, 2010), 17.

49. Legatum, 'Legatum Prosperity Index Report' (London: Legatum Institute, 2010), 81.

50. For an example of this worldview see John Knox, *The Races of Men: A Philosophical Inquiry into the Influence of Race over the Destinies of Nations* (London: Renshaw, 1862). For a classic discussion of these means of sorting human life see Stephen Jay Gould, *The Mismeasure of Man* (New York: Norton, 1981).

51. A fictional account anchored in reality that deals with this question is David Simon's landmark television series *The Wire*. In the series Baltimore's Police Department has political pressure placed on it to improve its crime-fighting. This policy results in a set of tragic-comic reversals where energy is expended to 'juke the stats' (alter the statistics to have them provide a better picture) that directly hinders the work of those who are 'good police'. For a more academic treatment of the question of statistical methodology and their utility for political power see Theodore M. Porter, 'Speaking Precision to Power: The Modern Political Role of Social Science', *Social Research* 73, no. 4 (2006): 1278–80.

52. A company called Benetech supported the work of the Truth and Reconciliation Commission (TRC). The support 'involved establishing analytical objectives, collecting data, designing and implementing an information management system'. TRC, 'Consolidated Final Report' (Monrovia: Republic of Liberia Truth and Reconciliation Commission, 2009), 86. For more on the TRC see Jonny Steinberg, 'A Truth Commission Goes Abroad: Liberian Transitional Justice in New York', *African Affairs* 110, no. 438 (2011).

53. R. Harrison Wagner, 'War and the State: A Synopsis', *International Theory* 2, no. 02 (2010): 287. Cf. Robert Egnell and Peter Haldén, 'Laudable, Ahistorical and Overambitious: Security Sector Reform Meets State Formation Theory' *Conflict, Security & Development* 9, no. 1 (2009).

54. Talal Asad, 'Thinking About Terrorism and Just War', *Cambridge Review of International Affairs* 23, no. 1 (2010): 7. Gilman, Nils 'Deviant Globalization' *Long Now* Talk, 3 May 2010.

55. This is from his influential 1958 inaugural lecture at Oxford. See Isiah Berlin, *Liberty* (Oxford: Oxford University Press, 2002).

56. Robert H. Jackson, *Quasi-States: Sovereignty, International Relations, and the Third World* (Cambridge: Cambridge University Press, 1990), 27. For more literature on sovereignty see Jens Bartelson, *A Genealogy of Sovereignty* (Cambridge: Cambridge University Press, 1995); R.B.J. Walker, *Inside/Outside: International Relations as Political Theory* (Cambridge: Cambridge University Press, 1993); Stephen D. Krasner, *Sovereignty: Organized Hypocrisy* (Princeton: Princeton

University Press, 1999); *Problematic Sovereignty* (New York: Columbia University Press, 2001); Richard A. Falk, *Human Rights and State Sovereignty* (Teaneck: Holmes & Meier, 1981).

57. Jackson, *Quasi-States*, 29.

58. Carl Schmitt, *Der Leviathan in Der Staatslehre Des Thomas Hobbes* (Stuttgart: Klett-Cotta, 1995), 72–3. The emphasis is mine.

59. This connects to the idea of sovereignty as constituted by the 'Responsibility to Protect'. A tendency in the 'Responsibility to Protect' discourse is to present earlier forms of sovereignty as only entailing rights and not responsibilities. For a text correcting this oversight see Luke Glanville, 'The Antecedents of "Sovereignty as Responsibility"', *European Journal of International Relations* 17, no. 2 (2011).

60. Anthony F. Norpah, 'Minutes of the DAMC Meeting Held on Oct. 25, 2005 in the Cabinet Room at the Executive Mansion' (Monrovia 2005).

61. James C. Scott, *Seeing Like a State: How Certain Schemes to Improve the Human Condition Have Failed* (New Haven: Yale University Press, 1998), 65–71.

62. Interview with DDRR Technical Coordinator, UNDP, Liberia, Monrovia, May 8, 2009.

63. Defense Advisory Committee (DAC), 'AFL Restructuring Plan Revised' (Monrovia 2004), 9.

64. For more on the DDR process see Kathleen M. Jennings, 'The Struggle to Satisfy: DDR through the Eyes of Ex-Combatants in Liberia', *International Peacekeeping* 14, no. 2 (2007); Albert Caramés and Eneko Sanz, 'DDR 2008: Analysis of Disarmament, Demobilisation and Reintegration (DDR) Programmes in the World During 2007' (Barcelona: School for a Culture of Peace, Autonomous University of Barcelona, 2008); Jeremy M. Weinstein and Macartan Humphreys, 'Disentangling the Determinants of Successful Demobilization and Reintegration' (Center for Global Development, 2005).

65. UNDDR, 'Liberia Country Programme' United Nations Disarmament, Demobilization and Reintegration Center, www.unddr.org/countryprogrammes.php?c=52#framework.

66. Interview with ex-combatant, Monrovia, 9 Jan. 2007.

67. 'Comprehensive Peace Agreement between the Government of Liberia and the Liberians United for Reconciliation and Democracy (LURD) and the Movement for Democracy in Liberia (MODEL) and Political Parties' (Accra, 2003).

68. For a close description of the timeline of the process see Sean McFate, 'Outsourcing the Making of Militaries: Dyncorp International as Sovereign Agent', *Review of African Political Economy* 35, no. 118 (2008). For a critique of the use of contractors for this kind of programme see Kwesi Aning, Thomas Jaye, and Samuel Atuobi, 'The Role of Private Military Companies in US-Africa Policy,' ibid.

69. For more on vetting see Sean McFate, 'The Art and Aggravation of Vetting in Post–Conflict Environments', *Military Review*, July–Aug. 2007, 79–87. For an assessment of the entire SSR process see Mark Malan, *Security Sector Reform in Liberia: Mixed Results from Humble Beginnings* (Strategic Studies Institute, United States Army War College, 2008).

70. R&V Section, 'Recruiting & Vetting Standard Operating Procedure: SSR Liberia' (Monrovia: DynCorp International, 2006), 56.

71. R&V Section, 'Recruiting & Vetting Report and Analysis, January 18th–June 1st' (Monrovia DynCorp International, 2006), 37.

72. R&V Section, 'Recruiting & Vetting Standard Operating Procedure,' 62.

73. Ibid.,' 142.

74. Ibid.

75. Said, *Orientalism*, 234.

76. Frederik Rosén, 'Off the Record: Outsourcing Security and State Building to Private Firms and the Question of Record Keeping, Archives, and Collective Memory,' *Archival Science*, no. 8 (2008).

77. For instance, 'There is a certain abstract reality to an obvious clustering of linguistic attributes and sociocultural traits among the many peoples counted as Kru, Grebo, or Krahn. But these similarities in one sense have been imposed on the data by linguists, historians and anthropologists.' Frederick McEvoy, 'Understanding Ethnic Realities among the Grebo and Kru Peoples of West Africa', *Africa: The Journal of the International African Institute* 47, no. 1 (1977): 66.

78. Landau, 'Empires of the Visual,' 150. On the role of anthropology under colonialism see Cohn, *Colonialism and Its Forms of Knowledge*; Talal Asad, ed. *Anthropology & the Colonial Encounter* (London: Ithaca Press, 1973); Henrika Kuklick, 'Tribal Exemplars: Images of Political Authority in British Anthropology, 1885–1945', in *Functionalism Historicized: Essays on British Social Anthropology*, ed. George W. Stocking (Madison: University of Wisconsin Press, 1984); James Ferguson, *Expectations of Modernity: Myths and Meanings of Urban Life on the Zambian Copperbelt* (Berkeley: University of California Press, 1999); Talal Asad, 'From the History of Colonial Anthropology to the Anthropology of Western Hegemony', in *The Anthropology of Politics: A Reader in Ethnography, Theory, and Critique*, ed. Joan Vincent (Malden, MA: Blackwell Publishers, 2002); Johannes Fabian, *Time and the Other: How Anthropology Makes Its Object* (New York: Columbia University Press, 2002).

79. Patrick Porter, *Military Orientalism: Eastern War through Western Eyes* (New York: Columbia University Press, 2009), 154–5.

80. Jim Gant, 'One Tribe at a Time: A Strategy for Success in Afghanistan' (Los Angeles: Nihe Sisters Imports, 2009), 8.

81. Landau, 'Empires of the Visual,' 161.

82. For a similar argument about the necessity of the World Bank to construct Lesotho as an economy that is not embedded in the capitalist labour relations of South Africa see James Ferguson, *The Anti-Politics Machine: 'Development,' Depoliticization, and Bureaucratic Power in Lesotho* (Minneapolis: University of Minnesota Press, 1994).

83. Josef Teboho Ansorge, 'Spirits of War: A Field Manual', *International Political Sociology* 4, no. 4 (2010): 369.

11. RESISTANCE ON OUR PLANETARY SHIP OF STATE

1. R. Buckminster Fuller, *Operating Manual for Spaceship Earth* (Carbondale: Southern Illinois University Press, 1969).

2. This is treated in Plutarch's *Lives*. For a more recent version see Harold W. Noonan, *Personal Identity* (London: Routledge, 1989), 131.

3. Hobbes's account is in *De Corpore* (II, 7, 2). For a recent treatment of it see Christopher Hughes, 'Same-Kind Coincidence and the Ship of Theseus', *Mind* 106, no. 421 (1997): 54.

4. Jean Baudrillard, *Simulacra and Simulation* (Ann Arbor: University of Michigan Press, 1994).

5. James Ferguson, *Global Shadows: Africa in the Neoliberal World Order* (London: Duke University Press, 2006), 65.

6. 'Deviant globalization is inextricably linked to and bound up with mainstream globalization.' Nils Gilman, Jesse Goldhammer, and Steven Weber, eds, *Deviant Globalization: Black Market Economy in the 21st Century* (New York: Continuum, 2011), 2.

7. For a comprehensive assessment of the history of the idea of the self see Jerrod Seigel, *The Idea of the Self: Thought and Experience in Western Europe since the Seventeenth Century* (Cambridge: Cambridge University Press, 2005).

8. Evgeny Morozov, *The Net Delusion: How Not to Liberate the World* (London: Allen Lane, 2011), 161.

9. Volkszählungsurteil, 65 BVerfGE 1, 68–9 (1983).

10. Spiros Simitis, 'Reviewing Privacy in an Information Society', *University of Pennsylvania Law Review* 135(1986–1987): 746.

11. Yves-Alexandre de Montjoye et al., 'Unique in the Crowd: The Privacy Bounds of Human Mobility', *Scientific Reports* 3 (2013).

12. Computer scientists have been referring to a nymity slider as the transition from anonymity, pseudonymity, and verinimity—representing different levels of identifying information. See Ian Goldberg, 'A Pseudonymous Communications Infrastructure for the Internet' [PhD Thesis, Berkeley] (2000), 38. To my knowledge this paper is the first time *nymity* is proposed as a legal principle.

13. See www.gov.uk/request-cctv-footage-of-yourself
14. See http://www.foxnews.com/politics/2014/03/01/california-allows-minors-to-deleted-social-media-posts-with-erase-law/
15. Court of Justice of the European Union, Press Release No. 70/14, Judgment in Case C-131/12, Google Spain SL, Google Inc. v Agencia Española de Protección de Datos, Mario Costeja González www.curia.europa.eu/jcms/jcms/P_127116/

APPENDIX

1. GStA, Rep. 77, Tit. 343, vol. no. 107a.

BIBLIOGRAPHY

AAA Commission on the Engagement of Anthropology with the U.S. Security and Intelligence Communities (CEAUSSIC), 'Final Report on the Army's Human Terrain System Proof of Concept Program', 73, 2009.

Ackerman, Bruce A, *We the People*, Cambridge, MA: Belknap Press of Harvard University Press, 1991.

Adas, Michael, 'From Avoidance to Confrontation: Peasant Protest in Precolonial Southeast Asia', *Comparative Studies in Society and History* 23, no. 2 (1981): 217–47.

———. *Machines as the Measure of Men: Science, Technology, and Ideologies of Western Dominance*, Ithaca: Cornell University Press, 1989.

Adler, Emanuel, and Vincent Pouliot, 'International Practices', *International Theory* 3, no. 01 (2011): 1–36.

Agamben, Giorgio, *State of Exception*, Chicago: The University of Chicago Press, 2005.

Aid, Matthew M, *The Secret Sentry: The Untold History of the National Security Agency*, New York: Bloomsbury Press, 2009.

Alexander, Jeffrey C., 'Marxism and the Spirit of Socialism: Cultural Origins of Anti-Capitalism (1982)', *Theses Eleven* 100, no. 1 (2010): 84–105.

———. *The Performance of Politics: Obama's Victory and the Democratic Struggle for Power*, Oxford: Oxford University Press, 2010.

Allen, Francis Olcott, ed, *The History of Enfield Connecticut*, Vol. III, Lancaster: The Wickersham Printing Co., 1900.

Alter, Adam L., Daniel M, Oppenheimer, Nicholas Epley, and Rebecca N. Eyre, 'Overcoming Intuition: Metacognitive Difficulty Activates Analytic Reasoning', *Journal of Experimental Psychology: General* 136, no. 4 (2007): 569–76.

Aly, Götz, and Karl Heinz Roth, *Die Restlose Erfassung: Volkszählen, Identifizieren, Aussondern Im Nationalsozialismus*, Berlin: Rotbuch Verlag, 1984.

Aly, Götz, Karl Heinz Roth, Edwin Black, and Assenka Oksiloff, *The Nazi Census:*

BIBLIOGRAPHY

Identification and Control in the Third Reich, Politics, History, and Social Change. Philadelphia: Temple University Press, 2004.

American Anti-Slavery Society, *American Slavery as It Is: Testimony of a Thousand Witnesses*, New York: The American Anti-Slavery Society, 1839.

Amoore, Louise, and Marieke De Goede, 'Governance, Risk and Dataveillance in the War on Terror', *Crime, Law & Social Change* 43, no. 2–3 (2005): 149–73.

Amoore, Louise, and Alexandra Hall, 'Taking People Apart: Digitised Dissection and the Body at the Border', *Environment and Planning D: Society and Space* (2009).

Anderson, Margo J., *The American Census: A Social History*, New Haven: Yale University Press, 1988.

Anderson, Margo J., and Stephen E. Fienberg, *Who Counts?: The Politics of Census-Taking in Contemporary America*, 1st pbk. ed., New York: Russell Sage Foundation, 2001.

Anderson, Matthew S., 'Samuel Bentham in Russia, 1779–1791', *American Slavic and East European Review* 15, no. 2 (1956): 157–72.

Aning, Kwesi, Thomas Jaye, and Samuel Atuobi, 'The Role of Private Military Companies in US–Africa Policy', *Review of African Political Economy* 35, no. 118 (2008): 613–28.

Ansorge, Josef Teboho, 'Spirits of War: A Field Manual', *International Political Sociology* 4, no. 4 (2010): 362–79.

Arendt, Hannah, *Elemente Und Ursprünge Totaler Herrschaft: Antisemitismus, Imperialismus, Totale Herrschaft*. München: Piper, 1986.

———. *The Origins of Totalitarianism*, New York: Schocken Books, 2004.

Aristotle, *The Complete Works of Aristotle*, edited by Jonathan Barnes 2 vols Princeton: Princeton University Press, 1984.

Army, US, 'HTS Components', http://humanterrainsystem.army.mil/components.html.

Arthur, W. Brian, 'Competing Technologies, Increasing Returns, and Lock-in by Historical Events', *The Economic Journal* 99, no. 394 (1989): 116–31.

Asad, Talal, ed., *Anthropology & the Colonial Encounter*, London: Ithaca Press, 1973.

———. 'From the History of Colonial Anthropology to the Anthropology of Western Hegemony', In *The Anthropology of Politics: A Reader in Ethnography, Theory, and Critique*, edited by Joan Vincent, Malden, MA: Blackwell Publishers, 2002.

———. 'Thinking About Terrorism and Just War', *Cambridge Review of International Affairs* 23, no. 1 (2010): 3—24.

Ascher, Marcia, and Robert Ascher, *Mathematics of the Incas: Code of the Quipu*. Mineola, New York: Dover Publications, 1997.

Baehr, Peter, 'The "Iron Cage" and the "Shell as Hard as Steel": Parsons, Weber, and the Stahlhartes Gehäuse Metaphor in the Protestant Ethic and the Spirit of Capitalism', *History and Theory* 40, no. 2 (2002): 153–69.

Bagby, Cali, '"I'd Say a Good Percentage of Iraqis Are Already in the Database"', *KVAL.com*, 7 Nov. 2009.

Bamford, James, 'Who's in Big Brother's Database?', *The New York Review of Books* 56, no. 17 (2009).

Bardini, Thierry, *Junkware*, Minneapolis: University of Minnesota Press, 2011.

Barkawi, Tarak, 'Peoples, Homelands, and Wars? Ethnicity, the Military, and Battle among British Imperial Forces in the War against Japan', *Comparative Studies in Society and History* 46, no. 1 (2004): 134–63.

Barnett, Michael, and Raymond Duvall, 'Power in International Politics', *International Organization* 59, no. 01 (2005): 39–75.

Bartelson, Jens, *A Genealogy of Sovereignty*, Cambridge: Cambridge University Press, 1995.

Bartky, Ian R., 'The Adoption of Standard Time', *Technology and Culture* 30, no. 1 (1989): 25–56.

Bates, David, 'Political Theology and the Nazi State: Carl Schmitt's Concept of the Institution', *Modern Intellectual History* 3, no. 3 (2006): 415–42.

Batson, Douglas E., *Registering the Human Terrains: A Valuation of Cadastre*, NDIC Press, 2008.

Baudrillard, Jean, *Simulacra and Simulation*, Ann Arbor: University of Michigan Press, 1994.

Bauman, Zygmunt, 'On Postmodern Uses of Sex', in *Love and Eroticism*, edited by Mike Featherstone, 19–34, London: Sage, 1999.

Bayly, C. A., *The Birth of the Modern World, 1780–1914: Global Connections and Comparisons*, Malden: Blackwell Publishers, 2004.

———. *Empire and Information: Intelligence Gathering and Social Communication in India, 1780–1870*, Cambridge: Cambridge University Press, 1996.

Bell, Catherine M., *Ritual Theory, Ritual Practice*, New York: Oxford University Press, 1992.

———. *Ritual: Perspectives and Dimensions*, New York: Oxford University Press, 1997.

———. *Teaching Ritual*, Oxford: Oxford University Press, 2007.

Bell, Duncan, *The Idea of Greater Britain: Empire and the Future of World Order, 1860–1900*, Princeton: Princeton University Press, 2007.

———. 'Writing the World: Disciplinary History and Beyond', *International Affairs* 85, no. 1 (2009): 3–22.

Benjamin, Walter, 'Einbahnstraße', in *Gesammelte Schriften* Frankfurt am Main: Suhrkamp Verlag, 1929.

———. *Illuminationen: Ausgewählte Schriften 1*, Frankfurt am Main: Suhrkamp Verlag, 1974.

Bennett, Colin J., 'What Happens When You Book an Airline Ticket? The Collecting and Processing of Passenger Data Post-9/11', in *Global Surveillance and Policing: Borders, Security, Identity*, edited by Elia Zureik and Mark B. Salter, 113–38, London: Willan Publishing, 2005.

BIBLIOGRAPHY

Bennett, Lance W., and Robert M Entman, *Mediated Politics: Communication in the Future of Democracy*, Cambridge: Cambridge University Press, 2001.

Bentham, Jeremy, *The Panopticon Writings*, London: Verso, 1995.

———. 'Panopticon', in *The Complete Works of Jeremy Bentham*, edited by John Bowring, vol. 4, Edinburgh: William Tait, 1843.

Berlin, Isiah, *Liberty*, Oxford: Oxford University Press, 2002.

Bertillon, Alphonse, *Signaletic Instructions: Including the Theory and Practice of Anthropometrical Identification*, translated by R. W. McClaughry, Chicago: The Werner Company, 1896.

Bester, Coetzee, 'The Management of Information in Development Projects: A Proposed Model for Enhancing Community Participation in Democracy and Policy Making in Africa', *European View* 7, no. 1 (2008): 33–44.

Biometrics Identity Management Agency (BIMA), 'Biometrics Glossary 5.0', 2010.

Blackstone, William. *Commentaries on the Laws of England*, http://avalon.law.yale.edu/18th_century/blackstone_bk4ch15.asp.

Blair, Ann M., *Too Much to Know: Managing Scholarly Information before the Modern Age*, New Haven: Yale University Press, 2010.

Blaise, Clark, *Time Lord: Sir Sandford Fleming and the Creation of Standard Time*, New York: Pantheon Books, 2000.

Boehlich, W, ed., *Der Berliner Antisemitismusstreit*, Frankfurt am Main, 1965.

Bookchin, Murray, 'Towards a Liberatory Technology', in *Post-Scarcity Anarchism*, edited by Murray Bookchin, Edinburgh: AK Press, 2004.

Borges, Jorge Luis, 'On Exactitude in Science', translated by Andrew Hurley, in *Collected Fictions*, London: The Penguin Press, 1999.

Boyne, Roy, 'Post-Panopticism', *Economy and Society* 29, no. 2 (2000): 285–307.

Branch, Jordan, 'Mapping the Sovereign State: Technology, Authority, and Systemic Change', *International Organization* 65, no. 01 (2011): 1–36.

Breasted, James Henry, *Ancient Records of Egypt*, Vol. IV, Chicago: University of Chicago Press, 1906.

Bremmer, Ian, *The J Curve: A New Way to Understand Why Nation's Rise and Fall*, New York: Simon and Schuster, 2006.

Britz, Johannes J., 'Making the Global Information Society Good: A Social Justice Perspective on the Ethical Dimensions of the Global Information Society', *Journal of the American Society for Information Science and Technology* 59, no. 7 (2008): 1171–83.

Brown, Wendy, *Walled States, Waning Sovereignty*, New York: Zone Books, 2010.

Burcham, L. Neil, and Jason L. Turner, 'Guide B-602: Identify Pigs by Ear Notching', Las Cruces, NM: NM State University Cooperative Extension Service, College of Agricultural, Consumer and Environmental Sciences, 2011.

Burger, Richard L., Craig Morris, Ramiro Matos Mendieta, Joanne Pillsbury, and Jeffrey Quilter, *Variations in the Expression of Inka Power: A Symposium at*

Dumbarton Oaks, 18 and 19 October 1997, Washington, DC: Dumbarton Oaks Research Library and Collection, 2007.

Burkert, Walter, René Girard, Jonathan Z. Smith, and Robert Hamerton-Kelly, *Violent Origins*, Stanford: Stanford University Press, 1987.

Buzan, Barry, Ole Waever, and Jaap de Wilde, *Security: A New Framework for Analysis*, London: Lynne Riener, 1998.

Campanella, Tommaso, *City of the Sun: A Poetical Dialogue*, Berkeley: University of California Press, 1992.

Campbell, David, *Writing Security: United States Foreign Policy and the Politics of Identity*, Minneapolis: University of Minnesota Press, 1992.

Caplan, Jane, '"This or That Particular Person": Protocols of Identification in Nineteenth-Century Europe', in *Documenting Individual Identity: The Development of State Practices in the Modern World*, edited by Jane Caplan and John Torpey, 49–66. Princeton: Princeton University Press, 2001.

Caplan, Jane, and John C. Torpey, *Documenting Individual Identity: The Development of State Practices in the Modern World*, Princeton: Princeton University Press, 2001.

Caramés, Albert, and Eneko Sanz, 'DDR 2008: Analysis of Disarmament, Demobilisation and Reintegration (DDR) Programmes in the World During 2007', Barcelona: School for a Culture of Peace, Autonomous University of Barcelona, 2008.

Carr, Matt, 'Slouching Towards Dystopia: The New Military Futurism', *Race & Class* 51, no. 13 (2010): 13–32.

Castells, Manuel, *The Rise of the Network Society: The Information Age*, Chichester: Wiley-Blackwell, 2010.

Chamayou, Gregoire, '"Every Move Will Be Recorded": A Machinic Police Utopia in the Eighteenth Century', Max Planck Institute For the History of Science, http://www.mpiwg-berlin.mpg.de/en/news/features/feature14.

Chandler, David, 'The Revival of Carl Schmitt in International Relations: The Last Refuge of Critical Theorists?', *Millennium* 37, no. 1 (2008): 27–48.

Chandrasekaran, Rajiv, *Imperial Life in the Emerald City: Inside Iraq's Green Zone*, New York: Vintage Books, 2007.

Chiapello, Eve, 'Die Geburt Des Kapitalismus Aus Der Idee Der Doppelten Buchfuehrung', *WestEnd: Neue Zeitschrift für Sozialforschung* 4, no. 2 (2007): 64–95.

Choi, Charles Q., 'Military to Adopt NFL's Instant Replay Technology', *LiveScience. Com*, 1 June 2010.

Chow, Rey, *The Age of the World Target: Self-Referentiality in War, Theory, and Comparative Work*, London: Duke University Press, 2006.

Clarke, Roger, 'Dataveillance: Delivering 1984', in *Framing Technology: Society, Choice and Change*, edited by Lelia Green and Roger Guinery, London: Routledge, 1994.

———. 'Introduction to Dataveillance and Information Privacy, and Definitions of Terms', http://www.anu.edu.au/people/Roger.Clarke/DV/Intro.html.

BIBLIOGRAPHY

Clausewitz, Carl von, *Vom Kriege*, München: Cormoran Verlag, 2000.

Clendinnen, Inga, *The Cost of Courage in Aztec Society*, Cambridge: Cambridge University Press, 2010.

——. *The Cost of Courage in Aztec Society: Essays on Mesoamerican Society and Culture*, Cambridge: Cambridge University Press, 2010.

cnn.com. 'Clinton's Gift to Internet Age: Only 2 E-Mails', http://edition.cnn.com/2004/TECH/internet/01/28/clinton.email.reut/.

Cohn, Bernard S., *Colonialism and Its Forms of Knowledge: The British in India*, Princeton: Princeton University Press, 1996.

'Comprehensive Peace Agreement between the Government of Liberia and the Liberians United for Reconciliation and Democracy (LURD) and the Movement for Democracy in Liberia (MODEL) and Political Parties', Accra, Ghana, 2003.

Connelly, Matthew, *Fatal Misconception: The Struggle to Control World Population*, Cambridge: Harvard University Press, 2008.

Conrad, Joseph, *Heart of Darkness*, New York: Bendford Books, 1996.

Cooper, Frederick, and Ann Laura Stoler, *Tensions of Empire: Colonial Cultures in a Bourgeois World*, Berkeley: University of California Press, 1997.

Corbusier, Le, *The Radiant City: Elements of a Doctrine of Urbanism to Be Used as the Basis of Our Machine-Age Civilization*, New York: Orion Press, 1967.

Cosgrove, Denis, *Geography and Vision: Seeing, Imagining and Representing the World*, London: I.B. Tauris, 2008.

Court of Justice of the European Union, 'Press Release No. 70/14, Judgment in Case C-131/12, Google Spain SL, Google Inc. v Agencia Española de Protección de Datos', Mario Costeja González, www.curia.europa.eu/jcms/jcms/P_127116/

Cusset, François, *French Theory: How Foucault, Derrida, Deleuze, & Co. Transformed the Intellectual Life of the United States*, Minneapolis: University of Minnesota Press, 2008.

Davidson, Herbert E., and W.E. Parker, *Classified Illustrated Catalog of the Library Bureau. A Handbook of Library and Office Fittings and Supplies*, Boston: Library Bureau, 1891.

Davis, Mike, *Planet of Slums*, London: Verso, 2007.

Defense Advisory Committee (DAC), 'AFL Restructuring Plan Revised', Monrovia, 2004.

De Landa, Manuel, *War in the Age of Intelligent Machines*, New York: Zone Books, 1991.

Derrida, Jacques, *Specters of Marx: The State of the Debt, the Work of Mourning, and the New International*, New York: Routledge, 1994.

Detienne, Marcel, and Jean Pierre Vernant, *Cunning Intelligence in Greek Culture and Society*. Hassocks: Harvester Press, 1978.

Diamond, Larry, 'Liberation Technology', *Journal of Democracy* 21, no. 3 (2010): 69–83.

Diemand-Yauman, Connor, Daniel M. Oppenheimer, and Erikka B. Vaughan, 'Fortune Favors the Bold (*and the Italicized*): Effects of Disfluency on Educational Outcomes', *Cognition* 118, no. 1 (2011): 111–15.

Dillon, Michael, and Julian Reid, 'Global Liberal Governance: Biopolitics, Security and War', *Millennium—Journal of International Studies* 30, no. 1 (2001): 41–66.

DiMaggio, Paul J., and Walter W. Powell, 'The Iron Cage Revisited: Institutional Isomorphism and Collective Rationality in Organizational Fields', *American Sociological Review* 48, no. 2 (1983): 147–60.

Dirks, Nicholas B, *Castes of Mind: Colonialism and the Making of Modern India*, Princeton, N.J.: Princeton University Press, 2001.

Division, L1 Identity Solutions: Biometrics. 'Portable Multimodal Enrollment and Recognition Device: The Handheld Interagency Identity Detection Equipment', http://www.l1id.com/HIIDE, 2009.

Dohrn-van Rossum, Gerhard, *History of the Hour: Clocks and Modern Temporal Orders*, Chicago: University of Chicago Press, 1996.

Dostal, Robert J., 'Time and Phenomenology in Husserl and Heidegger', Chap. 5 in *The Cambridge Companion to Heidegger*, edited by Charles B Guignon, 141–69, Cambridge: Cambridge University Press, 1993.

Douglas, Mary, *Purity and Danger: An Analysis of Concepts of Pollution and Taboo*, London: Routledge & K. Paul, 1966.

Douhet, Giulio, *The Command of the Air*. Usaf Warrior Studies, Washington, DC: Office of Air Force History, 1983.

Drew, Christopher, 'Military Is Awash in Data from Drones', *New York Times*, 10 Jan. 2010.

Durkheim, Emile, *The Elementary Forms of Religious Life*, translated by Karen E. Fields, New York: Free Press, 1995.

Edgerton, David, *The Shock of the Old: Technology and Global History since 1900*, London: Profile Books, 2008.

Edwards, Paul N., *The Closed World: Computers and the Politics of Discourse in Cold War America*, Cambridge: MIT Press, 1996.

Egnell, Robert, and Peter Haldén, 'Laudable, Ahistorical and Overambitious: Security Sector Reform Meets State Formation Theory', *Conflict, Security & Development* 9, no. 1 (2009): 27–54.

Eilstrup-Sangiovanni, Mette, and Calvert Jones, 'Assessing the Dangers of Illicit Networks: Why Al-Qaida May Be Less Threatening Than Many Think', *International Security* 33, no. 2 (2008): 7–44.

Eisenstein, Elizabeth L, *The Printing Press as an Agent of Change: Communications and Cultural Transformations in Early Modern Europe*, Cambridge: Cambridge University Press, 1979.

Ellis, Stephen, *The Mask of Anarchy: The Destruction of Liberia and the Religious Dimension of an African Civil War*, London: Hurst, 1999.

Elster, Jon, *The Cement of Society: A Study of Social Order*, Cambridge: Cambridge University Press, 1989.

Ely, John Hart, *Democracy and Distrust: A Theory of Judicial Review*, Cambridge: Harvard University Press, 1980.

Engels, Friedrich, *Der Deutsche Bauernkrieg*. Leipzig: Verlag der Expedition des 'Volksstaat', 1870.

——. 'On Authority', In *Philosophy of Technology: An Anthology*, edited by Val Dusek and Robert C Sharff. Oxford: Blackwell Publishing, [1873] 2003.

Engerman, David, *Modernization from the Other Shore: American Intellectuals and the Romance of Russian Development*, Cambridge: Harvard University Press, 2003.

Fabian, Johannes, *Time and the Other: How Anthropology Makes Its Object*, New York: Columbia University Press, 2002.

Falk, Richard A., *Human Rights and State Sovereignty*, Teaneck: Holmes & Meier, 1981.

Fanon, Frantz, *The Wretched of the Earth*, London: Penguin, 2001.

Febvre, Lucien Paul Victor, and Henri–Jean Martin, *The Coming of the Book: The Impact of Printing, 1450–1800*, translated by David Gerard, London: Verso, 2010.

Feenberg, Andrew, *Alternative Modernity: The Technical Turn in Philosophy and Social Theory*, Berkeley: University of California Press, 1995.

——. *Alternative Modernity: The Technical Turn in Philosophy and Social Theory*, London: University of California Press, 1995.

Ferguson, James,. *The Anti-Politics Machine: 'Development,' Depoliticization, and Bureaucratic Power in Lesotho*, Minneapolis: University of Minnesota Press, 1994.

——. *Expectations of Modernity: Myths and Meanings of Urban Life on the Zambian Copperbelt*, Berkeley: University of California Press, 1999.

——. *Global Shadows: Africa in the Neoliberal World Order*, London: Duke University Press, 2006.

Finnemore, Martha, 'Review: Norms, Culture, and World Politics: Insights from Sociology's Institutionalism', *International Organization* 50, no. 2 (1996): 325–47.

Flood, Christopher, *Political Myth: A Theoretical Introduction*, New York: Garland Pub. Inc., 1996.

Flynn, James R, *What Is Intelligence?* Cambridge: Cambridge University Press, 2007.

Flyvbjerg, Bent, *Making Social Science Matter: Why Social Inquiry Fails and How It Can Succeed Again*, Cambridge: Cambridge University Press, 2001.

Fosdick, Raymond B, 'The Passing of the Bertillon System of Identification', *Journal of the American Institute of Criminal Law and Criminology* 6, no. 3 (1915): 363–9.

Foster, Hal, 'Preface', in *Vision and Visuality*, edited by Hal Foster, ix–xiv, Seattle: Bay Press, 1988.

Foucault, Michel. *Discipline and Punish: The Birth of the Prison*, New York: Pantheon Books, 1977.

BIBLIOGRAPHY

————. *Power/Knowledge: Selected Interviews and Other Writings 1972–1977*, edited and translated by Colin Gordon, Brighton, Sussex: Harvester Press, 1980.

————. *The History of Sexuality*, New York: Vintage Books, 1988.

————. *Society Must Be Defended: Lectures at the Collège De France, 1975–76*, translated by David Macey, New York: Picador, 2003.

————. *Security, Territory, Population: Lectures at the Collège De France, 1977–1978*, translated by Arnold Ira Davidson, Houndmills: Palgrave Macmillan, 2007.

Frazer, James George, *The Golden Bough: A Study in Magic and Religion*, Harmondsworth: Penguin Books, 1996.

Freud, Sigmund, 'Der Moses Des Michelangelo', *Imago. Zeitschrift für Anwendung der Psychoanalyse auf die Geisteswissenschaften* III (1914): 15–36.

————. *Jenseits Des Lustprinzips*, Beihefte Der Internationalen Zeitschrift Für Psychoanalyse, Nr. 2, 2nd ed. Zürich: Internationaler Psychoanalytischer Verlag, 1921.

Friedman, Lawrence M., *Crime and Punishment in American History*, New York: Basic Books, 1993.

Fuller, R. Buckminster, *Operating Manual for Spaceship Earth*, Carbondale: Southern Illinois University Press, 1969.

Galison, Peter, 'The Ontology of the Enemy: Norbert Wiener and the Cybernetic Vision', *Critical Inquiry* 21, no. 1 (1994): 229–66.

Gallup, 'Global Wellbeing Surveys Find Nations Worlds Apart', Gallup.com, http://www.gallup.com/poll/126977/global-wellbeing-surveys-find-nations-worlds-apart.aspx.

Galton, Francis, *Finger Prints*, London: Macmillan and Co., 1892.

Galula, David, *Counterinsurgency Warfare: Theory and Practice*. New York: Praeger, 1964.

Gandy, Oscar H, Lance W Bennett, and Robert M Entman, *Dividing Practices: Segmentation and Targeting in the Emerging Public Sphere*, Cambridge: Cambridge University Press, 2000.

Gannon, Charles, *Rumors of War and Infernal Machines: Technomilitary Agenda-Setting in British and American Speculative Fiction*, Liverpool: Liverpool University Press, 2005.

Gant, Jim, 'One Tribe at a Time: A Strategy for Success in Afghanistan', Los Angeles: Nine Sisters Imports, 2009.

Ghamari-Tabrizi, Sharon, *The Worlds of Herman Kahn*, Cambridge, MA: Harvard University Press, 2005.

Gibson, William, and Michael Swanwick, 'Dogfight', *Omni*, 7, no. 10 (1985).

Giddens, Anthony, *The Consequences of Modernity*, Stanford: Stanford University Press, 1990.

————. *The Nation-State and Violence*, Berkeley: University of California Press, 1987.

Gilman, Nils, *Mandarins of the Future: Modernization Theory in Cold War America*, Baltimore: Johns Hopkins University Press, 2003.

Gilman, Nils, Jesse Goldhammer, and Steven Weber, eds., *Deviant Globalization: Black Market Economy in the 21st Century*, New York: Continuum, 2011.

Gilroy, Paul, *The Black Atlantic: Modernity and Double Consciousness*, London: Verso, 1993.

Ginzburg, Carlo, 'Morelli, Freud and Sherlock Holmes: Clues and Scientific Method', *Hist Workshop J* 9, no. 1 (1 Jan. 1980): 5–36.

Gladwell, Malcolm, 'Small Change: Why the Revolution Will Not Be Tweeted', *The New Yorker*, 4 Oct. 2010.

Glanville, Luke, 'The Antecedents of "Sovereignty as Responsibility"', *European Journal of International Relations* 17, no. 2 (2011): 233–55.

Glass, D. V., *Numbering the People: The Eighteenth-Century Population Controversy and the Development of Census and Vital Statistics in Britain*, Farnborough: D.C. Heath, 1973.

Gleick, James, *The Information: A History, a Theory, a Flood*, New York: Pantheon Books, 2011.

Godelier, Maurice, *The Mental and the Material: Thought, Economy, and Society*, London: Verso, 1988.

Goody, Jack, *The Logic of Writing and the Organization of Society*, Cambridge: Cambridge University Press, 1986.

Gorman, Siobhan, 'NSA Officers Spy on Love Interests', *The Wall Street Journal*, 23 Aug. 2013.

Gould, Stephen Jay, *The Mismeasure of Man*, New York: Norton, 1981.

Gowa, Joanne, *Ballots and Bullets: The Elusive Democratic Peace*, Princeton: Princeton University Press, 2000.

Graham, Bradley, 'Poindexter Resigns but Defends Programs: Anti-Terrorism, Data Scanning Efforts at Pentagon Called Victims of Ignorance', *Washington Post*, 13 Aug. 2003.

Graham, Stephen, 'The Urban "Battlespace"', *Theory, Culture & Society* 26, no. 7–8 (1 Dec. 2009), 278–88.

Grebmer, Klaus von, Marie T. Ruel, Purnima Menon, Bella Nestorova, Tolulope Olofinbiyi, Heidi Fritschel, Yisehac Yohannes, et al., 'Global Hunger Index, the Challenge of Hunger: Focus on the Crisis of Child Undernutrition', Bonn, Washington DC, Dublin: Welthungerhilfe, International Food Policy Research Institute, Concern Worldwide, 2010.

Gregory, Derek, *The Colonial Present: Afghanistan, Palestine, and Iraq*, Malden, MA: Blackwell, 2004.

———. '"The Rush to the Intimate" Counterinsurgency and the Cultural Turn', *Radical Philosophy*, no. 150 (2008).

Grewal, David Singh, *Network Power: The Social Dynamics of Globalization*, New Haven: Yale University Press, 2008.

Groebner, Valentin, 'Describing the Person, Reading the Signs in Late Medieval and

Renaissance Europe: Identity Papers, Vested Figures, and the Limits of Identification, 1400–1600', in *Documenting Individual Identity: The Development of State Practices in the Modern World*, edited by Jane Caplan and John C. Torpey, 15–27, Princeton: Princeton University Press, 2001.

Groot, Roger D., 'Petit Larceny, Jury Lenity and Parliament', in *The Dearest Birth Right of the People of England: The Jury in the History of the Common Law*, edited by John W. Cairns and Grant McLeod, 47–61, Oxford: Hart Publishing, 2002.

Gugerli, David, *Suchmaschinen. Die Welt Als Datenbank*, Frankfurt am Main: Suhrkamp, 2009.

Gugerli, David, and Daniel Speich, *Topografien Der Nation: Politik, Kartografische Orndung Und Landschaft Im 19. Jahrhundert*, Zürich: Chronos Verlag, 2002.

Habermas, Jürgen, *Technik Und Wissenschaft Als 'Ideologie'*, Frankfurt am Main: Suhrkamp, 1989 [1968].

Hacking, Ian, *The Taming of Chance*, Cambridge: Cambridge University Press, 1990.

Haggerty, Kevin D., 'Tear Down the Walls: On Demolishing the Panopticon', in *Theorizing Surveillance: The Panopticon and Beyond*, edited by David Lyon, 23–45, Cullompton, Devon: Willan Publishing, 2006.

Hall, Phyllis A., 'The Appreciation of Technology in Campanella's "the City of the Sun"', *Technology and Culture* 34, no. 3 (1993): 613–28.

Haraway, Donna, 'A Cyborg Manifesto: Science, Technology, Socialist-Feminism in the Late Twentieth Century', in *Simians, Cyborgs and Women: The Reinvention of Nature*, edited by Donna Haraway, 149–81, New York: Routledge, 1991.

Harris, Shane, 'Tia Lives On', *National Journal*, 23 Feb. 2006.

Hasbrouck, Edward, 'What's in a Passenger Name Record (PNR)?', http://www.hasbrouck.org/articles/PNR.html.

Hayek, F.A., 'The Use of Knowledge in Society', *The American Economic Review* 35, no. 4 (1945): 519–30.

Hayles, Katherine N., *How We Became Posthuman: Virtual Bodies in Cybernetics, Literature, and Informatics*, Chicago: University of Chicago Press, 1999.

Headrick, Daniel, *The Tools of Empire: Technology and European Imperialism in the Nineteenth Century*, Oxford: Oxford University Press, 1981.

Healy, Timothy J., 'Five Years after the Intelligence Reform and Terrorism Prevention Act: Stopping Terrorist Travel', edited by Terrorist Screening Center Director, Federal Bureau of Investigation, 2009.

Heath, Richard, *The English Peasant. Studies: Historical, Local, and Biographic*, London: T. Fisher Unwin, 1893.

Heide, Lars, *Punch-Card Systems and the Early Information Explosion, 1880–1945*, Baltimore: Johns Hopkins University Press, 2009.

Heidegger, Martin, *Contributions to Philosophy: From Enowning*, Bloomington: Indiana University Press, 1999.

———. 'Das Rektorat, 1933/34: Tatsachen Und Gedanken', in *Die Selbstbehauptung Der Deutschen Universität*. Frankfurt a. M.: Vittorio Klosterman, 1983.

BIBLIOGRAPHY

———. *Die Technik Und Die Kehre*, Pfullingen: Günther Neske, 1962.

———. *Sein Und Zeit*, Tübingen: Max Niemeyer Verlag, 2001 [1926].

Heidegger, Martin, and Erhart Kästner, *Briefwechsel, 1953–1974*, edited by Heinrich W Petzet, Frankfurt a. M.: Insel Verlag, 1986.

Hewitt, Rachel, *Map of a Nation: A Biography of the Ordnance Survey*, London: Granta Books, 2011.

Himmelfarb, Gertrude, 'The Haunted House of Jeremy Bentham', in *Ideas in History: Essays Presented to Louis Gottschalk by His Former Students*, edited by Richard Herr and Harold Parker, Durham: Duke University Press, 1965.

Hirst, Paul, *Space and Power: Politics, War and Architecture*, Cambridge: Polity Press, 2005.

Hobart, Michael E., and Zachary S. Schiffman, *Information Ages: Literacy, Numeracy, and the Computer Revolution*, Baltimore: Johns Hopkins University Press, 1998.

Höglund, Johan, 'Electronic Empire: Orientalism Revisited in the Military Shooter', *Game Studies: The International Journal of Computer Game Research* 8, no. 1 (2008).

Hölderlin, Friedrich, 'Patmos', in *Friedrich Hölderlin: Die Gedichte*, edited by Jochen Schmidt, 350–60, Frankfurt a.M.: Insel Verlag, [1800–5] 2001.

Holmes, Jamie, 'Identification, Please', *Foreign Policy*, http://www.foreignpolicy.com/articles/2011/03/08/identification_please.

Holston, James, *The Modernist City: An Anthropological Critique of Brasília*, Chicago: University of Chicago Press, 1989.

Hom, Andrew R., 'Hegemonic Metronome: The Ascendancy of Western Standard Time', *Review of International Studies* 36 (2010): 1145–70.

Hoogstrate, A.J., H. Van Den Heuvel, and E. Huyben, 'Ear Identification Based on Surveillance Camera Images', *Sci Justice* 41, no. 3 (2001): 167–72.

Horace, *Horace, the Odes*, edited by Robert Bly and J.D. McClatchy, Princeton: Princeton University Press, 2002.

Hornborg, Alf, *The Power of the Machine: Global Inequalities of Economy, Technology, and Environment*, Oxford: Rowman & Littlefield Publishers, 2001.

Hughes, Christopher, 'Same-Kind Coincidence and the Ship of Theseus', *Mind* 106, no. 421 (1997).

Hunt, James D., *An American Looks at Gandhi: Essays in Satyagraha, Civil Rights, and Peace*, New Delhi: Promilla & Co. Publishers, 2005.

Husserl, Edmund, 'Die Krisis Der Europäischen Wissenschaften', in *Gesammelte Werke*, edited by H.L. Van Breda, 1–193, The Hague: Martinus Nijhoff, 1962 [1937].

Hutchings, Kimberly, 'Happy Anniversary! Time and Critique in International Relations Theory', *Review of International Studies* 33 (2007): 71–89.

———. *Time and World Politics: Thinking the Present*, Manchester: Manchester University Press, 2008.

BIBLIOGRAPHY

ICRC, 'Liberia: Opinion Survey and in-Depth Research', Geneva: International Committe of Red Cross, 2009.

International Monetary Fund, 'Liberia: Interim Poverty Reduction Strategy Paper', Washington DC: IMF, 2007.

Igo, Sarah Elizabeth, *The Averaged American: Surveys, Citizens, and the Making of a Mass Public*, Cambridge: Harvard University Press, 2007.

Jackson, Robert H., *Quasi-States: Sovereignty, International Relations, and the Third World*, Cambridge: Cambridge University Press, 1990.

Jay, Erin Flynn, 'Mapping the Human Terrain', *Geospatial Intelligence Forum* 7, no. 4 (2009).

Jay, Martin, *Downcast Eyes: The Denigration of Vision in Twentieth-Century French Thought*, Berkeley: University of California Press, 1994.

Jennings, Kathleen M., 'The Struggle to Satisfy: DDR through the Eyes of Ex-Combatants in Liberia', *International Peacekeeping* 14, no. 2 (2007): 204–18.

Johnson, Robert, 'The Pashtun Way of War: A Contested History, 1809–2010', in *Orientalism at War*, edited by Tarak Barkawi and Keith Stanski, Oxford: University of Oxford, 2010.

Joseph, Anne M., 'Anthropometry, the Police Expert, and the Deptford Murders: The Contested Introduction of Fingerprinting for the Identification of Criminals in Late Victorian and Edwardian Britain', in *Documenting Individual Identity: The Development of State Practices in the Modern World*, edited by Jane Caplan and John Torpey, Princeton: Princeton University Press, 2001.

Kafka, Franz, 'In Der Strafkolonie', in *Das Urteil Und Andere Erzählungen*, 98–126, Frankfurt am Main: Fischer Taschenbuch Verlag, 1935.

Kain, R. J. P., and Elizabeth Baigent, *The Cadastral Map in the Service of the State: A History of Property Mapping*, Chicago: University of Chicago Press, 1992.

Kaplan, Martha, 'Panopticon in Poona: An Essay on Foucault and Colonialism', *Cultural Anthropology* 10, no. 1 (1995): 85–98.

Keegan, John, *The Face of Battle*, New York: Penguin, 1978.

Kelly, Duncan, *The State of the Political: Conceptions of Politics and the State in the Thought of Max Weber, Carl Schmitt, and Franz Neumann*, Oxford: Oxford University Press, 2003.

Kern, Stephen, *The Culture of Time and Space, 1880–1918*, Cambridge: Harvard University Press, 2003.

Kertzer, David I., *Ritual, Politics, and Power*, New Haven: Yale University Press, 1988.

Kertzer, David I., and Dominique Arel, *Census and Identity: The Politics of Race, Ethnicity, and Language in National Census*, Cambridge: Cambridge University Press, 2002.

Keynes, John Maynard, *A Treatise on Money*, Vol. 2, New York: Harcourt, 1930.

Kittler, Friedrich A., *Aufschreibesysteme 1800/1900*, München: Fink, 1985.

Knox, John, *The Races of Men: A Philosophical Inquiry into the Influence of Race over the Destinies of Nations*, London: Renshaw, 1862.

BIBLIOGRAPHY

Kohno, Tadayoshi, Adam Stubblefield, Aviel D. Rubin, and Dan S. Wallach, 'Analysis of an Electronic Voting System', in *IEEE Symposium on Security and Privacy*, 2004.

Krajewski, Markus, *Restlosigkeit: Weltprojekte Um 1900*, Frankfurt am Main: Fischer Taschenbuch Verlag, 2006.

———. *Zettelwitschaft: Die Geburt Der Kartei Aus Dem Geiste Der Bibliothek*, Berlin: Kulturverlag Kadmos, 2002.

Krasner, Stephen D., *Problematic Sovereignty*, New York: Columbia University Press, 2001.

———. *Sovereignty: Organized Hypocrisy*. Princeton: Princeton University Press, 1999.

Kuklick, Henrika, 'Tribal Exemplars: Images of Political Authority in British Anthropology, 1885–1945', in *Functionalism Historicized: Essays on British Social Anthropology*, edited by George W. Stocking, 59–82, Madison: University of Wisconsin Press, 1984.

Kurland, Philip B., and Ralph Lerner, *The Founders' Constitution*, 5 vols, vol. 5, Indianapolis: Liberty Fund, 2000.

Lacoue-Labarthe, Philippe, *Heidegger, Art, and Politics: The Fiction of the Political*, Oxford: B. Blackwell, 1990.

Ladewig, Paul, *Politik Der Bücherei*, Leipzig: Ernst Wiegandt Verlagsbuchhandlung, 1912.

Landau, Paul S, 'Empires of the Visual: Photography and Colonial Administration in Africa', in *Images & Empires: Visuality in Colonial and Postcolonial Africa*, edited by Paul S. Landau and Deborah D. Kaspin, Berkeley: University of California Press, 2002.

Landes, David S., *Revolution in Time: Clocks and the Making of the Modern World*, Cambridge, MA: Belknap Press, 2000.

Landow, George P., ed., *Hyper/Text/Theory*, Baltimore: Johns Hopkins University Press, 1994.

Latham, Michael, *Modernization as Ideology: American Social Science and 'Nation Building' in the Kennedy Era*, Chapel Hill: University of North Carolina Press, 2000.

Latour, Bruno, *Science in Action: How to Follow Scientists and Engineers through Society*, Cambridge: Harvard University Press, 1987.

Layne, Christopher, 'Kant or Cant: The Myth of the Democratic Peace', *International Security* 19, no. 2 (1994): 5–49.

Lederer, Emil, 'On the Sociology of World War', *European Journal of Sociology* 47, no. 02 (2006): 241–68.

Lee, Keekok, '*Homo Faber*: The Unity of the History and Philosophy of Technology', in *New Waves in Philosophy of Technology*, edited by Jan Kyrre Berg Olsen, Evan Selinger and Søren Riis, 13–39, New York: Palgrave Macmillan, 2009.

Legatum, 'Legatum Prosperity Index Report', London: Legatum Institute, 2010.

BIBLIOGRAPHY

'Leitsätze Zum Urteil Des Ersten Senats Vom 11. März 2008', in *1 BvR 2074/05*, edited by Bundesverfassungsgericht, 2008.

Lelyveld, Joseph, *Great Soul: Mahatma Gandhi and His Struggle with India*, New York: Alfred A Knopf, 2011.

Lemov, Rebecca, 'Towards a Data Base of Dreams: Assembling an Archive of Elusive Materials, C. 1947–61', *Hist Workshop J* 67, no. 1 (2009): 44–68.

Lenin, V.I., '(Reply by N. Lenin to Rosa Luxemburg) One Step Forward, Two Steps Back', Marxists Internet Archive, http://www.marxists.org/archive/lenin/works/1904/sep/15a.htm

Levitt, Jeremy I., *The Evolution of Deadly Conflict in Liberia: From 'Paternaltarianism' to State Collapse*, Durham: Carolina Academic Press, 2005.

The Lex Scripta of the Isle of Man; Comprehending the Ancient Ordinances and Statute Laws. From the Earliest to the Present Date, Douglas: G. Jefferson, 1819.

Li, Darryl, 'A Universal Enemy?: "Foreign Fighters" and Legal Regimes of Exclusion and Exemption under the "Global War on Terror"', *Columbia Human Rights Law Review* 41, no. 2 (2010): 355–428.

Lincoln, Bruce, *Discourse and the Construction of Society: Comparative Studies of Myth, Ritual, and Classification*, Oxford: Oxford University Press, 1989.

Linebaugh, Peter, and Marcus Buford Rediker, *The Many-Headed Hydra: Sailors, Slaves, Commoners, and the Hidden History of the Revolutionary Atlantic*, Boston: Beacon Press, 2000.

Longfellow, Henry Wadsworth, *Poems and Other Writings*, New York: Library of America, 2000.

Luhmann, Niklas, *Die Gesellschaft Der Gesellschaft I*, Frankfurt am Main: Suhrkamp, 1997.

Lyon, David, 'Surveillance after September 11, 2001', in *The Intensification of Surveillance: Crime, Terrorism, and Warfare in the Information Age*, edited by Kristie Ball and Frank Webster, London: Pluto Press, 2003.

Macgregor, John, *The History of the British Empire from the Accession of James the First*, London: Chapman and Hall, 1852.

MacIsaac, David, 'Voices from the Central Blue: The Air Power Theorists', in *Makers of Modern Strategy: From Machiavelli to the Nuclear Age*, edited by Peter Paret, 624–47, Oxford: Oxford University Press, 1986.

Madden, Mike, 'Barack Obama's Super Marketing Machine', Salon.com, http://www.salon.com/news/feature/2008/07/16/obama_data/

Malan, Mark, *Security Sector Reform in Liberia: Mixed Results from Humble Beginnings*, Strategic Studies Institute, United States Army War College, 2008.

Marcuse, Herbert, *One-Dimensional Man*, New York: Routledge Classics, 2007.

Markoff, John, 'Chief Takes over at Agency to Thwart Attacks on U.S.', *The New York Times*, 13 Feb. 2002.

Martin, Henri-Jean, *The History and Power of Writing*, Chicago: University of Chicago Press, 1994.

Martin, Matt J., and Charles W. Sasser, *Predator: The Remote-Control Air War over Iraq and Afghanistan*. Minneapolis: Zenith Press, 2010.

Marx, Leo, *The Machine in the Garden: Technology and the Pastoral Ideal in America*, Oxford: Oxford University Press, 1964.

———. 'Technology: The Emergence of a Hazardous Concept', *Technology and Culture* 51, no. 3 (2010): 561–77.

McCormick, John P., *Carl Schmitt's Critique of Liberalism: Against Politics as Technology*, Cambridge: Cambridge University Press, 1997.

McCoy, Alfred, *Policing America's Empire: The United States, the Philippines, and the Rise of the Surveillance State*, Madison: The University of Wisconsin Press, 2009.

McChrystal, Stanley, 'It Takes a Network', *Foreign Policy*, online edition, 22 Feb. 2011, www.foreignpolicy.com/articles/2011/02/22/it_takes_a_network

McEvoy, Frederick, 'Understanding Ethnic Realities among the Grebo and Kru Peoples of West Africa', *Africa: The Journal of the International African Institute* 47, no. 1 (1977): 62–80.

McFate, Sean, 'The Art and Aggravation of Vetting in Post-Conflict Environments', *Military Review*, July–Aug. (2007): 79–87.

———. 'Outsourcing the Making of Militaries: Dyncorp International as Sovereign Agent', *Review of African Political Economy* 35, no. 118 (2008): 645–59.

McGinniss, Joe, *The Selling of the President, 1968*, New York: Trident Press, 1969.

McKeown, Adam, *Melancholy Order: Asian Migration and the Globalization of Borders*, New York: Columbia University Press, 2008.

McLuhan, Marshall, *The Gutenberg Galaxy; the Making of Typographic Man*, Toronto: University of Toronto Press, 1962.

Melber, Ari, 'Year One of Organizing for America: The Permanent Field Campaign in a Digital Age', in *techPresident Special Report*, 2010.

Messner, Dirk, *The Network Society: Economic Development and International Competitiveness as Problems of Social Governance*, London: Frank Cass, 1997.

Mirowski, Philip, *Machine Dreams: Economics Becomes a Cyborg Science*, Cambridge: Cambridge University Press, 2002.

Mitchell, Arnold, *The Nine American Lifestyles: Who We Are and Where We're Going*, New York: Macmillan, 1983.

Mitchell, Timothy, *Colonising Egypt*, Cambridge: Cambridge University Press, 1988.

———. *Rule of Experts: Egypt, Techno-Politics, Modernity*, Berkeley: University of California Press, 2002.

Monk, Daniel Bertrand, 'Hives and Swarms: On the "Nature" of Neoliberalism and the Rise of the Ecological Insurgent', in *Evil Paradises: Dreamworlds of Neoliberalism*, edited by Mike Davis and Daniel Bertrand Monk, 262–73, New York: The New Press, 2007.

Monmonier, Mark S., *Bushmanders & Bullwinkles: How Politicians Manipulate Electronic Maps and Census Data to Win Elections*, Chicago: University of Chicago Press, 2001.

————. *How to Lie with Maps*, Chicago: University of Chicago Press, 1996.

Montjoye, Yves-Alexandre de, Cesar A, Hidalgo, Michel Verleysen, and Vincent D. Blondel, 'Unique in the Crowd: The Privacy Bounds of Human Mobility', *Scientific Reports* 3 (2013).

Moorstedt, Tobias, *Jeffersons Erben: Wie Die Digitalen Medien Die Politik Verändern* Frankfurt am Main: Suhrkamp, 2008.

Morozov, Evgeny, *The Net Delusion: How Not to Liberate the World*, London: Allen Lane, 2011.

Müller, Jan-Werner, *A Dangerous Mind: Carl Schmitt in Post-War European Thought*, New Haven: Yale University Press, 2003.

Multi-National Force in Iraq, Offical Website, 'Unmanned Aerial System First to Fire Missiles in Combat', http://www.mnf-iraq.com/index.php?option=com_content &task=view&id=25656&Itemid=128

Mumford, Lewis, *The Myth of the Machine*, New York: Harcourt, 1967.

Murra, John V., *The Economic Organization of the Inka State*, Greenwich: JAI Press, 1980.

Murray, Shailagh, and Matthew Mosk, 'Under Obama, Web Would Be the Way', *Washington Post*, 10 Nov. 2008.

Nandy, Ashis, *The Intimate Enemy: Loss and Recovery of Self under Colonialism*, Oxford: Oxford University Press, 1988.

National Commission on Terrorist Attacks upon the United States, *The 9/11 Commission Report: Final Report of the National Commission on Terrorist Attacks Upon the United States*, 1st ed., New York: Norton, 2004.

Netz, Reviel, *Barbed Wire: An Ecology of Modernity*, Middletown, CT: Wesleyan University Press, 2004.

Neumann, Solomon, *Die Fabel Von Der Jüdischen Masseneinwanderung: Ein Kapitel Aus Der Preussischen Statistik*, 2nd ed., Berlin 1880.

Neurath, Otto, *Anti-Spengler*, München: G.D.W. Callwey, 1921.

Nevers, Renée de, *Comrades No More: The Seeds of Political Change in Eastern Europe*, Cambridge MA: The MIT Press, 2003.

Nielsen, Rasmus Kleis, 'Mundane Internet Tools, Mobilizing Practices, and the Coproduction of Citizenship in Political Campaigns', *New Media & Society* (2010).

Noonan, Harold W., *Personal Identity*, London: Routledge, 1989.

Norpah, Anthony F., 'Minutes of the DAMC Meeting Held on October 25, 2005 in the Cabinet Room at the Executive Mansion', Monrovia, 2005.

Norris, Pippa, *Digital Divide: Civic Engagement, Information Poverty, and the Internet Worldwide*, Cambridge: Cambridge University Press, 2001.

Northrup Grumman, 'An AAQ-37 Eo Das for the F-35', http://www.es.north-ropgrumman.com/solutions/f35targeting/assets/eodasvideo.html

Nye, Joseph S., and Robert O Keohane, 'Power and Interdependence in the Information Age', *Foreign Affairs* 77, no. 5 (1998): 81–94.

BIBLIOGRAPHY

Oakeshott, Michael, *Rationalism in Politics*, New York: Basic Books, 1962.

Odysseos, Louiza, and Fabio Petito, *The International Political Thought of Carl Schmitt*, Abingdon: Routledge, 2008.

OED, 'Information, *n.*', Oxford English Dictionary, http://www.oed.com:80/Entry/95568

Oliver, Michael, *The Politics of Disablement: A Sociological Approach*, New York: St. Martin's Press, 1990.

Ong, Walter J., *Orality and Literacy: Technologizing the Word*, Oxford: Routledge, 2002.

———. *Orality and Literacy: The Technologizing of the Word*, London: Routledge, 1991.

Osborn, Tracy, Scott D. McClurg, and Benjamin Knoll, 'Voter Mobilization and the Obama Victory', *American Politics Research* 38, no. 2 (1 Mar. 2010): 211–32.

Pang, Laikwan, '"China Who Makes and Fakes": A Semiotics of the Counterfeit', *Theory, Culture & Society* 25, no. 6 (2008): 117–40.

Perla, Peter P., *The Art of Wargaming: A Guide for Professionals and Hobbyists*, Annapolis: Naval Institute Press, 1990.

Petty, William, 'The Political Anatomy of Ireland', in *Economic Writings*, 1691.

Pickles, John, *A History of Spaces: Cartographic Reason, Mapping and the Geo-Coded World*, New York: Routledge, 2004.

Plato, *Republic*, Oxford: Oxford University Press, 1998.

Policy Development and Evaluation Service, IDP Advisory Team, 'Real-Time Evaluation of UNHCR's IDP Operation in Liberia', Geneva: United Nations High Commissioner for Refugees (UNHCR), 2007.

Porter, Patrick, *Military Orientalism: Eastern War through Western Eyes*, New York: Columbia University Press, 2009.

Porter, Theodore M., 'Speaking Precision to Power: The Modern Political Role of Social Science', *Social Research* 73, no. 4 (2006): 1273–94.

———. *The Rise of Statistical Thinking, 1820–1900*, Princeton: Princeton University Press, 1986.

Portinaro, Pier Paolo, 'Kulturpessimismus Und Die Grenzen Der Entzauberung. Diagnosen Zur Technik, Kultur Und Politik Nach Der Jahrhundertwende', in *Kultur Und Kulturwissenschaften Um 1900*, edited by Rüdiger vom Bruch, Friedrich Wilhelm Graf and Gangolf Hübinger, 175–96, Stuttgart: Franz Steiner Verlag Wiesbaden, 1989.

Pun, K. H., and Y. S. Moon, 'Recent Advances in Ear Biometrics', paper presented at the Sixth IEEE International Conference on Automatic Face and Gesture Recognition, 2004.

Putnam, Robert, *Bowling Alone: The Collapse and Revival of American Community*, New York: Simon & Schuster, 2000.

Rattray, R.S., 'Ashanti Law and Constitution', in *Readings in African Law*, edited by

Neville Rubin and Eugene Cotran, 78–81, New York: Frank Cass & Company Limited, 1970.

Reid, Julian, 'Politicizing Connectivity: Beyond the Biopolitics of Information Technology in International Relations', *Cambridge Review of International Affairs* 22, no. 4 (2009): 607–23.

Rhodes, Neil, and Jonathan Sawday, 'Paperworlds: Imagining the Renaissance Computer', in *The Renaissance Computer: Knowledge Technology in the First Age of Print*, edited by Neil Rhodes and Jonathan Sawday, 1–17, New York: Routledge, 2000.

Roeder, Ethan, Data Manager for Obama for America, Telephone Interview, 16 Jan. 2009.

Roscher, Max, *Die Kabel Des Weltverkehrs Hauptsächlich in Volkswirtschaftlicher Hinsicht*, Berlin: Puttkammer & Mühlbrecht, 1911.

Rosén, Frederik, 'Off the Record: Outsourcing Security and State Building to Private Firms and the Question of Record Keeping, Archives, and Collective Memory', *Archival Science*, no. 8 (2008): 1–14.

Rosen, Stanley, 'Technē and the Origins of Modernity', in *Technology in the Western Political Tradition*, edited by Arthur M Melzer, Jerry Weinberger and Richard M Zinman, 69–84, Ithaca: Cornell University Press, 1993.

Rousseau, Jean-Jacques, 'On Social Contract or Principles of Political Right', translated by Alan Ritter and Julia Conaway Bondanella, in *Rousseau's Political Writings: New Translations, Interpretive Notes, Backgrounds, Commentaries*, 84–173, New York: W.W. Norton, 1988 [1762].

Said, Edward, *Orientalism*, London: Penguin Books, 2003.

Said, Edward W., *Orientalism*, 1st Vintage Books ed., New York: Vintage Books, 1979.

———. *Orientalism*, New York: Pantheon Books, 1978.

Saletan, William, 'Ghosts in the Machine: Do Remote-Control War Pilots Get Combat Stress', *Slate*, 11 Aug. 2008.

Salter, Mark B., *Rights of Passage: The Passport in International Relations*, Boulder: Lynne Rienner Publishers, 2003.

Saussure, Ferdinand de, *Course in General Linguistics*, revised ed., London: Fontana, 1974.

Schelling, Thomas C., *Arms and Influence*, New Haven: Yale University Press, 1966.

———. *The Strategy of Conflict*, Cambridge: Harvard University Press, 1960.

Schmidt, Eric, and Jared Cohen, 'The Digital Disruption: Connectivity and the Diffusion of Power', *Foreign Affairs* 89, no. 6 (2010).

Schmitt, Carl, 'Das Zeitalter Der Neutralisierungen Und Entpolitisierungen', in *Der Begriff Des Politischen*, 79–95, Berlin: Duncker & Humblot, [1929] 2002.

———. *Der Leviathan in Der Staatslehre Des Thomas Hobbes*, Stuttgart: Klett-Cotta, 1995 [1938].

———. *Politische Theologie II: Die Legende Von Der Erledigung Jeder Politischen Theologie*, Berlin: Duncker & Humblot, 1996.

———. *Politische Theologie: Vier Kapitel Zur Lehre Von Der Souveränität*, Berlin: Duncker & Humblot, 2004 [1922].

Schultz, George P., 'New Realities and New Ways of Thinking', *Foreign Affairs* 63, no. 4 (1985).

Schumpeter, Joseph. 'The Analysis of Economic Change', in *Essays on Entrepeneurs, Innovations, Business Cycles and the Evolution of Capitalism*, edited by Richard V Clemence, 134–49, New Brunswick: Transactions Publishers, 2000.

Scott, James C., *The Art of Not Being Governed: An Anarchist History of Upland Southeast Asia*, New Haven: Yale University Press, 2009.

———. *Decoding Subaltern Politics: Ideology, Disguise, and Resistance in Agrarian Politics*, Asia's Transformations, New York: Routledge, 2013.

———. *Seeing Like a State: How Certain Schemes to Improve the Human Condition Have Failed*, New Haven: Yale University Press, 1998.

R&V Section, 'Recruiting & Vetting Report and Analysis, January 18th–June 1st', Monrovia DynCorp International, 2006.

———. 'Recruiting & Vetting Standard Operating Procedure: SSR Liberia', Monrovia: DynCorp International, 2006.

Seigel, Jerrod, *The Idea of the Self: Thought and Experience in Western Europe since the Seventeenth Century*, Cambridge: Cambridge University Press, 2005.

Sengoopta, Chandak, *Imprint of the Raj: How Fingerprinting Was Born in Colonial India*, Oxford: Macmillan, 2003.

Seward, Josiah Lafayette, *A History of the Town of Sullivan, New Hampshire, 1777–1917*, Keene, NH: Sentinel Printing Co., 1921.

Shane, Scott, *Dismantling Utopia: How Information Ended the Soviet Union*, Chicago: I.R. Dee, 1995.

Shils, Edward, *Center and Periphery: Essays in Macrosociology*, Chicago: University of Chicago Press, 1975.

Shils, Edward, and Michael Young, 'The Meaning of the Coronation', in *Center and Periphery: Essays in Macrosociology*, edited by Edward Shils, 135–52, Chicago: University of Chicago Press, 1956 [1975].

Shirky, Clay, *Cognitive Surplus: Creativity and Generosity in a Connected Age*, London: Penguin, 2010.

———. *Here Comes Everybody*, London: Allen Lane, 2008.

———. 'The Political Power of Social Media', *Foreign Affairs* 90, no. 3 (2011).

Sieber-Lehmann, Claudius, *Spätmittelalterlicher Nationalismus*, Göttingen: Vandenhoek und Ruprecht, 1995.

Silverman, Barry, 'Human Terrain Data What Should We Do with It?', *Departmental Papers (ESE)* (2007).

Silverman, Barry, David Pietrocola, Nathan Weyer, Ransom Weaver, Nouva Esomar,

BIBLIOGRAPHY

Robert Might, and Deepthi Chandrasekaran, 'NonKin Village: An Embeddable Training Game Generator for Learning Cultural Terrain and Sustainable Counter-Insurgent Operations', *Agents for Games and Simulations: Lecture Notes in Computer Science*, 5920 (2009): 135–54.

Simitis, Spiros, 'Reviewing Privacy in an Information Society', *University of Pennsylvania Law Review*, 135 (1986–7).

Simmel, Georg, 'Die Grossstradt Und Das Geistesleben', in *Jahrbuch Der Gehe-Stiftung Zu Dresden, Vol. 9*, edited by K. Bücher, Dresden: von Zahn & Jaensch, 1903.

Simon, Jonathan, 'The Ideological Effects of Actuarial Practices', *Law & Society Review* 22, no. 4 (1988): 771–800.

Singer, P.W., *Wired for War: The Robotics Revolution and Conflict in the 21st Century*, New York: The Penguin Press, 2009.

Skinner, Quentin, *Liberty before Liberalism*, Cambridge: Cambridge University Press, 1998.

———. *Visions of Politics, Regarding Method*, 3 vols, vol. 1, Cambridge: Cambridge University Press, 2002.

Smeaton, Chase J., 'Cropping Animals' Ears', *Folklore* 17, no. 1 (1906): 72–3.

Smith, George, *The Hebrew People*, New York: Carlton & Phillips, 1856.

Smith, Jonathan Z., 'The Bare Facts of Ritual', *History of Religions* 20, no. 1/2 (1980): 112–27.

Smith, Roger, 'The Long History of Gaming in Military Training', *Simulation Gaming* 41, no. 1 (2010): 6–19.

Sola Pool, Ithiel de, *Technologies of Freedom: On Free Speech in an Electronic Age*, Cambridge: Harvard University Press, 1983.

Solove, Daniel J., 'Privacy and Power: Computer Databases and Metaphors for Information Privacy', *Stanford Law Review* 53, no. 6 (2001): 1393–462.

———. *Understanding Privacy*, Cambridge, MA: Harvard University Press, 2008.

Solove, Daniel J., Marc Rotenberg, and Paul M. Schwartz, *Privacy, Information, and Technology*, New York: Aspen Publishers, 2006.

'Standard Time and Measures', *Science* 9, no. 205 (1887): 7–8.

Steinberg, Jonny, 'A Truth Commission Goes Abroad: Liberian Transitional Justice in New York', *African Affairs* 110, no. 438 (2011): 35–53.

Stewart, Alexander, *Twixt Ben Nevis and Glencoe: The Natural History, Legends, and Folk-Lore of the West Highlands*, Edinburgh: William Paterson, 1885.

Stiegler, Bernard, *Technics and Time*, Stanford: Stanford University Press, 1998.

Stirland, Sarah Lai, 'Obama's Secret Weapons: Internet, Databases and Psychology', WIRED Blog Network, http://blog.wired.com/27bstroke6/2008/10/obamas-secret-w.html

Strong, Tracy B., '"What Have We to Do with Morals? Nietzsche and Weber on History and Ethics"', *History of the Human Sciences* 5, no. 3 (1992): 9–18.

BIBLIOGRAPHY

Suchman, Lucy A., *Human-Machine Reconfigurations: Plans and Situated Actions*, Cambridge: Cambridge University Press, 2007.

Tacitus, 'The Annals', http://classics.mit.edu/Tacitus/annals.8.xii.html

Taussig, Michael, *Mimesis and Alterity: A Particular History of the Senses*, New York: Routledge, 1993.

Taylor, Frederick Winslow, *The Principles of Scientific Management; and Shop Management*, London: Routledge/Thoemmes Press, 1993.

Tellewoyan, Joseph, *The Years the Locusts Have Eaten: Liberia, 1816–2004*, Philadelphia: Xlibris Corporation, 2006.

Thomas, Martin, *Empires of Intelligence: Security Services and Colonial Disorder after 1914*, Berkeley: University of California Press, 2008.

Thompson, Mark, 'Discourse, "Development" & the "Digital Divide": ICT & the World Bank', *Review of African Political Economy* 31, no. 99 (2004): 103–23.

Tilly, Charles, *Coercion, Capital, and European States, AD 990–1990*, Cambridge: Blackwell, 1990.

Tocqueville, Alexis de, *Democracy in America*, Cambridge: Sever and Francis, 1862.

Todorov, Tzvetan, *The Conquest of America: The Question of the Other*, Norman: University of Oklahoma Press, 1999.

Torpey, John, 'The Great War and the Birth of the Modern Passport System', in *Documenting Individual Identity: The Development of State Practices in the Modern World*, edited by Jane Caplan and John Torpey, 256–70, Princeton: Princeton University Press, 2001.

Torpey, John C., *The Invention of the Passport: Surveillance, Citizenship, and the State*, Cambridge: Cambridge University Press, 2000.

Toynbee, Arnold Joseph, *Lectures on the Industrial Revolution in England*, Kessinger Publishing, 2004 [1884].

Travis, Alan, and Richard Norton-Taylor, 'Private Firm May Track All Email and Calls: "Hellhouse" of Personal Data Will Be Created, Warns Former DPP', *The Guardian*, 31 Dec. 2008.

Truman, Harry S., 'Inaugural Address', 1949.

Turner, Lucien M., 'Ethnology of the Ungava District, Hudson Bay Territory', in *Eleventh Annual Report of the Bureau of Ethnology to the Secretary of the Smithsonian Institution*, edited by J.W. Powell, 167–360, Washington: Government Printing Office, 1894.

Turner, Victor Witter, *The Drums of Affliction: A Study of Religious Processes among the Ndembu of Zambia*, Oxford: Clarendon, 1968.

———. *The Forest of Symbols; Aspects of Ndembu Ritual*, Ithaca: Cornell University Press, 1967.

———. *The Ritual Process*, London: Routledge & Kegan Paul Ltd, 1969.

Tyson, Ann Scott, 'A Historic Success in Military Recruiting', *Washington Post*, 14 Oct. 2009.

BIBLIOGRAPHY

UNDDR, 'Liberia Country Programme', United Nations Disarmament, Demobilization and Reintegration Center, http://www.unddr.org/countryprogrammes.php? c=52—framework

UNDP, 'Human Development Report', New York: United Nations Development Programme, 2009.

UNHCR, 'Liberia: Regional Operations Profile—West Africa', http://www.unhcr. org/cgi-bin/texis/vtx/page?page=49e484936

United States Dept. of the Army, and United States Marine Corps, *The U.S. Army/ Marine Corps Counterinsurgency Field Manual: U.S. Army Field Manual No. 3–24: Marine Corps Warfighting Publication No. 3–33.5*, University of Chicago Press ed., Chicago: University of Chicago Press, 2007.

United States Marine Corps, *Small Wars Manual*, Honolulu, Hawaii: University Press of the Pacific, 2005 [1940].

Urton, Gary, *Signs of the Inka Khipu: Binary Coding in the Andean Knotted-String Records*, Austin: University of Texas Press, 2003.

Urton, Gary, and Carrie J. Brezine, 'Khipu Accounting in Ancient Peru', *Science* 309, no. 5737 (2005): 1065–7.

Varian, Hal, Joseph Farrell, and Carl Shapiro, *The Economics of Information Technology: An Introduction*, Cambridge: Cambridge University Press, 2004.

Vegetius Renatus, Flavius, *The Military Institutions of the Romans*, translated by John Clarke, edited by Thomas R. Phillips, Military Classics, Harrisburg, PA: The Military Service Publishing Company, 1944.

Virilio, Paul, *War and Cinema: The Logistics of Perception*, London: Verso, 1989.

Vleck, Jenifer L. Van, 'The "Logic of the Air": Aviation and the Globalism of the "American Century", *New Global Studies* 1, no. 1 (2007).

Wagner, R. Harrison, 'War and the State: A Synopsis', *International Theory* 2, no. 02 (2010): 283–7.

Walker, Peter, 'Database of Every Phone Call and Email "a Step Too Far"', *The Guardian*, 15 July 2008.

Walker, R.B.J., *Inside/Outside: International Relations as Political Theory*, Cambridge: Cambridge University Press, 1993.

Wallach, Wendell, and Colin Allen, *Moral Machines: Teaching Robots Right from Wrong*, Oxford: Oxford University Press, 2009.

Weber, Max, 'Die "Objektivität" Sozialwissenschaftlicher Und Sozialpolitischer Erkenntnis', in *Max Weber Schriften 1894–1922*, edited by Dirk Kaesler, 77–149, Stuttgart: Kroener, 2002 [1904].

———. 'Die Drei Reinen Typen Der Legitimen Herrschaft. Eine Soziologische Studie', in *Max Weber Schriften 1894–1922*, edited by Dirk Kaesler, 717–34, Stuttgart: Kroener, 2002 [1922].

———. 'Die Protestantische Ethik Und Der "Geist" Des Kapitalismus', in *Max Weber Schriften 1894–1922*, edited by Dirk Kaesler, 150–226, Stuttgart: Kroener, 2002 [1905/1920].

————. *The Protestant Ethic and the Spirit of Capitalism*, translated by Talcott Parsons, New York: Scribner, 1930.

————. *Schriften 1894–1922*, edited by Dirk Kaesler, Stuttgart: Kröner, 2002.

————. 'Science as a Vocation', in *Max Weber's 'Science as a Vocation'*, edited by Peter Lassman and Irving Velody, London: Unwin Hyman, 1989.

————. 'Vorbemerkung Zu Den "Gesammelten Aufsätzen Zur Religionssoziologie"', in *Max Weber Schriften 1894–1922*, edited by Dirk Kaesler, 557–72, Stuttgart: Kroener, 2002 [1920].

————. *Wirtschaft Und Gesellschaft*, Tübingen: J.C.B. Mohr, 1922.

————. 'Wissenschaft Als Beruf', in *Max Weber Schriften 1894–1922*, edited by Dirk Kaesler, 474–511, Stuttgart: Kroener, 2002 [1919].

Weinstein, Jeremy M., and Macartan Humphreys, 'Disentangling the Determinants of Successful Demobilization and Reintegration', Center for Global Development, 2005.

Westmoreland, William, *Address to the Association of the U.S. Army*, 1969.

Whitman, James Q., *Harsh Justice: Criminal Punishment and the Widening Divide between America and Europe*, New York: Oxford University Press, 2003.

Whitmore, William Henry, *The Colonial Laws of Massachusetts*, Boston: Published by order of the City Council of Boston, under the supervision of William H. Whitmore, Rockwell and Churchill, city printers, 1889.

Wieland, Georg Stephan, *Juristisches Hand-Buch*, Jena: Johann Gottfried Hanisch, 1762.

Wiener, Norbert, *Cybernetics: Or Control and Communication in the Animal and the Machine*, Cambridge: The MIT Press, 1948.

WikiLeaks, 'Collateral Murder', http://www.collateralmurder.com/

Wilcox, Dorvil Miller, *Records of the Town of Lee from Its Incorporation to A.D. 1801*, Lee: Press of the Valley Gleaner, 1900.

Wilentz, Sean, *Rites of Power: Symbolism, Ritual, and Politics since the Middle Ages*, Philadelphia: University of Pennsylvania Press, 1985.

Winichakul, Thongchai, *Siam Mapped: A History of the Geo-Body of a Nation*, Honolulu: University of Hawai'i Press, 1994.

Winner, Langdon, *The Whale and the Reactor: A Search for Limits in an Age of High Technology*, Chicago: The University of Chicago Press, 1986.

Wolters, Oliver, *History, Culture, and Region in Southeast Asian Perspective*, Singapore: Institute for Southeast Asian Studies, 1982.

Wright, Alex, *Glut: Mastering Information through the Ages*, Ithaca: Cornell University Press, 2007.

Wu, Tim, *The Master Switch: The Rise and Fall of Information Empires*, New York: Knopf, 2010.

Young, Robert J.C., *Colonial Desire: Hybridity in Theory, Culture and Race*, London: Routledge, 1995.

BIBLIOGRAPHY

Yuan, Li, Zhichun Mu, and Fan Yang, 'A Review of Recent Advances in Ear Recognition', paper presented at the Biometric Recognition: 6th Chinese Conference, CCBT 2011, Beijing, 2011.

Zeleny, Jeff, 'Obama Battles Block by Block to Get Voters to Polls', *New York Times*, 12 Oct. 2008.

Zetter, Kim, '22 Million E-Mails Missing from Bush White House Found', WIRED, http://www.wired.com/threatlevel/2009/12/220million-emails-found/

Zhang, Hui, Zhenan Sun, Tieniu Tan, and Jianyu Wang. 'Ethnic Classification Based on Iris Images', Paper presented at the Biometric Recognition: 6th Chinese Conference, CCBT 2011, Beijing, 2011.

INDEX